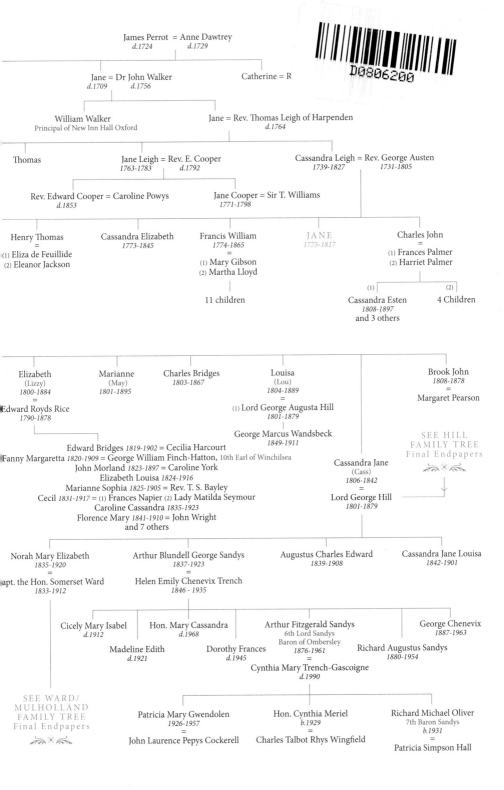

James Perrot = Anne Dawtrey
d.1724 / *d.1729*

Jane = Dr John Walker
d.1709 / *d.1756*

Catherine = R

William Walker
Principal of New Inn Hall Oxford

Jane = Rev. Thomas Leigh of Harpenden
d.1764

Thomas

Jane Leigh = Rev. E. Cooper
1763-1783 / *d.1792*

Cassandra Leigh = Rev. George Austen
1739-1827 / *1731-1805*

Rev. Edward Cooper = Caroline Powys
d.1853

Jane Cooper = Sir T. Williams
1771-1798

Henry Thomas
=
(1) Eliza de Feuillide
(2) Eleanor Jackson

Cassandra Elizabeth
1773-1845

Francis William
1774-1865
=
(1) Mary Gibson
(2) Martha Lloyd

JANE
1775-1817

Charles John
=
(1) Frances Palmer
(2) Harriet Palmer

11 children

(1) Cassandra Esten
1808-1897
and 3 others

(2) 4 Children

Elizabeth
(Lizzy)
1800-1884
=
Edward Royds Rice
1790-1878

Marianne
(May)
1801-1895

Charles Bridges
1803-1867

Louisa
(Lou)
1804-1889
=
(1) Lord George Augusta Hill
1801-1879
George Marcus Wandsbeck
1849-1911

Brook John
1808-1878
=
Margaret Pearson

SEE HILL
FAMILY TREE
Final Endpapers

Edward Bridges *1819-1902* = Cecilia Harcourt
Fanny Margaretta *1820-1909* = George William Finch-Hatton, 10th Earl of Winchilsea
John Morland *1823-1897* = Caroline York
Elizabeth Louisa *1824-1916*
Marianne Sophia *1825-1905* = Rev. T. S. Bayley
Cecil *1831-1917* = (1) Frances Napier (2) Lady Matilda Seymour
Caroline Cassandra *1835-1923*
Florence Mary *1841-1910* = John Wright
and 7 others

Cassandra Jane
(Cass)
1806-1842
=
Lord George Hill
1801-1879

Norah Mary Elizabeth
1835-1920
=
Capt. the Hon. Somerset Ward
1833-1912

Arthur Blundell George Sandys
1837-1923
=
Helen Emily Chenevix Trench
1846 - 1935

Augustus Charles Edward
1839-1908

Cassandra Jane Louisa
1842-1901

Cicely Mary Isabel
d.1912

Madeline Edith
d.1921

Hon. Mary Cassandra
d.1968

Dorothy Frances
d.1945

Arthur Fitzgerald Sandys
6th Lord Sandys
Baron of Ombersley
1876-1961
=
Cynthia Mary Trench-Gascoigne
d.1990

George Chenevix
1887-1963

Richard Augustus Sandys
1880-1954

SEE WARD/
MULHOLLAND
FAMILY TREE
Final Endpapers

Patricia Mary Gwendolen
1926-1957
=
John Laurence Pepys Cockerell

Hon. Cynthia Meriel
b.1929
=
Charles Talbot Rhys Wingfield

Richard Michael Oliver
7th Baron Sandys
b.1931
=
Patricia Simpson Hall

Dr Sophia Hillan was Assistant Director of the Queen's University of Belfast's Institute of Irish Studies. Her publications include, *In Quiet Places: Uncollected Stories, Letters and Critical Prose of Michael McLaverty* (1989); *The Silken Twine: A Study of the Works of Michael McLaverty* (1992) and *The Edge of Dark: A Sense of Place in the Writings of Michael McLaverty and Sam Hanna Bell* (2001). As a writer of fiction, she has been published in David Marcus's *New Irish Writing,* and his first *Faber Book of Best New Irish Short Stories, 2004–5*. She was a finalist for the Royal Society of Literature's first V.S. Pritchett Memorial Award (1999), and her short story, *Roses*, was featured as part of BBC Radio 4's *Defining Moments* series.

MAY, LOU & CASS

Jane Austen's
NIECES IN
IRELAND

SOPHIA HILLAN

BLACKSTAFF
PRESS
BELFAST

First published in 2011 by
Blackstaff Press
4c Heron Wharf, Sydenham Business Park
Belfast BT3 9LE
with the assistance of
The Arts Council of Northern Ireland

© Text, Sophia Hillan, 2011
© Photographs and images, see pages 283–4. The picture acknowledgements
on pages 283–4 constitute an extension of this copyright page.

Internal design by Two Associates
Typeset by www.sinedesign.net
Family Tree designed by Lisa Dynan, Belfast

Printed in Great Britain by the MPG Books Group

A CIP catalogue record for this book is available
from the British Library

ISBN 978-0-85640-868-7

www.blackstaffpress.com

To the memory of my mother and my brother,
who knew their Jane Austen

... And we think you had better not leave England. Let the Portmans go to Ireland, but as you know nothing of the Manners there, you had better not go with them. You will be in danger of giving false misrepresentations.

Jane Austen to her niece Anna, August 1814

CONTENTS

ACKNOWLEDGEMENTS

Over the five years in which this book has been in the making, I have had the expert assistance of a number of people, and to all of these I am indeed grateful. Patsy Horton, Managing Editor of Blackstaff Press, saw the potential in the project at an early stage and, despite the fragile economic climate affecting us all, championed it and saw it through to the end. To Patsy and to her colleagues, Julie Steenson, who copy-edited the book with style and grace, Helen Wright and Michelle Griffin, who worked with me on the illustrations with great understanding of the subject and Simon Coury, who read the proofs, special thanks are due.

The staff of Jane Austen's House Museum in Chawton, Hampshire could not have done more for me: Tom Carpenter, Louise West and Ann Channon made me welcome from the outset and gave me unlimited access not only to research facilities, but also to rare manuscripts and early editions. I was given the privilege of working with them, and with Isabel Snowden, among the personal possessions of Jane Austen and her family in the house where she lived and wrote most of her finest work: to do so has been one of the greatest pleasures of the last five years.

A short walk from the Jane Austen House, at the former home of her brother Edward Knight, once Chawton Great House, now Chawton House Library, I was most kindly permitted to consult unique editions, and was shown the room where family legend has it that Jane Austen sat and looked out over the grounds. Having stood there, I do not doubt it. I thank the Librarian, Jacqui Grainger, for showing it to me, and for all her kind assistance. Thanks are also due to the staff of the Hampshire Record Office in Winchester, where so many of Marianne Knight's letters, and the papers of Montagu Knight and James Edward Austen Leigh are kept. I am especially grateful to Nicola Pink, who helped enormously with finding rare images of members of the family and their homes.

The Knight sisters spent most of their childhood at Godmersham in Kent: I owe a great debt of thanks to the staff of the Centre for Kentish Studies at Maidstone, Julie Gregson and her colleagues. I was given invaluable and painstaking assistance by two people in particular: Helen Orme and Mark Ballard, to whom I am indebted for helping me so consistently and patiently through the Knatchbull and Rice archives. Though I did not meet Margaret Hammond, whose earlier work on the Rice archive proved very helpful to me, I am most grateful to her. I am sorry that the sudden death of Henry Rice, who most kindly answered my queries, means I cannot thank him: I do thank Mrs Rice, his widow, for the help that she gave in his stead. In Kent, too, I was privileged to meet Margaret Wilson, whose meticulous work on the life, letters and diaries of Fanny Knight (later Lady Knatchbull) has been a boon: I thank Margaret, a most generous scholar, for her careful attention to my many queries, which few but she could have answered.

In Ireland, I carried out most of my work in Belfast's Linen Hall Library, founded when Jane Austen was not yet thirteen years old. For all the assistance and support I have been given by the Librarian, John Killen, and his kind and most helpful colleagues, I am very grateful. The Public Record Office of Northern Ireland holds papers of the Downshire, Ward and Saunderson families: access to these was essential, and I thank the staff for all their help. In particular, I am also very grateful to the former Deputy Keeper of PRONI, A.P.W. Malcomson, who directed me very early in my research towards a key document in the Granard Papers. The staff of both the National Archives and the National Library in Dublin answered my queries quickly and fully: I owe special thanks to the Duty Archivist in the Department of Manuscripts of the National Library of Ireland, Avice-Claire McGovern, who helped me find Lord George Hill's copy of Brian Merriman's Gaelic epic, 'The Midnight Court'. My thanks are also due to Michelle Ashmore, Picture Library Executive of the National Museums Northern Ireland at Cultra, Holywood, who gave me access to photographs by James Glass of nineteenth-century Donegal. I had first seen these reproduced in a study of Irish photography by my former colleague at Queen's University's Institute of Irish Studies, W.A. Maguire. I am indeed sorry that Bill's recent passing means I cannot now thank him as I would have wished. I thank, instead, his widow Joan, my former colleague at the Institute of Irish Studies. I can and do thank my former Director at the Institute of Irish Studies, R.H. Buchanan, not only for introducing me to the work of E. Estyn Evans, founder of the Institute and editor of the only modern edition of Lord George's *Facts from Gweedore*, but also for identifying for me the location of Isle O'Valla, where Jane Austen's great-niece lived in County Down. I am also grateful to Ronnie's wife, Rhoma, who photographed the house; to his successor at the Institute, my colleague Brian Walker, who kindly read the manuscript and gave me guidance on points of Irish history; and to Lord and Lady Dunleath for granting permission to use extracts from *Ballywalter Park* (1985), and for providing me with the images of Somerset and Norah Ward. In Donegal, I was greatly assisted by the Archivist of the Donegal County Archives in Lifford, Niamh Brennan, who gave me access to the first *Gweedore Hotel Book*. Patricia Doherty, proprietor of An Chúirt, the Gweedore Court Hotel and Heritage Centre, kindly allowed me to consult the second *Gweedore Hotel Book,* wonderfully discovered during her renovations of the old hotel, once Lord George Hill's pride and joy. Susan McCaffrey of Donegal Ancestry in Ramelton gave me invaluable assistance in finding death certificates for Lord George, his wife and sisters-in-law. Also in Gweedore, I was given generous access to rare texts concerning Lord George and Father James McFadden by Tony McHugh, of Comharchumann Fordartha in Derrybeg, to whom I must also express my gratitude. Concerning Lord George Hill and his work in Donegal, I have been greatly aided by the kindness and generosity of Margaret Bonar in sharing with me evidence uncovered during her own invaluable research. I was introduced to Margaret Bonar's scholarship by the present owners of Ballyare, Lord George's house in Donegal, Roy and Noreen Greenslade, who have most kindly given of their time and unique knowledge of the subject. It is thanks to my friends Angélique Day and her husband Fergus Hanna Bell that I met Roy and Noreen Greenslade. I must also express my gratitude to Angélique not only for the hospitality she and her family have extended to me in Donegal but also, as all scholars of Irish Studies must, for her great work in editing, with Patrick McWilliams, the *Ordnance Survey Memoirs* of the early 1830s, which give a unique and comprehensive picture of the Donegal Jane Austen's nieces knew.

In present-day Donegal, I owe a debt of thanks to my brother Shane and his wife Patricia, who most kindly gave me the use of their house while I worked on the book. One of their own books in that lovely house, Hugh Dorian's *The Outer Edge of Ulster*, helped me greatly at the outset of my research. From that same house, with the friends who made me so welcome in their home when I was researching the book in England, Kevin and Bernadette McLean, I set out one day to find the graves of Marianne and Louisa: it was Bernadette who discovered them first, and Kevin who took the remarkable photographs of those almost forgotten headstones, sadly obscured by weeds and débris. Other friends who made me welcome in Donegal, and gave generously of their own time to help me with my research, were Brendan and Jenny Meegan, who travelled to check sources in Bunbeg, where Brendan was able to photograph the plaque to Lord George in Bunbeg's Church of Ireland church. It is also to Brendan that I owe the photograph of Ballyare (now Ballyarr) House, the Knight sisters' last home.

I must thank my sister Anne, my sister-in-law Sheelagh and my brothers Shane and Edward, with their families, for their extra support during the period of illness which held back the book's progress in 2008. I cannot begin to thank my children, John and Judith, for all they have done and continue to do for me: nonetheless, I do. The book is dedicated to the memory of my eldest brother, Séamus (1944–1987), and my mother, Anne Judith (1915–2010), to whom I owe my lifelong delight in the novels of Jane Austen.

INTRODUCTION

Daughters of the House

'A single woman, with a very narrow income, must be a ridiculous, disagreeable, old maid! the proper sport of boys and girls; but a single woman, of good fortune, is always respectable, and may be as sensible and pleasant as anybody else.'

EMMA

In an upper room of a house in an English village, inside a glass case, sits a small pair of white satin dancing slippers. The house, in the village of Chawton in Hampshire, was the last home of Jane Austen, and the slippers belonged to her niece, Marianne, who would be the last person to record first-hand memories of the author. She is remembered on a stained-glass window in St Nicholas' Church in Chawton, yet Marianne is not buried there. Far across the Irish Sea, in a deserted hilltop graveyard in the windswept county of Donegal, an almost forgotten headstone, overgrown with nettles and wild flowers, marks the place where this English gentlewoman was laid to rest. How did Marianne Austen, and her two younger sisters, Louisa and Cassandra Jane, come to be buried so far from the genteel English household of their birth? In the lives of the three sisters, known in the family as May, Lou and Cass, the plots of Jane Austen's extraordinary novels were echoed to an uncanny degree, with shades of *Persuasion*, *Pride and Prejudice* and *Sense and Sensibility* permeating their real lives. Yet, some of what befell the Knight sisters was beyond even the realm of their aunt's extensive imagination.

Born on 15 September 1801, Marianne Austen was the seventh child of eleven, and third daughter to Jane's second brother Edward. By the time of her death in Ireland in 1895, she had become Marianne Knight. Like Jane Austen, however, she was never married. Her change in surname came about through her father's adoption of the name on his inheritance of the estate of a distant relative. Marianne, known to her family as 'Aunt May', would outlive all of her generation. In that little churchyard at the top of a hill in Donegal, Ireland's most northerly county, she rests beside her younger sister Louisa, one headstone listing towards the other. A few miles away, in the market town of Letterkenny, is the grave of their youngest sister of all, Cassandra Jane.

Yet, in the lives and letters of these overlooked women, dismissively recorded on one Austen family tree as 'three others, Knights of Chawton', there is a story which provides a unique link between the Regency world of England so wittily and economically delineated by Jane Austen, and that of turbulent nineteenth-century Ireland.[1] The Knight sisters lived through Ireland's Great Famine of 1845–47 and the subsequent Land Wars of the closing decades of the century. By the time Marianne died in 1895, the Victorian era was coming to a close and Ireland was within twenty years of the uprising in 1916 which would signal the end of its link with the British Empire.

At the time of Jane's death in 1817, the girls were still young and, although some commentators have therefore doubted the veracity of their memories, there is no doubt that they had every opportunity to spend time with their aunt. They played with her as children, sewed and read with her as young girls and, within their trusted circle, recorded their unique memories.[2] Moreover, she observed them astutely and quite without sentiment, as her letters to her sister Cassandra show. In 1808, arriving to visit the family, she sent this unvarnished report of her sister-in-law Elizabeth and her then five youngest children – Lizzy, Marianne, Charles, Louisa and Cassandra Jane – all under nine years old:

> I cannot praise Elizabeth's looks, but they are probably affected by a cold. Her little namesake has gained in beauty in the last three years, though not all that Marianne has lost. Charles is not quite so lovely as he was. Louisa is much as I expected, and Cassandra I find handsomer than I expected, though at present disguised by such a violent breaking-out that she does not come down after dinner. She has charming eyes and a nice open countenance, and seems likely to be very lovable. Her size is magnificent.[3]

Jane's sister-in-law Elizabeth was a beautiful and well-born woman, and the devoted mother of eleven children. In that quick pen-picture of 1808, perhaps rather enjoying the temporary loss of her sister-in-law's looks to a cold, Jane assesses her family with a clinical detachment, anticipating her portraits of the young Gardiners in *Pride and Prejudice*, the Bertrams in *Mansfield Park*, and Mary Musgrove's unruly little boys in *Persuasion*. Edward, though not the only brother to provide her with nieces and nephews to observe, was the only one to present her, from 1793 onwards, with such a large number of useful models and, even more importantly, to give her the opportunity to see at first hand how the landed gentry and their aristocratic connections lived from day to day.

With her sister Cassandra, Jane made regular visits to their brother's estate at Godmersham Park in Kent after he took possession of it in 1798. From 1808 onward, Edward and his family often spent the spring and summer months at his second home in Chawton, where he allowed his sisters and mother to live after 1809. There, Jane saw May, Lou and Cass grow out of babyhood, and shared with them some of the most vivid experiences of the last extraordinary eight years of her life, the time of her greatest productivity and the very beginning of her fame. Louisa, born in 1804, received extra attentions as Jane's goddaughter. She was named in the will Jane made in the final months of her life, and a needlecase specially made for her, wrapped in a paper inscribed 'With Aunt Jane's love', was so carefully kept that it can be seen today, exhibited alongside Marianne's dancing slippers.[4] Louisa's younger sister Cassandra, suffering a painful illness at eight and a half, received particular praise for her fortitude from her dying aunt. Marianne was not quite sixteen at the time of Jane Austen's death. By then, although Jane had not been impressed with her looks when she was seven years old, May's dark eyes and slight build reminded her uncle James Austen's family most poignantly of their loss, and inspired in Jane's future first biographer, Marianne's cousin James Edward, even deeper feelings.[5] In temperament, too, they had much in common, and Marianne was known in the family for her merry, lively wit and even temper. Throughout her long life, she had need of those qualities, for the greatest resemblance between Marianne Knight and Jane Austen may have lain not in a physical similarity, but in their powers of endurance and patience. As an unmarried woman, like her aunt Jane, Marianne lived from early adulthood on the edges of other people's lives and found herself, through circumstances largely beyond her control, as uncertain of a place to live as her namesake Marianne in *Sense and Sensibility*.

In one way, the course of May, Lou and Cass's lives was dictated by the changing times in which they lived. Even as Jane Austen lay dying, and the girls were still in the schoolroom, the Georgian world into which they had all been born, and for which they were assiduously prepared, was already disappearing. The Knight sisters, like their aunt, knew well and observed carefully the rules of mannered Georgian society where, as Amanda Vickery has observed, 'a gentlewoman's honour lay in the public recognition of her virtue, a gentleman's in the reliability of his word'.[6] In many ways, it was a very comfortable environment in which to grow up: the girls knew no want or deprivation, lived in delightful surroundings on the great estate of Godmersham, and were as well-educated as any other young ladies of their station. They were schooled not only in languages, music, dancing and art, but also in the nuances of polite behaviour. Propriety was everything, and a subtle code was learned: for all their privilege and position, they were to show courtesy to all, in whatever station in life, until or unless the rules by which they lived were breached. Edward Knight's daughters understood that their brothers would inherit, or serve their country in the army, navy or Church: the responsibilities of the daughters of the house were to guard their honour, respect their parents, nurture any members of the family requiring care and, if possible, make prudent marriages with gentlemen in a similar stratum of society. Following the battle of Waterloo in 1815, however, as Stella Tillyard observes, 'the prevailing tone of the age' was 'conservative, cautious and evangelical'.[7] Yet, there were good reasons for the change in the tone of the age:

> Everything that happened in the second decade of the nineteenth century must be set against the background of the French revolution and the wars to which it gave rise. The growth of evangelicalism, the changes in morality and in the nation's self-definition were all, in large part, reactions to a

notion of Frenchness and revolutionary France that Britain, or
more particularly, England, wished to define itself against.[8]

Certainly, the revolution in France in 1789, and that in America thirteen
years before, had rocked the certainties of the late eighteenth century. The
Austens were personally touched by the French revolution when the Comte
de Feuillide, husband of Jane's cousin Eliza, was executed on the guillotine;
and they suffered anxiety over Henry Austen's serving under Cornwallis in
Ireland during 1799, following what has been described as that country's
'forceful pacification'.[9] Henry never forgot the experience, and it may have
been his account of the country which made Jane so wary of Ireland that
she advised her niece Anna, daughter of her eldest brother James, not to
attempt to write about it. She knew nothing of the place or its ways, Jane told
her, and might give a false impression. How strange Jane Austen might have
found it to think of three others of her nieces making their way to live on that
incomprehensible island, where French ideas of liberty fired the imagination
not only of the poor and downtrodden, but also of members of the aristocracy
and the landed gentry. She might have been more puzzled still to learn that
the children of convicted rebels, prepared to attempt the overthrow of the
British establishment, would be the trusted friends of her family in Ireland.

By the mid-nineteenth century, little remained of life as the Georgians
had known it. Where Jane Austen's brothers had fought in the Napoleonic
wars, their sons and nephews would be called upon to fight for the Empire
as far away as the Crimea and India. Accepted levels of status in society were
to be challenged: marches and demonstrations, demands for greater parity
from the disgruntled, dissident or dispossessed would alarm the Knights of
Godmersham, especially when such upheavals affected their source of income,
or threatened the well-being of family members. Yet, none of it – the Peterloo
massacre, the rise of Chartism, the debate over Catholic Emancipation –
would prove as frustrating or as baffling as the struggle to understand what
was happening in Ireland. The Act of Union of Great Britain and Ireland,
with which the new century began, did not bring an end to rebellion and
discontent in Ireland. If anything, it signalled a new and more militant era.
'The abolition of the Irish parliament,' as Matthew Kelly has pointed out,

'earned the Ascendancy a stay of execution rather than a reprieve. Much of its direct political power had gone at a stroke; later reform legislation ... saw the bases of Ascendancy social and economic power wither away.'[10] Given her family's experiences, Jane Austen was quite justified in a certain wariness about this neighbouring island.

Yet, the fact that her three nieces did, for their different reasons, decide to live there made events in Ireland of paramount importance to the family. Failures of the harvest and consequent famine; insurrections and evictions; land acts and Home Rule debates became, as the century progressed, of increasing interest. Though the Knight sisters' lives were to present them with situations and circumstances uncannily close to those imagined by their aunt, theirs is ultimately a story which Jane Austen, determined as she was to keep her novels to tales of 'two or three country families in a village', might well have decided to leave alone. What they witnessed was, as she would have been the first to acknowledge, quite beyond her experience: Ireland could never be England, and England was what she and her family knew.

The extraordinary stories of these daughters of the house speak to the grace, courage and compassion instilled in them by their Georgian upbringing, and by the rare privilege of having Jane Austen as their aunt and early teacher. The values they learned in childhood at Godmersham and Chawton were to stand to all three, in their long years of exile in Ireland.

CHAPTER 1

'EVERYBODY IS RICH THERE'

Jane Austen and the Knights of Godmersham
1779–1817

Children of the same family, the same blood, with the same first associations
and habits, have some means of enjoyment in their power, which no
subsequent connections can supply.

MANSFIELD PARK

From the distance of two hundred years and considering her acknowledged
greatness as a writer, it may be difficult to appreciate that Jane Austen was a
single woman for whom a place in the family had to be found. The younger
daughter and seventh of eight children born to the Reverend George Austen
and his wife Cassandra Leigh, Jane had no money of her own. Her sister
Cassandra had the benefit of a small legacy from the fiancé who had died
before they could be married, and her mother had a small allowance.[1] Jane,
however, never knew wealth or lasting security in her adult life, and even fame,
which she did not seek, came only in the last few years before her death. Yet,
with access to her father's library in the Rectory of Steventon in Hampshire
where she grew up, with guidance from him and her scholarly brother James,
and piano lessons from the organist at nearby Winchester Cathedral, Jane
wanted for nothing. She could have said, with Elizabeth Bennet: 'We were
always encouraged to read, and had all the masters that were necessary.'[2] Her
nephew James Edward would later consider her 'not highly accomplished
according to the present standard', yet his daughter, Mary Augusta Austen
Leigh, believed that she was most accomplished, if self-deprecating.[3]

    This contented childhood at Steventon was interrupted only by an
interlude at boarding school, where her parents made the curious decision

to send her, at the age of six, with Cassandra. Jane almost died when 'putrid fever', the illness so vividly attributed to Marianne Dashwood in *Sense and Sensibility*, broke out at their first school. Surprisingly, this did not prevent her parents from sending both girls to yet another school in nearby Reading, from which they did not return until Jane was eleven years old. Yet, giving them an education may have been a matter of simple expediency to provide the girls with the means of earning a living. Neither their father, on the limited means of a clergyman, nor their mother, despite a well-connected family which included the Master of Balliol College, Oxford, could provide any guarantee of an inheritance, or even of a permanent home.[4] George Austen had been fortunate in winning a scholarship to university. He took his degree at St John's College, Oxford; his sons, James and Henry, would be enabled to attend the same university because of their mother's descent from one of the original benefactors of the college.[5] No such provision could be made for a girl, however bright. If she did not marry well, or earn her living by another means, she would be poor throughout her life. With considerable strength of will Jane, like her heroine Elizabeth Bennet, declined at least one offer of a comfortable marriage from Mr Harris Bigg-Wither whom, though he was a neighbour and the brother of a dear friend, she could not love.[6] As a consequence, it was only during the last eight years of her life, when Edward allowed his mother and sisters to live in what had been the bailiff's cottage at Chawton, that she had any security of tenure.

Edward was, within his own limits, a kindly brother to his sisters and mother. Sadly, it was by no means unusual, as *Sense and Sensibility* demonstrates, for brothers inheriting under the prevailing custom of primogeniture to overlook the unmarried or otherwise superannuated female members of their families. Indeed, for Marianne Knight, Edward's own third daughter and seventh of his eleven children, the position of the single woman without fortune meant that dependent status continued until she died, despite the fact that she devoted over half her life to the care of her father and his household, and most of the rest to the care of her brothers. In her ninetieth year she would find herself profoundly grateful to her nephew Montagu Knight for the offer of a 'refuge for [her] old age'.[7] For her, as for Jane, everything depended on the decision of one of the men in the family.

At Marianne's birth in 1801, however, this circumstance of her life could not have been anticipated. Her father, Edward Austen, was uniquely favoured among his siblings through his adoption by rich, childless relatives. His good fortune would not seem out of place in fiction and, indeed, a similar device was used by his sister to explain the case of Frank Churchill in her novel, *Emma*. A distant cousin, Thomas Knight of Kent, the benefactor who owned the living, or parish, of Steventon which George Austen held, married Catherine Knatchbull in May 1779. On their wedding journey, calling to the Rectory at Steventon to introduce the bride to the groom's cousins, they met and were so taken with the young Edward, who was then twelve, that they brought him with them on the rest of their journey and, when the family had almost forgotten the incident, surprisingly proposed to make him their heir. Two years after his marriage, Thomas Knight inherited the large estate of Godmersham Park, 'a handsome Palladian mansion ... about eight miles from Canterbury and set in a landscaped park in the Stour valley with wooded downland rising behind it'.[8] It was shortly afterwards that the proposal to adopt Edward was made, as Jane's brother Henry remembered:

> A letter arrived from Godmersham begging that little Edward might be allowed to spend his holydays there — and proposing to send for him. His Father was not however inclined to consent to Mr Knight's request, looking only to the consequences of so many weeks' idleness, and a probably falling behind in the Latin Grammar — but while he hesitated a few simple words from his Wife gently turned the scale — 'I think, my Dear, you had better oblige your cousins, and let the Child go' — And accordingly go he did ... Edward Austen returned from Godmersham ostensibly as much Edward Austen as ever, & remained for some years as such under the care of his natural Parents — By degrees however, it came to be understood in the family that Edward was selected from amongst themselves as the adopted son & heir of Mr Knight; and in further course of time he was taken more entire possession of, & sent to study in some German university.[9]

Edward seems to have joined the Knights as their formally adopted son in 1783. What his own feeling may have been is not recorded. His mother's shrewd assessment of him was that he was 'quite a man of Business', with 'an active mind, a clear head, & a sound judgement', suggesting a temperament well-suited to his new situation. To 'Classical Knowledge, Literary Taste, and the power of elegant composition,' she added, with the same detachment which induced her to urge her husband to give up their young son, 'he makes no pretentions'.[10] To the Austens, just as boarding school had been best for their little girls, this was the best provision they could make for their second son.

After a gentleman's education, including the then mandatory Grand Tour of Europe, Edward married in 1791, at the age of twenty-four. His bride, Elizabeth Bridges, then in her eighteenth year, was the daughter of a baronet, Sir Brook Bridges of Goodnestone Park, near Sandwich. The Bridges were an established family in Kent; following his adoption, Edward was considered an eligible prospect and was described by Elizabeth's mother, Lady Bridges, as 'a very sensible, amiable young man'.[11] In 1797, his fortunes rose further when his adopted mother invited him to move to Godmersham, proposing that she live in a smaller house in Canterbury.[12] Edward was reluctant at first, fearing that Mrs Knight would miss the home he knew she loved, and adding that he did not want her to make this sacrifice 'to enrich us'. With great fondness, she insisted. 'From the time that my partiality for you induced Mr Knight to treat you as our adopted child I have felt for you the tenderness of a mother,' she wrote, 'and never have you appeared more deserving of affection than at this time'.[13] Catherine Knight prevailed; Edward and his young family moved from their first Kent home at Rowlings to Godmersham in 1798, while his adopted mother, taking an income of £2,000 a year, retired as she had intended to Canterbury.

In a letter written to her elder sister Cassandra in early 1799, Jane Austen commented with characteristic irony on Mrs Knight's gesture:

> I am tolerably glad to hear that Edward's income is so good a one — as glad as I can at anybody's being rich besides You & me ... Mrs Knight giving up the Godmersham estate to Edward was no prodigious act of Generosity after all, it seems, for she has reserved herself an income out of it still; this ought to be

known, that her conduct may not be overrated. I rather think
Edward shows the most magnanimity of the two, in accepting
her Resignation with such Incumbrances ... [14]

The birth in 1793 of Edward and Elizabeth's first child, Fanny Catherine,
was followed the next year by that of her brother Edward, then by George
(1795) and Henry (1797). The family continued to grow following the
move to Godmersham, where William (1798), Elizabeth (1800), Marianne
(1801), Charles (1803), Louisa (1804), Cassandra Jane (1806) and finally
Brook John (1808) were born. The family naturally divided between the
five oldest children and the five youngest ones, whose natural leader
was Marianne. Elizabeth, or Lizzy, was the child in the middle: she
was close to Marianne, but also accepted as one of the older group.
    As Cassandra Austen was in regular demand to help her sister-in-
law at the time of her confinements, frequent opportunities arose for Jane
to observe the Godmersham life, and although she was not as popular
with Elizabeth as Cassandra, she was invited if her sister was unavailable.
Among the older boys, an early favourite was George, or 'Dordy' as he
styled himself when a child. 'My dear itty Dordy's remembrance of me is
very pleasing to me,' she wrote to Cassandra in 1798, 'foolishly pleasing,
because I know it will be over so soon. My attachment to him will be more
durable; I shall think with tenderness & delight on his beautiful and smiling
countenance & interesting Manners, till a few years have turned him into
an ungovernable, ungracious fellow.'[15] Time was to bear out her prophecy:
in the meantime, though occasionally tired by the sheer exuberance of the
growing boys and lively little girls, she continued to be involved with them,
learning to know them individually by entertaining and providing home
comforts for her nephews on their way to and from school at Winchester,
and spending time with her nieces at home. Writing to her sister Cassandra
during a visit to their cousins, the Cages, in late August 1805, she remarked:

> I have asked Sophie [Cage] if she has anything to say to Lizzy
> in acknowledgement of the little bird, and her message is that,
> with her love, she is very glad Lizzy sent it. She volunteers,

moreover, her love to little Marianne, with the promise of bringing her a doll next time she goes to Godmersham.[16]

As she approached her fourth birthday, dolls were favourite playthings of Marianne's: Jane's bond with her nieces and nephews was forged by her noticing, appreciating and remembering what each of the eleven was interested in, however briefly the interest lasted, and by her ability to keep up the acquaintance through letters and personal messages.

If, however, a little distance existed between the Austen sisters and their brother Edward's family it may have been because their economic circumstances were so very different. Edward alone had had the good fortune to be made wealthy and independent. His brothers, with the exception of his older brother, George Austen, were fortunate enough to have the benefit of university education, with its guaranteed entry to the professions, or to enter the navy and rise to distinction there, but they did not achieve the social *cachet* he enjoyed.[17] By contrast, his two unmarried sisters and his mother lived an almost nomadic existence after the Reverend George Austen retired in 1801, moving first to Bath and then, after his death, to Southampton. For Jane those years were less than happy; she found it difficult to settle and, with the notable exception of the tantalising fragment later known as *The Watsons*, almost impossible to work on her novels. 'Everybody who comes to Southampton finds it either their duty or pleasure to call upon us,' she wrote in 1808, with a certain weary resignation, to Cassandra at Godmersham.[18] There seemed little possibility of any material change in their circumstances until Edward made over to them the small house in the village of Chawton, not far from Steventon where Jane had been so happy. Jane loved the Chawton house almost immediately and, whatever she may have thought, voiced no envy of her brother's good fortune. Yet, as Claire Tomalin notes in her biography, the difference in their situations was so marked that the hairdresser who attended the Knight ladies automatically offered Jane a reduced rate, 'so obviously did she appear a poor relative'.[19] Her dry remark to Cassandra, however, soon after Edward's removal to Godmersham in 1798: 'People get so horridly poor & economical in this part of the World, that I have no patience with them. — Kent is the only place for happiness. Everybody is rich there,' may indicate more in its ironic understatement than a catalogue of complaints.[20] The Austen women were not well-off: after her father's death, and the cessation of his income, Jane and her mother and sister were left in reduced circumstances, their mother having only £210 per year, slightly more than one tenth of the income enjoyed by Edward's wealthy adopted mother, Catherine Knight. Among the Austen brothers, however, an arrangement was made: Henry, Francis and James agreed that each would give their mother £50 per year. Edward offered to contribute £100. Their mother now had £460 per year, which, while not wealth, and still very far from Mrs Knight's £2,000, was not poverty.[21]

Jane's wariness was to soften into appreciation of Catherine Knight's kindness, especially when, in the spirit of a patron, she gave her money on a regular basis, which Jane was very happy to accept: 'This morning brought me a letter from Mrs Knight, containing the usual Fee, & all the usual Kindness,' she wrote to Cassandra in the summer of 1808. 'She asks me to spend a day or two with her this week ... and I believe I shall go. — ... Her very agreeable present will make my circumstances quite easy. I shall reserve half for my Pelisse.'[22] They even came to share certain jokes, like the longstanding fiction that Jane was on the point of marrying the Rector of Chawton, the perpetually single Mr Papillon.[23]

While Catherine Knight's friendship and patronage made it easier for Jane Austen to follow her vocation, it may be that Edward's wife, Elizabeth, was less than encouraging to her younger sister-in-law.[24] James's daughter Anna had, like her Godmersham cousins, many opportunities to observe her aunts and other relatives; she had been sent to Steventon at the age of two for an extended stay after the death of her mother in 1795, and maintained close contact thereafter. She thought Edward's wife Elizabeth 'a very lovely woman, highly educated, though not I imagine of much natural talent. Her tastes were domestic,' she said, 'her affections strong, though exclusive, and her temper calculated to make Husband and children happy in their home'.[25] Where Cassandra and Jane were concerned, she believed that the former Elizabeth Bridges was not especially fond of Jane, distrusting her creativity, because 'a little talent went a long way with the Goodnestone Bridgeses of that period, & *much* must have gone a long way too far'. It may be that Elizabeth's 'strong, though exclusive' affections did not extend to Jane, or Jane's to her.[26]

Whether Anna was correct in her judgement or not, there is no doubt that Edward's children, though apparently unspoiled, enjoyed the comforts of a landed gentleman's family, which the Austens had not. Like the young Austens before them, however, they enjoyed games and theatricals, as Fanny described in a letter of January 1806 to her former governess, Miss Chapman:

> On Twelfth day we were all agreeably surprised with a sort of masquerade, all being dress'd in character, and then we were conducted into the library, which was all lighted up and at one end a throne, surrounded with a grove of Orange Trees, and other shrubs, and all this was totally unknown to us all! Was it not delightful? I should have liked you very much to have been of the party. Now I will tell you our different characters. Edward and I were a Shepherd King and Queen; Mama a Savoyarde with a Hurdy-Gurdy; Marianne and William her children with a Tambourine and Triangle; Papa and Aunt Louisa — Sir Bertram and Lady Beadmasc one hundred years old — Uncle H. Austen — a Jew; Uncle E — a Jewess; Miss Sharpe — a Witch; Elizabeth — a flowergirl; Sophia — a fruitgirl; Fanny Cage — a Haymaker; George— Harlequin; Henry — clown; and Charley a Cupid! Was it not a good one for him, sweet fellow! He had a little pair of wings and a bow and arrow! And looked charming.[27]

Fanny's vignette gives a charming glimpse of the family over two years before Jane described them so dispassionately, in the summer of 1808. Fanny, who would one day dismiss her aunt Jane as unrefined, was, in January 1806, a carefree child of almost thirteen; her brother Edward, who would later sell off the family home, an eleven-year-old boy. Their mother, Elizabeth, a full participant in the revelry, was already the mother of nine children, and would in November of that year give birth to Cassandra Jane, always known as Cassandra or, within the family, as Cass. William, carrier of the triangle, seven years old, would be one of only two members of the family to accompany Jane Austen on her last journey to Winchester in 1817. The flower girl Lizzy, almost six, and nearly two years older than Marianne with her tambourine, would come out in society the year Jane Austen died, and marry the following year, aged just eighteen. Little Charley, their Cupid, not yet three, would visit his aunt Jane in her last days at Winchester and would provide, as the Reverend Charles Austen of Chawton, a refuge for Marianne in the middle of her life.

No part seems to have been assigned on that happy Christmas to Louisa, Jane's goddaughter, then just over a year old. Yet, although she was not included in the pageant of January 1806, an impression of the infant Louisa has survived. Fanny describes her in her diaries as 'very pretty' with 'beautiful black eyes'. She was, however, a noisy child, which may explain her exclusion, as may her complete lack of inhibition: when Charles tried to say his prayers, Fanny wrote: 'He kneels down and she does too, gabbling all the time, quite naked.'[28] It is also worth noting the presence at the 1806 Twelfth Day party Edward's brother, 'Uncle H. Austen'. Henry Austen, Jane's favourite brother, had been posted with his regiment to Ireland in 1799, in the wake of the unsuccessful rising of the United Irishmen.[29] He so relished the occupation of Paymaster, and the company of such powerful figures as Lord Cornwallis, that he decided to go into banking with some of his regimental friends, and persuaded his family to invest in a bank at Alton in Hampshire. The collapse of this venture would prove to be the cause of great financial loss to his brother Edward.[30] Years later, Marianne would refer back to this collapse which, despite their good fortune in living at Godmersham, would leave all of the family with greatly reduced prospects.[31]

Although nobody could have guessed it at the time of that party in January 1806, the family's happiest days together were coming to a close. Elizabeth Austen, in her thirty-third year, seemed healthy: she gave birth without incident to Cassandra Jane later that year. Jane's letter to her sister Cassandra, yet again in attendance at Godmersham, reveals a certain amused weariness with the seemingly endless business of babies and their care:

> I really have very little to say this week & do not feel as if I
> should spread that little into the shew of much. I am inclined

for short sentences. Mary [their sister-in law, Mrs Francis Austen] will be obliged to you to take notice how often Eliz'th nurses her baby in the course of the 24 hours, how often it is fed & with what; — you need not trouble yourself to write the results of your observations, Your return will be early enough for the communication of them. — [32]

Despite Jane's lack of interest in the details, Elizabeth was undoubtedly a good mother to her children. A letter written to Lizzy from Chawton in September 1807, when Elizabeth and her husband went with Fanny and William to see Edward off to school at Winchester, makes it clear not only that Elizabeth disliked Chawton Great House, but also that she missed and was thinking with tenderness of her youngest children. She gives a clear picture of the children, as she saw them, and of Marianne, 'poor little May', in particular. She was not quite six, and nervous at her first experience on horseback, yet so quick with letters that Elizabeth could advise Lizzy, more than a year and a half Marianne's elder, to seek her help in deciphering their mother's handwriting.

You cannot think how much I miss you all. The house is quite dull & melancholy, & it appears already a long time since I have seen any of you. My little darling Cassandra, I am afraid she will forget me, I hope you talk to her of Mama sometimes that she may be accustomed to the sound, sweet Angel! How I long to kiss her fat soft neck and her little sweet lips. I am very glad she has cut another tooth, & I hope she will have four by the time I return home, & not look quite so pale as she did. How happy you must have been riding ... I should have liked to have seen you very much, I suppose you did not venture to trot or canter, but you will another time, so poor little May was afraid! I am not much surprised at it, as it was the first time ... This house is very cold and dreary, but it would be very comfortable if it was well filled with Children, their playing and prattling would enliven us very much. We all Breakfast together at half-past nine o'clock, your Brothers then go out; & amuse themselves generally with a nice little green Chaise which Edward gets into & William stands up behind, then they guide it down the hills as fast as they can, & enjoy it extremely, they have got a Trap, Bat and Ball, likewise. Wm. comes in about 12 and does a few lessons, afterwards he takes a walk with Fanny & me, whilst Papa and Edward ride, we dine at ½ past 4, walk in the evening, drink tea at 8 or before, and your Brothers generally go to bed soon after, not knowing what to do besides. I thought you should like to know how we pass our time, we shall soon have a little variety, for today your Grandmamma, and your Aunts Cassandra & Jane come to us which we shall like very much. I am afraid, my darling, you will not be much amused by this letter, for I am not in spirits to be entertaining. If you cannot read it, you must ask Marianne to help you, I know she is a clever little thing in reading letters, you must give her a great many loves and kisses from me, likewise my little angels, Charles, Louisa and Cassandra. Oh, how I wish you were all here, that I might kiss you myself, dear sweet little loves ... [33]

Whatever Elizabeth's true opinion of her sister-in-law may have been, or Jane's of her, they had Edward and the children in common, and maintained at all times the appearance of warmth. The Godmersham children were always glad to see their aunt, as Jane describes in an account of her welcome in June 1808. Elizabeth was expecting her child in November, and Jane was to bridge the gap soon to be left by the retirement of the girls' governess, Miss Anne Sharp, who would become instead a companion in the household, and a lifelong friend to Jane. 'Fanny and Lizzy met us in the hall with a great deal of pleasant joy,' she wrote. 'Elizabeth, who was dressing when we arrived, came to me for a minute attended by Marianne, Charles, and Louisa, and, you will not doubt, gave me a very affectionate welcome ...' Fanny was then very close to Jane who, while wholeheartedly trying to help her sister-in-law with the care of the exuberant children, was not above attempting to discover through her guileless niece any hint of a lack of enthusiasm on the part of Elizabeth.

'I cannot discover,' she wrote with what may have been mild disappointment, 'even through Fanny, that her mother is fatigued by her attendance on the children. I have, of course, tendered my services, and when Louisa [Bridges, the children's maternal aunt] is gone, who sometimes hears the little girls read, will try to be accepted in her stead. She will not be here many days longer ...'[34]

As intended, Jane took on some of the work of the children, hearing their reading, supervising their handwork and trying to make allowances for a lessening of her goddaughter's earlier prettiness: 'Louisa is not so handsome as I expected,' she wrote to Cassandra, 'but she is not quite well'. Before long, no one was quite well: the whole household came down with heavy colds, and Lizzy was in danger of being very ill 'with specks and a great deal of fever'.[35] Jane became homesick by the end of June and, as soon as the children were well enough recovered, she hoped to go back to Chawton. For the time remaining, she planned to 'eat Ice & drink French wine, & be above Vulgar Economy'. Homesick or not, she did not underestimate the luxuries available to her only at Godmersham. Jane had no qualms, however, about leaving Godmersham, for there was no suggestion that anything about Elizabeth's pregnancy was unusual. In fact, when she left in early July 1808, Jane wrote that her sister-in-law was 'considered ... more than usually active for her situation and size'.[36] In the autumn, Cassandra travelled to Godmersham to help Elizabeth with the birth of the expected child. In the end, despite all the careful preparation, the birth took place before Cassandra arrived, which amused Jane:

> Your letter this morning was quite unexpected, & it is well that it brings such good news, to counterbalance the disappointment to me of losing my first sentence, which I had arranged full of proper hopes about your Journey ... — We are extremely glad to hear of the birth of the Child, & trust everything will proceed as well as it begins; — his Mama has our best wishes, & he our second best for health & comfort — tho I suppose unless he has our best too, we do nothing for her. —We are glad it was all over before your arrival.[37]

The new baby, a healthy boy christened Brook John, and known ever afterwards as John, or Johnny, was born on 28 September 1808. His mother seemed so well, that Cassandra had less to do than expected. Like her sister, she made herself useful by hearing the children's lessons. 'Pray tell my little Goddaughter,' wrote Jane, 'that I am delighted to hear of her saying her lesson so well' and, a week later, she wrote to Cassandra with affection of her eldest niece, Fanny:

> I am greatly pleased with your account of Fanny; I found her in the summer just what you describe, *almost another Sister*, & could not have supposed that a niece could ever have been so much to me. She is quite after one's own heart; give her my best Love, & tell her that I always think of her with pleasure.[38]

This was to be the last time Fanny would ever be considered by anyone as a carefree young girl. On Monday, 10 October 1808, when little John was less than a fortnight old, Elizabeth Austen died unexpectedly. She seemed to have nothing more serious than a cold which, as the whole family had struggled with one throughout the summer, did not cause undue distress. No one suspected that she was suffering from puerperal fever, whose early symptoms resembled those of the common cold. 'Oh! The miserable events of this day!' wrote the distraught Fanny, in her journal. 'My mother, my beloved mother torn from us! After eating a hearty dinner, she was taken *violently* ill and expired (May God have mercy upon us) in ½ an hour!!!!'[39] Poor Fanny's literal description, with its incongruous description of the 'hearty dinner' and its many exclamation marks, underlines the fact that she was only fifteen years old and, like the rest of the household, in deep shock.

Help was soon at hand and two days later, Henry Austen arrived. The two eldest boys, Edward and George, were taken to stay with their uncle James at Steventon, and arrangements were made for the funeral on the following Monday, 17 October. Jane received the news from her sister two days after Elizabeth's death. She wrote the next morning of her shock and distress, her novelist's mind fully picturing the scene, and her attachment to the children clear, not only in her imaginative concern, but also in her sincere wish to look after Edward and George herself:

> I have received your letter, & with most melancholy anxiety was it expected, for the sad news reach'd us last night, but without any particulars; ... — We have felt, we do feel for you all — as you will not need to be told — for you, for Fanny, for Henry, for Lady Bridges, & for dearest Edward, whose loss and whose sufferings seem to make those of every other person nothing — God be praised! That you can say what you do of him — that he has a religious Mind to bear him up, & a Disposition that will gradually lead him to comfort. — My dear, dear Fanny! — I am so thankful that she has you with her! — You will be everything to her, you will give her all the consolation that human aid can give. — May the Almighty sustain you all —& keep you my dearest Cassandra well — but for the present I dare say you are equal to everything — You will know that the poor Boys are at Steventon, perhaps it is best for them, as they will have more means of exercise and amusement there than they cd have with us, but I own myself disappointed with the arrangement; — I should have loved to have them with me at such a time.[40]

In 1808, Edward Knight's older children were barely in their teens, yet his eldest daughter Fanny was immediately considered fit to be not only a substitute mother to her ten younger siblings, but also the mainstay of her widowed father. Jane herself, despite her compassion for the whole family, naturally assumed it. 'Edward's loss is terrible,' she wrote to Cassandra five days after Elizabeth's death, '& must be felt as such, & these are too early days indeed to think of Moderation in grief, either in him or his afflicted daughter — but soon we hope that our dear Fanny's sense of Duty to that beloved Father will rouse her to exertion. For his sake, & as the most acceptable proof of Love to the spirit of her departed Mother, she will try to be tranquil and resigned ...'[41] A stoic sense of duty, such as she herself had always shown, was expected even of the little girls: 'Your account of Lizzy,' she replied to Cassandra, 'is very interesting.

Poor Child! One must hope the impression will be strong, & yet one's heart aches for a dejected mind of eight years old.' Jane was equally unsentimental about the facts of death, and her query: 'I suppose you see the Corpse, —: how does it appear?' may seem surprising, or even heartless, today. The Georgians, however, were unsqueamish and entirely pragmatic about both birth and death, and it was their accepted custom to view the remains before the closing of the coffin. In addition, proper mourning dress had to be worn. As Jane had already remarked to Cassandra before her sister-in-law's death: 'we must turn our black pelisses into new, for Velvet is to be very much worn this winter.'[42] Now, following Elizabeth's death, she used her eye for detail to remodel their winter fashions into mourning attire:

> I shall send you such of your mourning as I think most likely to be useful, reserving for myself your stockings and half the velvet — in which selfish arrangement I know I am doing what you wish. — I am to be in Bombazeen and Crape, according to what we are told is universal here; ... My Mourning however will not impoverish me, for my having my velvet Pelisse fresh lined and made up, I am sure I shall have no occasion this winter for anything new of that sort.[43]

Yet, practical and even light-hearted as her discussion of her mourning clothes may seem, there can be no doubt of the depth of Jane's feelings for her brother in his loss:

> I see your mournful party in my mind's eye under every varying circumstance of the day; — & in the Evening specially, figure to myself its sad gloom — the efforts to talk — the frequent summons to melancholy orders & cares — & poor Edward restless in Misery going from one room to the other — & perhaps not seldom upstairs to see all that remains of his Elizabeth.[44]

Within a few days, Jane was able to give the help she had wished when Edward and George were brought from Steventon to join their aunt and grandmother in Southampton. Edward was fourteen and George, at thirteen, was no longer 'itty Dordy'. The boys were very cold and miserable when they arrived, having chosen to travel on the outside of the coach without overcoats. Jane showed great sensitivity and encouraged them to settle down, play games, draw, make models, and choose their own style of mourning. Above all, she encouraged them to express their grief in their individual ways:

> They behave extremely well in every respect, showing quite as much feeling as one wishes to see, and on every occasion speaking of their father with the liveliest affection. His letter was read over by each of them yesterday, and with many tears; George sobbed aloud, Edward's tears do not flow so easily; but as far as I can judge they are both very properly impressed by what has happened ... George is almost a new acquaintance to me, and I find him in a different way as engaging as Edward. We do not want amusement; bilbocatch, at which George is indefatigable, spillikins, papers ships, riddles, conundrums, and cards, with watching the ebb and flow of the river, and now and then a stroll out, keep us well employed; and we mean to avail ourselves of our kind papa's consideration, by not returning to Winchester till the evening of Wednesday... Edward has an old black coat, which will save his having a second new one; but I find that black pantaloons are considered by them as necessary, and of course would not have them made uncomfortable by the want of what is usual on such occasions.[45]

Meanwhile, at Godmersham, fifteen-year-old Fanny had begun her new role, comforting her father and undertaking the overall supervision of the household. Henry and William, who were eleven and ten would, like their older brothers, return to their schools after the funeral. The very youngest children, five-year-old Charles, Louisa, nearly four, Cassandra Jane who was not quite two and the newborn John had their nurse, Susan Sackree, known to the family as Cakey. It was still not clear, however, who should take charge of Lizzy and Marianne. In one letter to Cassandra, written during the first

Christmas following Elizabeth's death, Jane sent a special message to seven-year-old Marianne, who had thrown her energies into making a present for her mother's bereaved brother, John Bridges: 'Pray let Marianne know, in private,' she wrote, 'that I think she is quite right to work a rug for Uncle John's Coffee urn, & that I am sure it must give great pleasure to herself now, & to him when he receives it.'[46] Jane herself took great satisfaction in needlework, the only accomplishment to which she admitted, and she understood that an absorbing occupation, and a private word of encouragement, might go a little way to assuage her niece's grief.

Her letter of 24 January 1809, equally bright and encouraging, sends 'best Love to dear little Lizzy and Marianne in particular'.[47] She had a particular reason for sending special love to them, for a solution had been found to the problem of their education and Jane, with first-hand experience, was in a position to understand how they might now feel. Like Jane and Cassandra twenty-seven years earlier, the two little girls were about to be sent away, at seven and nine, to board at Mrs Boyce's School at Wanstead in Essex. They left home on a miserable day at the end of January, sixteen weeks after their mother's death, and Jane felt for them. 'Here is such a wet Day as never was seen,' she wrote to Cassandra. 'I wish the poor little girls had better weather for their Journey; they must amuse themselves with watching the raindrops down the Windows. Sackree I suppose feels quite broken hearted.'[48] Sackree was indeed broken hearted: after Lizzy and Marianne went away to school, she wrote a heartfelt expression of grief, not only at the plight of the motherless baby, but also at her own loss: 'What tears have I shed over this Darling Child Night and day and the parting with the dear Little Girls has been all most too much for me but all this avails nothing.'[49]

Tender-hearted Sackree was correct in her assessment: no amount of grief or complaint would change matters. Even Jane, while expressing compassion for her nieces, does not appear to have thought it unfair or unusual to send the little girls away so soon. It may have been because she and Cassandra had endured, and survived, a similar early exile. Always practical, she preferred to consider how they might make the best of the situation rather than dwell on its cause. Of all the adults, only Sackree seems to have thought it strange that they were sent away so young, despite their protests and those of Fanny.

No attempt to bring them home seems to have been made for some time, apparently because no new governess had been appointed. Fanny's diary and letters record her repeated attempts to find someone suitable to educate a gentleman's daughters, further emphasising the difference in social status between her family and that of Jane and Cassandra who, like the Bennet girls in *Pride and Prejudice*, had never expected to have a governess.

Fanny's diary also shows, however, that a regular correspondence was kept up with the children while they were at school. On 17 June 1809, she wrote: 'Sent a letter by Fox to Fanny Cage at Ospringe, where she went to fetch the dearest little Girls Elizabeth and Marianne & arrived here about 9 quite well & happy.'[50] Like their brothers, they came home for the summer holidays: the boys went back to Winchester in September and by October 1809, Fanny's diary records: 'Papa, Uncle H., Charles & I went to Wanstead saw the dear girls all well.'[51] It was not until the end of 1810 that Fanny noted, in her summary of the year: 'Lizzy & Mne. leaving school at Christmas.'[52] It was April 1811 before a suitable new governess, Miss Allen, was brought to Godmersham to take over their education. Her beginning was not auspicious: she was shy and disinclined to make conversation. She improved, gradually, so that even Jane and Cassandra thought she might do very well, and Jane began to be hopeful that she would stay for a whole year.[53] In fact, she stayed until November 1812 when, abruptly, she was gone. 'Miss Allen after much vile behaviour treated Liz. so ill that it was resolved she should go away on Wedy. next,' Fanny wrote, grimly.[54] It is not clear whether Miss Allen proved unequal to the task of teaching the little girls, or whether they made her life so difficult that she could not carry out her tasks. While it may be tempting to imagine prefigurings of *Jane Eyre* or *The Turn of the Screw*, it seems wise to remember Jane Austen's note of caution shortly after Miss Allen arrived in April 1811: 'By this time I suppose she is hard at it, governing away — poor creature! I pity her, tho' they are my nieces.'[55] Jane knew the real Marianne and Lizzy so, as usual, was devoid of any sentimental glossing over of facts; and it is quite possible that, having been away for so long, and still aged only nine and eleven, they were difficult to manage. In the end, unlike Jane and Cassandra, they were not sent away again, for in 1814 a Miss Clewes was appointed. She was described by Fanny as 'quite a treasure' and by Jane as 'the governess they have been looking for these ten years'. In the end, she stayed until 1820, when Louisa was nearly sixteen and Cassandra almost fourteen, and was greatly missed when she left.

While Lizzy and Marianne were still away at school, however, and Louisa, Charles, Cassandra and John were safely in the nursery with Sackree, other pressing matters needed attention. Catherine Knight, Edward's adopted mother, had made her will in November 1808, and its contents were to be significant to her granddaughters. Mrs Knight was already an important figure in Jane's life. She had, almost uniquely, recognised the difficulty of the young woman's decision to devote herself to her art and, unprompted, acted as her first and only patron. Now, she made a kind gesture towards the girls of her family or, as Jane mischievously described them, Edward's 'Harem'.[56] Under the terms of her will, while all her remaining property was to be divided among her brothers Charles and Wyndham Knatchbull, she left legacies specifically to her granddaughters. Fanny was to have the sum of £2,000, and each of the younger girls £1,000.[57] The little girls might have been sent away from home, but they did now have some money belonging only to them.

It was at this time that Edward addressed the question of providing a home for his mother and sisters. Since the death of the Reverend George Austen in Bath on 21 January 1805, their new lodgings in Southampton had been adequate but not ideal. Jane's brother Francis, well established in the navy, had been stationed in Southampton, but had left for the Isle of Wight, so that a move seemed appropriate for Mrs Austen and her daughters. Edward offered them the choice of either a house in Wye, near Godmersham, or the house which had belonged to his Chawton bailiff, recently dead. They chose Chawton because of its proximity to Alton, where Henry Austen had a branch of his bank, and because of its situation within twelve miles of James Austen, in the original family home at Steventon. The Chawton house was inspected by Henry, and found to Jane's relief to contain 'six bed-chambers ... [and] Garrets for store-places'.[58] James's daughter Caroline thought the house 'delightful to children ... [and] ... altogether a comfortable and ladylike establishment'.[59] Her elder sister Anna, however, thought the house rather small and inadequate, though she acknowledged that it became, under the care of her aunts and grandmother, 'if not all that their home might & should have been, ... [still] such as fully satisfied the moderate desire of one, who had no taste for luxury or worldly state, and lived besides in the happy belief that what was decreed by those she loved must be wisest.'⁶⁰ What Anna does not say is that Edward, who frequently made the big house at Chawton available to his brothers and their families, thought the house of one of his servants quite adequate for his mother and sisters, and that he did not provide even that until they had been without the security of a permanent home for some years.

Though they were very pleased at the prospect of the house, they could not move at once. Cassandra's stay at Godmersham extended well into the New Year, so that she could help Fanny take over the running of the house and then, in the spring, both she and Jane had to tend their mother when she fell ill. It was not until 7 July 1809 that the move to Chawton was finally made, yet it proved immediately successful. Jane had found it almost impossible to write since 1800 when, near her twenty-fifth birthday in December of that year, her father had made the sudden announcement that the family would be leaving Steventon within a week, that her brother James was to take over the parish and that James's family would from now on live in Steventon Rectory. Jane, who had known no other home, fainted at the news.⁶¹ It was a traumatic time for her: not only her father's library, but also her own precious books and pianoforte were sold. Though she entered into her father's plan for his retirement with proper filial compliance, she was almost silenced by the shock, and had little inclination to work on her novels in either Bath or Southampton.⁶² It is all the more remarkable, therefore, that within a month of arriving in Chawton she began to revise her early novel *Sense and Sensibility*, which would be accepted for publication in 1810. She then started to plan *Mansfield Park* in February 1811. By the winter of that year, she was revising another early work, *First Impressions*, published as *Pride and Prejudice* in January 1813, by which time she was half way through the writing of *Mansfield Park*. *Emma* was begun a year later, in January 1814, and *Mansfield Park* published in May of that year. In March 1815, *Emma* was finished, and *Persuasion* begun in August.

Throughout this extraordinary period of creativity, Jane was in regular contact with Edward's family who, after 1813, tended to spend their summers at Chawton rather than Godmersham. Edward, despite his preference for Godmersham, did not neglect the upkeep of Chawton, making structural alterations to both the Great House and the cottage from 1809 onward. 'Chawton is not thrown away upon him,' Jane told her brother Francis in July 1813.[63] Yet, his first visit had been less than successful, as Elizabeth had written in 1807 to seven-year-old Lizzy. Fanny had been equally unimpressed. She found the Great House a warren of unnavigable corridors and rooms, and could hardly wait to get back to Kent. No one was eager to repeat the visit and the fact that Edward and his children made increasingly extended visits to Chawton from 1809 may owe much to the presence there of his mother and sisters. For the years between 1808 and 1813, Edward rented out Chawton Great House to a family named Middleton. Unlike Edward and Fanny the Middletons had fond memories of Chawton. John Charles Middleton had a family of six who were, like Edward's younger children, aged between five and fifteen. He also brought with him, as housekeeper, his sister-in-law, Miss Maria Beckford. Miss Beckford frequently called on the Austen ladies, and her niece, Charlotte-Maria Middleton, played with any visiting cousins. Many years later Charlotte-Maria, by then married to her own cousin, the Reverend Charles Beckford, recorded her impressions of Chawton:

> Our house Chawton House was a very ancient affair — Dogs instead of grates & Tapestry instead of Paper. An immense Hall —, of course a haunted gallery which no Servant wd. Pass alone, — but it was a charming place — one wing was modernised for Comfort — There were Staircases which gave us much fun & many tumbles — as in those happy days we were 6 children — I alas now the only one to remember it ... [64]

She remembered Jane and Cassandra too, and gives a rare picture of Jane, with none of the prejudice or partiality of a relative, in this most creative period of her life. Charlotte-Maria felt an affinity with the writer and remarked on the difference between her ease with children and her distance with strangers, concluding in retrospect that such distance was a device that allowed her to make valuable mental notes for her novels:

We saw her often. She was a most kind & enjoyable person to *children* but somewhat stiff and cold to strangers. She used to sit at Table at Dinner parties without uttering much probably collecting matter for her charming novels which in those days we knew nothing about — her Sister Cassandra was very lady-like but *very prim*, but my remembrance of Jane is that of her entering into all Children's Games & liking her extremely — we were often asked to meet her young nephews & nieces [when they were] at *Chawton with them.*[65]

Her description accords with the memories of Caroline, James's younger daughter, who observed the pattern of her aunts' daily life at Chawton, and leaves a memorable picture of the lively companion the Godmersham children must have known in those years: ready to play games, absorbed in needlework, sociable within her family, yet equally meticulous in the work of her mind:

I don't believe Aunt Jane observed any particular method in parcelling out her day but I think she generally sat in the drawing room until luncheon; when visitors were there, chiefly at work — she was fond of work — and she was a great adept at overcast and satin stitch — the peculiar delight of that day — general handiness and neatness were amongst her characteristics — She could throw the spillikens for us, better than anyone else, and she was wonderfully successful at cup and ball — She found a resource sometimes in that simple game, when she suffered from weak eyes and could not work or read for long together — ... After luncheon, my Aunts generally walked out — sometimes they went to Alton for shopping — often, one or other of them, to the Great House — as it was then called — when a brother was inhabiting it, to make a visit — or if the house were standing empty they liked to stroll about the grounds — sometimes to Chawton Park — a noble beech wood, just within a walk — but sometimes, but that was rarely, to call on a neighbour — They had no carriage, and their visitings did not extend far — there were a few families living in the village — but no great intimacy was kept up with any of them — they were upon *friendly* but rather *distant* terms, with all —[66]

Charlotte-Maria's impression of Jane's appearance is equally vivid, showing a lively, humorous, active woman at the peak of her powers: it is also at variance with surviving images, mostly based on Cassandra Austen's sketches: 'I remember her as a tall thin spare person,' Charlotte-Maria wrote, 'with very high cheek bones great colour — sparkling eyes not large but joyous & intelligent. The face by no means so broad & plump as represented.'[67]

Charlotte-Maria's memories, like the author's own letters, demonstrate Jane's ease with children and young people. There has never been any doubt, however, of the sharp edge of Jane Austen's wit, and one letter, describing a missed visit from the Middleton contingent, confirms the opinions of both Charlotte-Maria and Caroline on her reserve with adults: 'Before I set out [for Alton] we were visited by Mrs Edwards, and while I was gone Miss Beckford & Maria, & Miss Woolls & Harriet B. called, all of whom my Mother was glad to see & I very glad to escape.'[68] Her feelings towards the Middleton contingent had already been suggested in a droll letter to Cassandra of two years earlier: 'We shall have pease soon — I mean to have them with a couple of Ducks from Wood Barn and Maria Middleton towards the end of next week.'[69] If, as it appears from these recollections, Jane Austen let slip her reserve only with her family and, especially, with children, her nieces were even more fortunate than they supposed.

The removal of the Austens to Chawton in 1809 represented a new beginning for the whole family. The dynamic had changed. Mrs George Austen was almost seventy, and made it clear that she was prepared to resign as head of the family. She withdrew to her gardening, her sewing and her patchwork, favourite occupations which she shared with both daughters, and Cassandra Austen, assisted by the family's great friend Martha Lloyd, took over the management of the household. Jane took on the responsibility of making breakfast at nine o'clock, and had the keys of the cupboard which held the precious, expensive store of tea and sugar. 'That was her part of the household work,' Caroline wrote. 'The tea and sugar stores were under her charge — and the wine'. Before breakfast, however, Jane had another private ritual of her own. The selling of her first pianoforte, when the family removed from Steventon, had caused her great distress and it was a sign of her new happiness in Chawton that she wanted to play again. Caroline remembered her aunt's delight in choosing a new pianoforte for Chawton. She wanted 'as good a one as can be got for thirty guineas', and Jane herself told Cassandra, 'I will practise country dances, that we have some amusement for our nephews and nieces, when we have the pleasure of their company.'[70] Caroline described her joy:

> [She] ... began her day with music — for which I conclude she had a natural taste, as she thus kept it up — tho' she had no-one to teach; was never induced ... to play in company; and none of her family cared much for it. I suppose, that she might not trouble them, she chose her practising time before breakfast — when she could have the room to herself — ... Much that she played from was manuscript, copied out by herself — and so neatly and correctly, that it was as easy to read as print —[71]

Caroline's brother James Edward added: 'In the evening she would sometimes sing, to her own accompaniment, some simple old songs, the words and airs of which, now never heard, still linger in my memory.'[72] This Jane Austen – open, affectionate, thrifty and hard-working – was the aunt whom the Godmersham children knew from 1809 onwards when, without a mother, they naturally turned to the company of their family. Whatever coolness may have existed between Elizabeth Austen and her sister-in-law was now forgotten, and a new closeness developed. Yet, as the first sharpness of grief passed, and the children grew older and more independent, another shift took place. The unmentioned but obvious difference in their social positions was once more underlined when, in October 1812, Catherine Knight died. Edward was now obliged, under the terms of his adoptive father's will, to take the name of Knight. Jane's comment, in a letter to her friend Martha Lloyd of November 1812, was humorously guarded: 'We have reason to suppose the change of name has taken place, as we have to forward a Letter to Edward Knight Esq're from the Lawyer who has the management of our business. I must learn to make a better K.'[73] Fanny, almost twenty, declared herself incensed, writing furiously in her diary: 'Papa changed his name about this time in compliance with the will of the late Mr Knight and we are therefore all *Knights* instead of dear old *Austens*. How I hate it!!!!!'[74] There was no altering the fact, however, and from late 1812 onward, Edward Austen's family was known by the name of Knight.

It appeared, at first, that the connection between the Knights and Austens would be further strengthened when Edward decided to have Godmersham painted in the spring of 1813 and decamped with his entire family to Chawton. It was the first time the younger children had stayed there, and the two families were in constant contact, though Fanny remained as unimpressed as ever with Chawton Great House. 'We are half frozen at the cold uninhabited appearance of the old house,' she wrote in her diary.[75] The proximity of the Austens, however, was to make this long visit not only tolerable but also, in the end, unforgettable. 'I thought we never should get back again,' Fanny later told Miss Chapman, '& yet we were very comfortable at Chawton & enjoyed the society of our friends at the Cottage very much. Mrs Austen's house is very near ours & of course we met every day frequently'.[76] This was the year in which Jane Austen was in the final stages of writing *Mansfield Park*. Completed in July 1813, it was accepted for publication that November. It was also the period when the Knight girls, now all at home, were afforded unique insights into their aunt's working life. After seeing them almost daily, Jane then travelled back with them to Godmersham, staying until November, and taking in a visit to London on the way. Many years later, in 1856, Louisa would recall, most vividly, hearing a conversation between the Austen sisters about the plot of *Mansfield Park*, and would describe its author as she, not yet nine, had seen her:

> She had large dark eyes and a brilliant complexion, and long, long black hair down to her knees. She was very absent indeed.

She would sit silent awhile, then rub her hands, laugh to herself
and run up to her room ...[77]

Louisa's memory was told to Pamela, Lady Campbell, daughter of the
executed Irish rebel Lord Edward Fitzgerald. Lady Campbell, in 'extasies'
passed it on, in great excitement, to the then Lord Lieutenant of Ireland,
Lord Carlisle, adding the extraordinary revelation that Cassandra had tried
to persuade Jane to revise her plot: 'Miss Austen's sister Cassandra tried to
persuade her to alter the end of *Mansfield Park* and let Mr Crawford marry
Fanny Price,' Lady Campbell recounted, in astonishment. 'She [Louisa]
remembers their arguing the matter but Miss Austen stood firmly and would
not allow the change.'[78]

This unique glimpse of the authorial confidence of Jane Austen serves
as a useful reminder that the playful companion of the Knight children and
their friends did not permit interference in her work, even from a dear sister.
Louisa's account of her aunt suddenly seized by inspiration is echoed by
another recollection of that time, told many years later by her sister Marianne:

> I ... remember how Aunt Jane would sit quietly working beside
> the fire in the library, saying nothing for a good while, and then
> would suddenly burst out laughing, jump up and run across
> the room to a table where pens and paper were lying, write
> something down, and then come back to the fire and go on
> quietly working as before.[79]

These were the two Janes whom the girls were privileged to see – the aunt
who sewed, mended, and went quietly about normal daily activities; and
the artist, joyously inspired, oblivious of her surroundings or her company.
Their accounts demonstrate either their ability to remain unnoticed, or the
degree to which Jane trusted the children. Louisa must have been in the room
with her aunts to have heard the discussion about the ending of *Mansfield
Park*, perhaps when they were dressing, and brushing their hair – she may
have been young enough not to be considered a distraction. There were
limits, however. When it came to Jane's rare readings of the novels, neither

Marianne, at eleven, nor Louisa, at eight and a half, was included. Marianne remembered throughout her life sitting outside, excluded and disconsolate, with Charles, Louisa, Cassandra and John:

> I remember that when Aunt Jane came to us at Godmersham she used to bring the MS of whatever novel she was writing with her, and would shut herself up with my elder sisters in one of the bedrooms to read them aloud. I and the younger ones used to hear peals of laughter through the door, and thought it very hard that we should be shut out from what was so delightful ...[80]

Though Marianne believed this occurred at Godmersham, Elizabeth Jenkins suggests in her biography that this memory may in fact refer to the family's visit to Chawton in the autumn of 1812, as Fanny recalls her aunt reading to her there from the manuscript of *Pride and Prejudice*. 'The room in Chawton House where Jane usually sat with the children,' Jenkins writes, 'is one over the porch, lined with panelling and known as the Oak Room.'[81] Whether Marianne's memory is of Chawton or not, the Oak Room, used in Jane Austen's time as a ladies' withdrawing room after dinner, is still there. Even today, the sense of peace and tranquillity in the little alcove above the window, looking out over the park and beyond to the countryside, makes it easy to believe that Jane Austen did, as family tradition maintains, sit there to observe the world. It is equally possible to believe that she read in that room to the older girls, Fanny and Elizabeth, while Marianne sat on the stairs outside with the little ones, baffled and disappointed, listening to the laughter. Though Marianne does not say, and probably could not know, whether it was *Pride and Prejudice* or *Mansfield Park* which was being read, it is certain that Jane Austen did read from *Pride and Prejudice* to at least one of her elder nieces not only during the autumn of 1812, but also during the Chawton visit in the spring of 1813. 'A[un]t Jane spent the morning with me & read P&P to me,' Fanny recorded in her diary for 5 June 1813.[82] The fact that she had been inspired several weeks earlier to write a letter to her aunt in the guise of Mr Darcy's sister, Georgiana, suggests that readings may have taken place even before June.[83] The atmosphere for the children must have been extraordinary. Young though they were, Marianne and Louisa did not fail to perceive that their aunt was uniquely gifted, and it was this perception, undimmed by the passing of many years, which distinguished their later recollections from those of the increasingly conventional and censorious Fanny. Their chances of seeing Jane at work that year were greatly increased by a happy accident. The family remained at Chawton until September 1813, though Edward had not intended to stay quite so long. As Fanny told Miss Chapman, the painting of the house at Godmersham had taken longer than was thought, '& the smell would not go off sooner'.[84] If the renovations had gone according to plan, Marianne and Louisa might never have had their unforgettable glimpses of Jane Austen in the act of creation.

Jane herself seems to have enjoyed the long visit greatly, though writing to her brother Francis during the summer, she was as detached as ever in her assessment of character. Edward might have become a great landowner, but Jane declined to see him differently. To her, he was still one of the Austens of Steventon Rectory:

> The pleasure to us of having them here is so great, that if we were not the best Creatures in the World we should not deserve it. — We go on in the most comfortable way, very frequently dining together, & always meeting in some part of every day. — Edward is very well & enjoys himself as thoroughly as any Hampshire born Austen can desire. Chawton is not thrown away upon him. — He talks of making a new garden; the present is a bad one & ill situated, near Mr Papillon's; — he means to have the new, at the top of the Lawn behind his own house. — We like to have him proving and strengthening his attachment to the place by making it better. — He will soon have all his children about him, Edward, George and Charles are collected already, & another week brings Henry and William. — It is the custom at Winchester for Georges to come away a fortnight before the Holidays, when they are not to return any more; for fear they should overstudy themselves just at last, I suppose.[85]

The little nudge at the chronic indolence of George, her petted 'itty Dordy' of some years before, suggests that she understood him rather well. George, rather like his uncle Henry Austen, Jane's favourite brother, never quite did what everyone one else did, and only rarely what was expected. He continued this pattern throughout his life – his nephew Lord Brabourne, Fanny's son and first editor of Jane Austen's letters, would later sum him up as 'one of those men who are clever enough to do almost anything, but live to their lives' end very comfortably doing nothing.'[86] Despite this, or perhaps because of it, Jane loved him. She was rather less impressed, however, with another aspect of his behaviour that summer, when he and his slightly younger brother Henry, or Harry, as the family knew him, 'showed more interest in one of the servants at the Great House than was considered desirable by their careful aunts.'[87] Young men of the Austen family, brought up in the Rectory at Steventon, did not dally with servants. The young gentlemen brought up in the Great House at Godmersham, however, no longer Austens but Knights, clearly felt quite at liberty to do so.

That interesting summer eventually came to an end, and Jane travelled with the Knights to Godmersham for what would be, though no one could have guessed it, her last visit there. On 14 September, after the servants and household had been sent ahead into Kent, Edward set out for London with Jane, Fanny, Lizzy and Marianne, who was to have her twelfth birthday the next day. They were rather confined in their coach, 'all 4 within, which was a little crowd'. Jane wrote to Francis on 25 September:

> My Br., Fanny, Lizzy, Marianne and I composed this division of the family, and filled his carriage, inside and out. Two post-chaises under the escort of George conveyed eight more across the country, the chair brought two, two others came on horseback, and the rest by the coach — and so by one means or another we all are removed. It puts me in mind of the account of St Paul's shipwreck, where all are said by different means to reach the shore in safety.[88]

Despite the discomfort of the journey, a playful letter to Cassandra from their first stop, Henry's house in Henrietta Street near Covent Garden, shows that Jane's buoyant mood of the summer had continued. 'I am going to write nothing but short sentences,' she declared, possibly poking fun at the staccato style of delivery favoured by some of the popular actors of the time, for they had attended the first play of their visit, a very light comedy, the previous night:

> There shall be two full stops in every line. Layton and Shear's
> is Bedford House. We mean to get there before breakfast if it's
> possible. For we feel more and more how much we have to do.
> And how little time. This house looks very nice.[89]

A hairdresser called, and attempted to style Jane's hair in the latest fashion: 'Mr Hall was very punctual yesterday & curled me out at a great rate,' she told Cassandra. Though less than impressed by the hairdresser's attempts, Jane submitted with good humour to the transformation as part of the novelty of the holiday. 'I thought it looked hideous,' she confided, 'and longed for a snug cap instead, but my companions silenced me by their admiration.'[90] With greater enthusiasm, she went shopping, a favourite Austen occupation when circumstances allowed, and this outing was made all the more delightful when she received, most unexpectedly, a present of £5 from 'kind, beautiful Edward'.

The whole party was to go again that night to the theatre in Covent Garden. First, however, everyone had to pay a visit to Mr Spence, the dentist, which no one enjoyed, especially as they were told they would have to return the next day to deal with 'a very sad hole between two of [Lizzy's] front teeth'. No one else was due to undergo treatment, which must have been a relief to Marianne, on the eve of her birthday. Once free of Mr Spence, they had their evening out. Theatre had always been a source of joy for the Austens of Steventon, and the habit had passed on to the next generation, with games and charades throughout the winter, and entertainments all through the twelve days of Christmas. The girls had chosen the play – a comedy from 1764 named *Midas: an English Burletta*. It would not have been Jane's first choice, she confessed to Cassandra, but it was Marianne's birthday and she was content that the girls were happy and excited. The performance the night before, *Don Juan*, or *The Libertine Destroyed*, had concluded its music and pantomime with a 'spectacular Representation of the Infernal regions'. They had travelled by coach to see it from a private box, right on the stage, at the Lyceum Theatre, in the grounds of Exeter House in the Strand. Lizzy and Marianne were delighted. 'They revelled last night in *Don Juan*,' she told Cassandra, 'whom we left in Hell at ½ past eleven. — We had Scaramouche and a Ghost — and were delighted; — I speak of them; my delight was very tranquil.' In the end, *Midas* did not thrill the girls quite as much as the wicked *Don Juan*: '& I must say,' Jane conceded, 'that I have seen nobody on the stage who has been a more interesting Character than that compound of Cruelty & Lust.'[91]

On the following day, they were all once again at the dentist, where Lizzy suffered torment and Marianne, on her birthday, had the unpleasant discovery that, after all, she too was to be treated. Jane, as a consequence, flatly refused to let the 'lover of Teeth and Money and Mischief' examine her:

> Poor Marianne had two taken out after all, the two just beyond the eye teeth, to make room for those in front. — When her doom was fixed, Fanny, Lizzy and I walked into the next room, where we heard each of the two sharp hasty Screams ... He had before urged the expediency of L & M's being brought to town in the course of a couple of Months to be farther examined, & continued to the last to press for their all coming to him. — My Br would not absolutely promise. — The little girls' teeth I can suppose in a critical state ... I would not have had him look at mine for a shilling a tooth & double it.[92]

By the next day all excitements, good and bad, were over, and the entire party was back at Godmersham. This visit, lasting until November, was a happy one for Jane. As *Mansfield Park* had been accepted for publication, she could relax for a while and, unusually for her, enjoy 'the luxury of meals especially brought to her on trays, and a fire lit in her bedroom before breakfast'.[93] She attended a ball, the last of her life. She found herself with a little less energy for the growing children and, though she tried not to think ill of them, continued to find herself disappointed in her older nephews. In particular, she thought Edward and her former favourite, George, now nineteen and eighteen, had grown very bloodthirsty: 'Now those two boys who are out with the foxhounds,' she wrote to Cassandra, 'will come home and disgust me again by some habit of luxury or some proof of sporting mania — unless I keep it off by this prediction.'[94] Yet no prediction in the world could have stopped the boys becoming young men and, for the Knights, becoming young men meant hunting and shooting. Inevitably, and rather more obviously than their sisters, they were growing away from her. It may have been this consciousness that the family was rapidly growing up which caused Jane's letters, generally so bright, witty and resolutely cheerful, to take on a more serious tone. In late 1814 Fanny had written to Jane of a rather sporadic attachment to a young neighbour, Mr Plumptre, and received sobering, even grave advice:

> You like him well enough to marry, but not well enough to wait.
> — The unpleasantness of appearing fickle is certainly great —
> but if you think you want Punishment for past Illusions, there
> is it — and nothing can be compared to the misery of being
> bound without Love, bound to one, & preferring another. That
> is a Punishment which you do not deserve.[95]

Fanny had now entered her twenties and, as with her brothers, her aunt could foresee her inevitable moving away: 'You can hardly think what a pleasure it is to me, to have such thorough pictures of your Heart. — Oh! What a loss it will be when you are married.'[96] Fanny was not yet seriously attached, however, and still had charge of a large family, with the help only of the governess, Miss Clewes. Together, they managed, more or less, to contain the high spirits of the youngest children. 'Miss Clewes & my sisters are not particularly pleased at our absence, as you may imagine,' she wrote to Miss Chapman, when she had taken a short trip to Bath with her father, '& indeed, I quite hate to leave them for so long.'[97]

Even when the family was at Chawton, which they visited for May and part of June 1814, it was clear that priorities had shifted. Lizzy was now fourteen and a half, and had to begin to prepare for her coming out into society: 'Lizzy goes on a little with her dancing,' wrote Fanny, 'but the poor girl is sadly quite disadvantaged, as we cannot get a Master. Jeffery attends us now for Music, & she gets on very well with singing — instrumental music she has now given up.'[98] By 1815, a dancing master had been secured, and Lizzy was finally having lessons. Fanny, too, was studying music, as were Marianne and Louisa, now thirteen and ten, and the whole family, with all their servants, enjoyed a great celebration in May 1815 for the coming of age of the eldest of the Knights, Edward:

> I had Meyer for the Harp, which I began last summer with Mr Jeffery & which I continue to enjoy very much. He is now here giving Marianne & Louisa lessons on the Pianoforte, and he thinks the latter will make a fine performer in time ... I am not sure whether you recollected that the 10th of this month was the day Edwd came of age — we had grand doings on the occasion — at least very pleasant doings, for it is always delightful to see a number of people happy & I believe that was most thoroughly the case. We had a ball for the servants and tenants, & as the Laundry was not thought large enough, the beds were taken down in the Nursery for them to dance there, & the servants ornamented the room very prettily with handfuls of Lavender and Lilacs & at the upper end E. K. in gold letters surrounded with boughs & lamps. I had the honour of opening the Ball with Mr Therer [?] and I believe they danced till 1 o'clock, & then supped in the Servants' Hall & Lobby ... The next day the poor people danced before the Servants' Hall door, & afterwards danced on the green in front of the house — we counted above 200 people, & I never witnessed a more gratifying sight, than the glimpses of dancers & smokers ... They gave several rounds of cheers, & I think their hurrahs might almost have been heard at Chilham ... &

> we had also 'God Save the King' in fine style. We do not go
> to Chawton this year, & I am thoroughly enjoying this sweet
> spring in Kent — the woods are already in high beauty, & the
> Flower garden is coming on rapidly ... Lizzy & Marianne join
> me in kind remembrance ... [99]

The last sentence of that account may be the most telling. The focus of the Knight family, and especially that of Fanny and her younger charges, was concentrated almost exclusively on Kent and on their lives in the Great House at Godmersham. Chawton figured less and less. Neither Jane nor Cassandra was part of the great celebration of Edward's coming of age.

During those years from 1813 to 1815, however, Jane had her own pre-occupations, and they were delightful to her. She had gone home from her last visit to Godmersham in November 1813 refreshed and renewed, and had spent that unusually harsh winter most productively, beginning *Emma* soon after the New Year, 1814. May that year saw the publication of *Mansfield Park* and by November the first edition was sold out. *Emma*, which was completed in March 1815, was published at the end of December by John Murray, described by Jane to Cassandra as 'a rogue of course, but a civil one'.[100] She started work on *Persuasion* in August 1815, and completed it in August 1816. Her professional life could not have been better.

In her personal life, however, matters became rather more difficult after 1815. Her brother Henry, who had ably assisted Jane in the process of publication, became seriously ill in London during November of that year, and Jane nursed him back to health. Moreover, the bank in which he had been a partner since 1802 failed on 15 March 1816, and Henry was declared bankrupt. The consequence for the wider family was severe, though less so for Henry. He decided almost immediately that he would become a clergyman, and was ordained by the end of the year, securing with relative ease a curacy at Bentley near Chawton where he was soon known for the eloquence of his sermons.[101] It was not quite so straightforward for those in the family with investments in the failed bank, especially Edward, who lost £20,000. Jane herself lost £13, no small sum to her.[102] To make matters worse, Edward had been contesting a law suit since 1814, brought by some of Catherine Knight's relatives, a Mr and Miss Hinton and their nephew James Baverstock, who had challenged his right to the Knight estate. To have lost the suit would have cost him up to two-thirds of his income and, while in the end he did not lose, he was obliged to cut down many trees in Chawton Park to raise the £15,000 he needed to extricate himself from the case. This, in conjunction with Henry's failed banking venture, cost Edward and all of his children dearly, putting the onus on all of them to marry, if they could, into money.[103] The family was remarkably forgiving. Edward, the greatest loser by Henry's failed venture, bore it, as Caroline Austen later wrote, in a 'spirit of forbearance and generosity'.[104] In December 1816, Jane wrote to her nephew James Edward, who, like his half-sister Anna, had begun to try his hand at fiction: 'Uncle Henry writes very superior sermons — You & I must try to get hold of one or two, & put them into our Novels:— it would be a fine help to a volume.'[105] Indeed, when she wrote her will, in April 1817, leaving almost all she had to Cassandra, she made sure there was a legacy of £50 for her brother.

It was during this difficult period that Jane became conscious of feeling unwell. Through the spring and summer of 1815, she experienced intermittent back pain, unusual weakness and inexplicable fatigue.[106] Her illness progressed, even as her work began to take on its own momentum. There were other stresses, too, for the collapse of Henry's venture was compounded by another disappointment. Jane's maternal uncle, James Leigh Perrot, died on 28 March 1817. He was a wealthy man, and it had long been assumed, and indeed expected, that he would provide in his will for his sister Cassandra, Mrs George Austen, and her daughters. In the event, Mrs Austen was not named in the will. James Austen, Jane's eldest brother, father of James Edward, Anna and Caroline, was the main beneficiary, and £1,000 was to be left to any of Mr Leigh Perrot's nieces and nephews who should outlive his wife.[107] 'Single women,' Jane would write soon afterwards to Fanny, 'have a dreadful propensity for being poor'. It was a theme to which she returned in her novels, with increasingly ironic compassion, beginning with the dispossessed Bennet and Dashwood girls of her early novels, and moving from her delineation in *Emma* of the precarious position of Jane Fairfax and Miss Bates, to the desperate plight of Mrs Smith in *Persuasion*. Now, feeling increasingly unwell, she could not find that saving detachment. Her great refuge had always been in her talent and, though as late as January 1817 she had begun a new novel, later known as *Sanditon*, she had laid it aside by 18 March, unable to write and too ill even to walk.[108] The shock of her uncle's will, coming so soon afterwards, was very great. Jane knew that Edward, with eleven children of his own and an unexpectedly reduced income, could scarcely do more for them than he was already doing. Moreover, while she had faith in her own talent, she was not only too ill to work, but all too well aware that the rewards of authorship were likely to be uncertain. Cassandra, who had gone as soon as she learned of their uncle's death to the Leigh Perrot house to help her widowed aunt, received to her surprise a most uncharacteristic letter from Jane, imploring her to return. Jane herself was abashed at such weakness, as she wrote to her brother Charles:

> I am ashamed to say that the shock of my Uncle's Will brought on a relapse, & I was so ill on Friday & thought myself so likely to be worse that I could not but press for Cassandra's returning with Frank after the funeral last night, which she of course did, & either her return, or my having seen Mr Curtis, or my Disorder's chusing to go away, have made me better this morning. I live upstairs for the present & am coddled. I am the only one of the Legatees who has been so silly, but a weak Body must excuse weak nerves. My Mother has borne the forgetfulness of her extremely well; — her expectations for herself were never beyond the extreme of moderation, & she thinks with you that my Uncle always looked forward to surviving her. — She desires her best Love & many thanks for your kind feelings; and heartily wishes that her younger Children had more, & all her Children something immediately.[109]

While the Leigh Perrot will was causing such havoc in the minds of their Austen relatives, young Edward Knight and his interesting brother George, who had tried the navy and decided it did not suit him, were about to set out on the Grand Tour of Europe, just as their father had done. Henry and William were in their late teens, Henry with his regiment in France, and

William about to begin to study for the Church. Charles, by then fourteen, was at school at Winchester; lively John, at eight and a half, was proving almost too much for his sisters and governess; and Lizzy, at seventeen, was about to enter society, as Fanny wrote to Miss Chapman:

> Edward & George too are going abroad for a longer time in April, so we shall be quite deserted. George made a short trial in the navy last Autumn, but it disagreed with his health, which is not very strong. You will imagine how much we shall miss them ... Wm is decided for the Church ... Charles is at Winchester & John is still at home, though we are beginning to think it time to send him to School. I think you heard of an accident he had nearly two years ago with an arrow in his eye, poor child — the sight can never be recovered but he suffers no pain & it is not much disfigured & his other eye is very strong, I hope he will not experience any material inconvenience from the loss of it ... Miss Clewes is still with us ... Lizzy has left the Schoolroom, & is grown a very fine girl (though I say it that should not say it) — she has been to one ball, but she is not to be considered as regularly out till the Races, which I hope she will attend, as Isabella Deedes is also to make her appearance at that time. Sophia Cage tho' about the same age is not strong enough ... to be of the party this year ... My other Sisters grow of course & I think improve. Cassandra has been confined lately with an inflammation in one knee but it has improved & they are all really well at present.[110]

It seems unusual that neither Marianne nor Louisa is mentioned by name in this letter, though Marianne in March 1817 was fifteen and a half, and should surely have been receiving dancing lessons, for she too would soon be old enough to go into society. Cassandra Jane, however, had received a special message from Jane, probably the last she ever had from her. Knowing Cassandra had been ill, and in pain, Jane encapsulated the young girl's character, a mixture of charm, sweetness and a certain dogged patience of which she would have need in her adult life: 'What a comfort that Cassandra should be so recovered! — It is more than we had expected. — I can easily believe she was very patient & very good. I always loved Cassandra, for her fine dark eyes & sweet temper.'[111] Shortly afterwards, Fanny wrote to Jane, bringing her up to date with the details of her own latest unfortunate romance, with Mr James Wildman of nearby Chilham Castle. In her reply of 13 March 1817, advising her to wait for the right man, her aunt kindly wrote as though Fanny were just a young woman, not mistress of a vast establishment, and quite as though she herself were not increasingly ill:

> By your description he cannot be in love with you, however he may try at it, & I could not wish the match unless there were a great deal of Love on his side ... Single women have a dreadful propensity for being poor — which is one very strong argument in favour of Matrimony, but I need not dwell on such arguments with you, pretty Dear, you do not want inclination. — Well, I shall say, as I have often said before, Do not be in a hurry; depend upon it, the right Man will come at last; you will in the course of the next two or three years, meet with somebody more generally unexceptionable than anyone you have yet known, who will love you as warmly as ever He did, & who will so completely attach you, that you will feel you have never really loved before.[112]

Fanny would soon bear out this prediction, though her aunt would not see it. Fanny could not know how ill she was, and Jane spoke little in this letter of her own health, telling her: 'I am got tolerably well again, quite equal to walking about & enjoying the Air; & by sitting down & resting a good while between my Walks, I get exercise enough.'[113] She moved quickly to the subject of Fanny's brother William, who had been visiting at Chawton: 'Wm & I are the best of friends. I love him very much — Everything is so natural about him, his affections, his Manners & his Drollery. He entertains & interests us extremely.' As a ten-year-old he had sat beside her working at cross stitch, and had made a footstool for the cottage of which Jane had said, 'We shall never have the heart to put our feet on it.'[114] Nine years later, she was pleased to find him just as congenial, no doubt a pleasant surprise after her disappointment in his older brothers Edward and George.

A certain ruthlessness in Fanny's developing character, however, did not escape Jane's notice, however unwell she may have felt. It was demonstrated by her first requiring the unfortunate Mr Wildman to read all of her aunt's then published work, and then reporting his subsequent critical remarks. 'You are the oddest Creature!' Jane wrote, 'nervous enough in some respects, but in others perfectly without nerves! — Quite unrepulsible, hardened & impudent.'[115] Jane would not live to see Fanny marry in three years' time. Fortunately, she did not live to see her become the Victorian matriarch who would one day dismiss her and her work as coarse and unrefined. Yet, this insight of March 1817 may indicate that she would have been less surprised by Fanny's criticism of her than some of her loyal readers were to be.

Jane's illness worsened and her family, always at their best in time of crisis, stepped in. She wrote to her friend, the former Godmersham governess Anne Sharp, on 22 May: 'I have kept my bed since the 13 of April, with only removals to a Sopha.'[116] Feeling a little better at the time of writing this letter, she mentioned that she was about to travel to Winchester in the hope of expert medical help, 'to see what Mr Lyford can do to re-establishing me in tolerable health'. Never at a loss for wry observation, having commented how kind her entire family had been to her in her time of illness, she added: 'In short, if I live to be an old Woman I must expect to wish I had died now, blessed in the tenderness of such a Family, & before I had survived either them or their affection.'[117] The three who were nearest, James, Henry and Francis, ensured that one of them, or members of their families, visited daily. Yet, it is a sad fact that, while Mrs Austen and her daughters were trying to absorb the fact that there would be no material improvement in their circumstances, and while Jane was writing her last will and testament in April 1817, most of the Godmersham family were caught up in preparations for holidays and celebrations of their own. Six days before Jane travelled to Winchester in the vain hope of recovery of 'tolerable health', Edward Knight left for a fortnight's holiday in Paris, bringing Fanny, Lizzy and George, with two of their late mother's family. It was James Austen, himself gravely ill, who lent his carriage for Jane's last journey. Young William Knight, who had so captured his aunt's heart earlier in the year, accompanied her to Winchester, riding outside the carriage on one side, with his mercurial uncle Henry Austen on the other. Their lodgings were at 8 College Street, and Charles Knight, next door at the College, did his best to visit his aunt, as Jane wrote to her nephew James Edward on 27 May 1817:

> Thanks to the kindness of your Father & Mother in sending me their Carriage, my Journey hither on Saturday was performed with very little fatigue, & had it been a fine day I think I shd have felt none, but it distressed me to see Uncle Henry & Wm K— who kindly attended us on horseback, riding in rain almost all the way.— We expect a visit from them tomorrow, & hope they will stay the night, and on Thursday, which is Confirmation & a Holiday, we are to get Charles out to breakfast. We have had but one visit yet from him poor fellow, as he is in Sickroom, but he hopes to be out tonight. —[118]

During July 1817, Jane's health deteriorated sharply, and finally, in the early hours of the morning of 18 July, with her head on a pillow placed by her sister on her own lap, 'in quietness and peace', as James Edward later wrote, 'she breathed her last'.[119] Though Fanny had continued to write to Jane almost to the end, she did not attend the funeral on Thursday 24 July. Neither did Cassandra Austen, nor any of the girls, for it was not then the custom that women should be present. Nonetheless, they felt the enormity of her passing. 'Thursday was not so dreadful a day to me as you imagined,' Cassandra wrote afterwards to Fanny:

> Everything was done with the greatest tranquillity, & but that I was determined I would see the last & therefore was upon the list- en, I should not have known when they left the house. I watched the little mournful procession the length of the Street & when it turned from my sight & I had lost her for ever — even then I was not overpowered, nor so agitated as I am now in writing of it.[120]

Only Edward Knight and Francis Austen walked beside the coffin to Winchester Cathedral. Their eldest brother James was too ill to attend: his son James Edward, deeply affected, rode fourteen miles from Steventon to represent him. The service was conducted early to avoid a clash with Morning Prayer at ten o'clock: afterwards, Jane Austen was quietly interred in the North Aisle.

At Godmersham, on Sunday 20 July, Fanny recorded in her journal: 'Evening church. Liz. Mne. & I did not go, in consequence of a letter from Papa announcing my poor dear Aunt Jane Austen's death at 4 on Friday morning.'[121] Three weeks later, she wrote to Miss Chapman to inform her of their loss. There is no doubt that she was greatly grieved; there is equally no doubt that she was by then quite in command of her emotions and, indeed, more concerned with the present and future than with the past, or the dead:

> The papers will have informed you of the sad loss we have lately sustained, & you will, I am sure, have felt for us, & will be glad to hear that my Grandmamma & Aunt Cassandra bear their loss with great fortitude, & that their health is not affected by the anxiety they have undergone. Did you hear of our little trip to Paris in May? Papa, Lizzy & I with my Aunts Louisa & Charlotte (Mrs John Bridges) went there with Edward & George & spent a fortnight very pleasantly ... I believe John still at Eltham, but we are not quite certain — he will certainly go somewhere before Mich'mas, as he gets too unmanageable for home, like most boys of this age. Cakey wished very much to take him today — I hope he will not be troublesome if you are so good as to admit him to visit you ... We have of course not attended the races, but we are going to an Ashford Ball next Thursday, when Lizzy is to be considered out. Wm is at home & is a good deal grown. Charles is also at home in his Winchester holiday. But Sackree will tell you about her darling ... Lizzy & Marianne write with me in kind remembrance ...[122]

What Fanny did not say to Miss Chapman, indeed probably could not yet know, was that Lizzy had just met in Paris the man with whom she would fall in love, just as she herself had, without realising it, already met the man she would marry in 1820. Marianne, who would be out in society the following year, was herself only five years away from receiving a proposal. For Marianne, Louisa and Cassandra Jane Knight – May, Lou and Cass – the very situations which Jane Austen had conjured in her imagination would shortly be presented to them in reality, and they would have, more than any of their family, a chance to understand in their own lives the prescient truth of her work.

CHAPTER 2

'Goodbye from the Cowhouse'

Two Weddings, a Scandal and a Refusal
1817–1826

'He is just what a young man ought to be,' said she, 'sensible,
good-humoured, lively. And I never saw such happy manners!
So much ease, with such perfect good breeding!'
'He is also handsome,' replied Elizabeth, 'which a young man ought likewise
to be if he possibly can. His character is thereby complete.'

PRIDE AND PREJUDICE

Following her aunt's death, Lizzy's début was deferred, though not for long.
The ball in Ashford in Kent where she came out took place in mid-August,
scarcely a month after Jane's death. As it happened, the ball did not launch
Lizzy in the usual way within her social set. A chance meeting had already
decided her future, as her granddaughter, Evelyn Templetown, later described:

> They first met in Paris in 1817. Mr Knight had taken his two
> elder daughters, Fanny and Elizabeth, there for a period of
> enjoyment. Edward Rice had been there for the same reason
> for some considerable time. He was a friend of Elizabeth's
> brother George who, while staying with his father and sisters,
> took him to call. 'How remarkably pretty your sister is,' said
> Edward as they left the house – it was love at first sight!¹

The 'period of enjoyment' was the trip taken in May 1817, shortly before
Jane went to Winchester in her last hope of recovery. On their return in early
June, when the full import of her illness became known, there was, for a

time, a turning away from pleasure and social engagement. By the end of the summer of 1817, however, despite their bereavement, the Godmersham family had almost completely resumed normal life.

Edward Royds Rice, ten years older than Lizzy and in a position to marry, was quickly certain of his feelings. 'He followed up the acquaintance when they all returned to Kent,' recorded Evelyn Templetown, 'and soon proposed. Elizabeth refused him. She was only seventeen and very happy at home.'[2] Lizzy, despite the sudden death in the family circle and her father's recent legal and financial struggles, was indeed happy: she had just left the school room, enjoyed a unique position in the family where she was equally at home with her older and the younger siblings, and had a particularly close relationship with Marianne, just twenty months her junior and soon to join her in society. She had long looked forward to the excitement of her first season. 'But she became deeply troubled,' according to Evelyn Templetown. 'She found herself deeply in love, and when Edward Rice again proposed, he was accepted.'[3]

Edward Austen Knight approved of Edward Rice, saw that he was in a position to give his daughter a comfortable establishment, and actively encouraged Lizzy to accept his proposal. Not everyone was quite so pleased. Fanny, who had carried the burden of looking after the family for nine years, was grieved that Elizabeth would now be leaving home.[4] The children's old nurse, Susanna Sackree, 'Cakey', who had wept when Marianne and Lizzy were sent off to school as young children, still felt deeply protective towards them. She was concerned to see Lizzy walk out alone with Edward Rice, and was oddly relieved that the young girl found it difficult to address her future husband by his Christian name. When he asked her to do so, a strange reprise of Emma Woodhouse's conversation with her fiancé, Mr Knightley, ensued: 'She replied that she had known him first as "Mr Rice" and liked that best. He retorted that she would think it odd if he called her sister Fanny "Miss Austen", but of course, "she must do as she likes" and so she did.'[5] It seems a pity that Jane was not there to comment on this match; she had known some of the Rices through her brother James, and there had once been a question of Edward's older brother, Henry Rice, having the living at Deane, near Steventon, one of two livings formerly held by the Reverend George Austen. Jane had held a decided opinion of Edward's mother, a redoubtable lady of French extraction known always as Madame Sarah Rice, and famous for her habit of wearing only white from head to toe. To Jane, even on slight acquaintance, Madame Sarah was 'a perverse and narrow-minded woman', not inclined 'to oblige those whom she does not love'.[6]

Lizzy's wedding took place just over a year after the meeting in Paris, on 6 October 1818. Like their cousin Anna's wedding a few years earlier – and quite unlike that imagined by Andrew Davies in the 1995 BBC adaptation of *Pride and Prejudice* – it was a very simple, understated affair:

> So quiet and simple was it in its arrangements that when the company returned to the house, the bridegroom went out shooting — and the bride, with her sister Marianne, 'walked all round the chicken-houses, and climbed up to the top of the cowhouses to say goodbye'.[7]

It was intended as Lizzy's farewell to childhood; yet, it was also Marianne's. After the two girls climbed down from the roof for the last time, and Lizzy set off with her new husband, Marianne was suddenly left, at seventeen, without her closest companion. Lizzy was to her as Cassandra had been to Jane and, like their aunts, they had seldom been parted. They had sat together as little children for their first painting, and had learned to read, write and ride together.[8] Again like Jane and Cassandra, they had been sent away to school together at just seven and nine. Far away from the rest of their family, they had only one another in the two years following their mother's sudden death and, when they were finally brought home, had combined to provoke a series of unfortunate governesses, before accompanying their aunt Jane to London for a painful visit to the dentist and a noisy, magical trip to the theatre. It was not until Jane decided to admit the thirteen-year-old Lizzy, but not the slightly younger Marianne, to her private readings that a difference was made between them. In fact, Jane's separation of the two girls signalled the beginning, if not of a relegation of Marianne, certainly of a tendency to overlook her which was to become more marked over the next seven years. Fanny was almost nine years older than Marianne: Louisa and Cassandra Jane were just fourteen and twelve when Lizzy married. As Jane had known and emphasised throughout her work, famously giving it as the opinion of the monstrous but socially astute Lady Catherine de Bourgh, it was of considerable benefit to a family with several girls if the older daughters married first, smoothing the paths of their younger sisters. No one was surprised that Miss Elizabeth Knight, acclaimed as the family beauty, had married so young – Jane herself had been known to praise Lizzy's looks to the detriment of Marianne.[9]

It was not, however, an opinion shared by everyone. In the year following Lizzy's wedding, when Marianne was herself out in society, her cousin, James Edward Austen, fell in love with her. Known in the family simply as Edward, he was three years older than his cousin. Whether coming from the old family home of Steventon, or from school in Winchester, he had been a frequent and welcome visitor at Chawton Cottage, famous for the ease of his manner, 'sitting in his quiet comfortable way making his delightful little sketches'.[10] In addition to his sketching and writing, he was also renowned within the family for his skilfully executed silhouettes which, without needing to draw them first, he made directly with special little scissors, 'the points ... an inch long, and the curved handles about three inches'.[11] By happy coincidence it was for this artistic young man, in a bid to lift his spirits after he had lost some chapters of a work in progress, that Jane described in similar terms her own unique and equally delicate art:

> Two Chapters & a half to be missing is monstrous! It is well that I have not been at Steventon lately, & therefore cannot be suspected of purloining them; — two strong twigs & a half towards a Nest of my own, would have been something. — I do not think however that any theft of that sort would be really useful to me. What should I do with your strong, manly, spirited sketches, full of Variety and Glow? — How could I possibly join them on to the little bit (two Inches wide) of Ivory on which I work with so fine a brush, as produces little effect after much labour?[12]

Jane enjoyed teasing this clever nephew: 'I give you Joy of having left Winchester,' she wrote on the last birthday of her life, 16 December 1816:

> Now you may own, how miserable you were there; now, it will all gradually come out — your Crimes & your Miseries — how often you went up by the Mail to London & threw away Fifty Guineas at a Tavern, & how often you were on the point of hanging yourself — restrained only ... by the want of a Tree within some miles of the City ... Adieu, Amiable.[13]

There was little chance of James Edward's throwing away fifty guineas anywhere, for money was in short supply. Although his father James had been the main beneficiary in the will of their uncle James Leigh Perrot, to the exclusion of Jane's family, the eventual disposition of the property at Scarlets in Berkshire had been left to the discretion of his widow, 'looked upon by her husband's relations as a capricious and uncertain person'.[14] Jane Leigh Perrot had the use of her husband's property and money for life and, like Jane's fictional tyrants Mrs Ferrars, Lady Catherine de Bourgh and Mrs Churchill, was quite prepared to use her power. 'The family,' as James Edward's daughter Mary Augusta later put it, 'could feel no assurance that she would leave the property to any of them.'[15]

Though James Edward, like his grandfather and uncles, was fortunate to be able to attend Oxford on a scholarship and, like his father and grandfather, considered entering the Church, Jane Leigh Perrot opposed his choice of career.[16] 'She would have preferred his being a smart young layman,' James Edward's daughter later wrote, 'and she threatened to do nothing for him in the future if he persisted in his choice.'[17] She could not cut him off entirely, as his father had ensured that, on his aunt's death, he would have a 'moderate fortune ... but,' as his daughter went on to say, 'she had the power to do a great deal more if she would'.[18] James Edward, however, like *Sense and Sensibility*'s Edward Ferrars, would not submit to her will. He knew where his own inclinations lay and, though generally quiet and agreeable, was also a young man of passion. 'The love of acting must have been very strong in the family,' his daughter later wrote, and like his father and Jane, who had revelled in writing and performing plays and charades for the Steventon Austens, James Edward loved the theatre. Even on his very limited allowance as a student, he tried to see a play every night if he found himself in London, seeking out performances in any town he was visiting and later astonishing his daughter with his knowledge of 'the quantity of theatres [which] then existed in the land'.[19]

Theatre was one passion. By 1819 Marianne Knight was another. At almost eighteen, she was at last enjoying the life of a young girl in society. Her uncle Charles Austen thought her a beauty, and told his brother James so: James Edward, at almost twenty-one, was simply entranced.[20] At the end of April 1819 his father, who was by then in the last year of his life, had a visit from his brother Edward, with Fanny and Marianne. Afterwards, James wrote to his son with the clear intention of dissuading him from his opinion. 'I am afraid you will not think me warm enough in the praise of Marianne's beauty,' he wrote. 'Pretty she certainly is — but not so very bewitching beautiful as I had been taught to expect from you and my brother Charles.' His daughter Caroline, at fourteen, went further, adding to her father's letter a waspishly ambivalent remark not unworthy of Jane Austen's Caroline Bingley: 'I cannot admire Marianne as much as you do. She is certainly very pretty, but I never saw her look anything like beautiful.' She added one concession, however, revealing in itself: 'Her greatest personal recommendation to me,' she said, 'is being very like poor Aunt Jane.'[21]

Fifty years later, James Edward would write that, after Jane Austen's death, all her brothers looked ever afterwards for her likeness in their daughters and nieces. Perhaps he too sought his aunt in Marianne. Caroline Austen may have genuinely thought Marianne less than beautiful: their father, however, in trying to curb his son's interest in Marianne may have been thinking of Mrs Leigh Perrot and her power of veto. In 1819 James Edward, still an undergraduate, could not afford to be in love; he was in no position to marry anyone, let alone an impecunious cousin. Moreover, his father James, knowing himself to be very ill, may have been anxious to avoid a confrontation with the capricious Mrs Leigh Perrot. No record has survived of Marianne's feelings. Sadly, they could have made no difference. Whether or not she returned the admiration of this gentle, cultured cousin who, with all the benefits of a shared history, might have been an ideal match for her, there was no hope of any development. For Edward Knight, following the crash of Henry's bank and the challenge to the estate, money was far from plentiful. The Knight sons would all be provided for, either through the property or through well-chosen professions, such as the army, the law, or the church. For the daughters, as for their aunts in Chawton, the choice was simple: they were to marry well, or to manage on the small allowance their father could make them, remaining forever dependent on their father and brothers. The hard fact was that, though Lizzy had married for love at eighteen, she had also married to the family's advantage. Neither Marianne nor James Edward could marry for love alone.

The matter may have been settled by the next loss to the family. James Austen, aged only fifty-six, entered his last illness in 1819, and James Edward came home from Oxford some weeks before Christmas to spend time with his dying father.[22] James Austen's death changed his son's position in the family, leaving him more than ever dependent on the good will of Mrs Leigh Perrot. It also took him away from Steventon and its proximity to Chawton, where he might have met or heard news of Marianne. James Edward took his degree in November 1820, left Oxford and, thereafter, he and Marianne seem to have reverted to their original relationship. He may not have forgotten her entirely, however: some verses surviving from that time indicate a certain despondency and just a hint of bitterness, not surprising in a young man who had recently lost his father, his childhood home and, perhaps, his first love. One of these poems was addressed to a boyhood friend, William Heathcote, a nephew of Mr Harris Bigg-Wither, whose proposal Jane had impulsively accepted one evening in 1802 and the next morning, upon reflection, rejected:

> William, A Muse I once possessed,
> A poor but willing maid,
> The inmate of a lightsome breast,
> Though not a weighty head.

... She's fled, or on this day of pride,
When, not for thee in vain,
Youth's quiet vista opens wide,
On manhood's active plain;

Thou sh'dst have heard her joy, her boast
Her pride from envy free,
At seeing in my friend, what most
Myself wd wish to be.[23]

Nine years later, James Edward would marry Miss Emma Smith, a young lady he met in the year in which he wrote that valedictory poem, 1822. Her aunt would describe him as 'a very agreeable companion, cheerful, lively, animated, ready to converse, willing to read out loud, never in the way and just enough of poetry and romance to please ... and yet not to overlook sober reason'.[24] Mrs Leigh Perrot, having by then forgiven James Edward for taking Orders 'so far at least as to say at times that she would still leave Scarlets to him, at other times that she would not, but would buy him a living instead', would be so pleased at his choice that she would double his allowance and announce her intention of leaving him not only Scarlets but also some money of her own.[25] Eventually, like Edward Knight, James Edward would take the name of his benefactress after her death and, in 1836, become James Edward Austen Leigh.[26]

Whatever life Marianne might have had with James Edward, comfortably settled like her sisters in her own establishment with a man of such similar background and interests, the opportunity was not repeated after 1819. James Edward's marriage and change of name were still far in the future in the year she came out and, at almost eighteen, elegant, accomplished, pretty and of good family, she was expected to make an early and advantageous match. Yet, Fanny, who had steered Lizzy's début so successfully, did not seem able to give Marianne the same attention. She was completely absorbed in establishing Lizzy in her role as a married woman, and expected Marianne to be equally so. Fanny accompanied the newlyweds to their new home at nearby Dane Court in Kent and, when Lizzy found she was expecting her first child, her eldest sister remained there well into the spring. 'Marianne left the schoolroom when Lizzy married,' Fanny wrote from Dane Court to Miss Chapman in March 1819, 'and went to one or two winter balls'. She did not, however, go on to describe a programme for Marianne's season as she had for Lizzy. Instead, she described Marianne's usefulness to the family, including their Deedes cousins with whom she had gone to stay at Sandling: 'She is now helping Louisa set up house, & I believe she will accompany Papa and me into Hampshire about the end of April for 3 or 4 months.'[27]

A perceptible change was occurring at Godmersham, signalled by Lizzy's wedding. With the imminent birth of Lizzy's first child, the focus of Fanny's attention tended even more towards Dane Court as Lizzy, remembering her mother's death, became increasingly anxious.[28] In December 1819, Fanny indicated her sense of the shift within the family when, in a letter to Miss Chapman, Lizzy was formally referred to as 'Mrs Edward Rice': Fanny would never again use the family pet name to her former governess. With the exception of John, she considered none of her charges as children any more, and it was this perception which would accelerate the change already begun. Edward and George, who had returned in July from their grand tour abroad, had not gone home to Godmersham: this marked a shift from another tradition, that of the family Christmas at home. Edward was at Dane Court, and George at Chawton, as was William. Charles was coming from Winchester, Henry going to his regiment at Nottingham, and tearaway John was on his way back from his tutor's house. 'Marianne,' she added, 'is staying at Sandling during this dispersion of the family, & the only ones at home are Louisa and Cassandra who are almost beyond being called children now, being 15 & 13.'[29]

With this first break, the Godmersham family was indeed beginning to disperse and Fanny who, at only twenty-seven, had been its head for so long seemed, like Anne Elliot, to feel the loneliness of the new situation. She had had her share of romantic attachments, notably with Mr Wildman and Mr Plumptre, about both of whom she had had several letters of sound advice from Jane. Mr James Wildman was a neighbour, and his name would recur a few years later in a different and troubling context. In November 1819, however, it was Mr Plumptre's name which came up, when Fanny heard unexpectedly from one of her Cage cousins that his recent marriage was less than happy, and that he avoided the mention of Fanny Knight's name.[30] Whether or not the knowledge of her former suitor's unhappiness awakened in Fanny a sense that she should have had or might yet have a life apart from her father and siblings, something changed. By September 1820, everything was changed, for in an announcement which seems to have come almost as a surprise to herself, she wrote to Miss Chapman: 'I have at present something to communicate ... I am engaged to be married to Sir Edward Knatchbull.'[31]

He was a widower and a distant relative: his father, Sir Edward Knatchbull, 8th Baronet, was first cousin to the same Catherine Knatchbull who, as Mrs Thomas Knight, had been Edward Austen's adoptive mother and Jane's trusted friend and patron. The 8th Baronet died in 1819, leaving his son in a position to take up his father's seat in Parliament, and to remarry. The Knatchbull family home was reasonably near Godmersham, nine miles away at Mersham le Hatch, near Ashford in Kent. Yet, while there had been social meetings throughout the years, there had never been until 1820 any indication of a special attachment. By the summer of that year, however, Sir Edward Knatchbull was a dinner guest of Edward Knight at Godmersham, and by the end of August he had proposed, writing not only to Fanny but also to her father. On the same day, 28 August 1820, Edward Knight accepted for his daughter by letter, thanking Sir Edward Knatchbull for 'the honourable distinction which you have shown her as well as the handsome and flattering terms in which your offer is contained.'[32] It was, for the family, another suitable and advantageous match. Within days, Sir Edward Knatchbull had introduced Fanny to his two eldest children, Mary Dorothea and Norton, who at thirteen and twelve, were almost of an age with Cassandra Jane and John Knight. This coincidence was not lost upon Fanny, who would shortly see a suitable and convenient way of completing the education of her youngest sister. Yet, as events would prove, she was not going to find it as easy to manage Mary, or any of her stepchildren, as she had her own siblings. In the summer of 1820, however, such problems lay ahead. By her own admission, Fanny accepted Sir Edward's proposal 'as much from a sense of duty as from inclination' and 'had made up [her] mind ... to grow attached to [him] in time.'[33] As the summer of their engagement progressed, however, she did become attached to him, even taking the trouble to assure Sir Edward that the whole Plumptre episode – including a recent visit from his wife and baby – had meant little to her.[34]

Though these were heady, sometimes alarming days for Fanny, there was one other member of the family for whom the marriage would have enormous consequences. For Marianne, while Lizzy's wedding had spelled the end of childhood, Fanny's altered her entire future. Fanny, shopping in 1818 for wedding clothes for Lizzy, had wondered 'when I should have to perform the same office for Marianne, little imagining it would be required for myself'.[35] Now, unexpectedly and joyously shopping for her own wedding, Fanny's plans for Marianne, who was not yet nineteen, no longer assumed an early marriage for her: 'Marianne is a dear good girl & is ready to assist me in every possible way —,' she wrote to her fiancé. 'I took her with me today for the first time to order dinner & I mean she should be in the room everyday in future whilst I am making this & other domestic arrangements.'[36] These were the same domestic arrangements which Fanny continued to find arduous and exhausting. Even in 1820, after twelve years' experience, she wrote that she had been struggling with household accounts, and had found the linen stores in 'a fine confusion'. The household was large: when Edward Knight stayed in Chawton in 1820, he had nineteen servants – and this was in his second home. He had gradually devolved to Fanny almost full responsibility for the running of the house, including not only the organisation of entertainment, but also the engagement and dismissal of staff, the management of linen and other household stores, the purchasing of household necessities and the regular payment of wages. With Fanny's wedding imminent, Marianne was now expected to learn all this between August and October. Far from enjoying the round of engagements and outings which Fanny had considered essential for Lizzy, even within a month of her aunt's death, Marianne seems to have spent the summer of 1820 preparing to take over as her father's housekeeper. Perhaps only half in earnest, Fanny described her in one letter as 'idle', though it is hard to see how she could have found time to be so, and seems to have pressed her at once into making cravats for Sir Edward.[37]

It had been taken for granted in the previous generation that Jane Austen and her sister Cassandra would care for their mother and that, as in *Sense and Sensibility*, their brothers need have little responsibility in the matter beyond the provision of gifts of money and, after several rootless years, a house. Similarly, it seems to have been assumed that Marianne, at nineteen, would simply take over where Fanny left off. While Fanny had herself stepped into her mother's role at only fifteen, she had had a great deal of help from the generation above, and was constantly encouraged to meet other young people and to think of her own future, as was Lizzy. However much Marianne might have worn her white dancing slippers in the brief period of girlhood allowed to her between the weddings of her two sisters, there seems to have been little opportunity after Fanny's engagement for her to go dancing. Fanny herself indicated as much to Miss Chapman in September 1820, in what reads like a description of her final handing over of responsibility to Marianne:

> I have been very little at this dear place since April, when we all went into Hampshire for three months. Mrs Edward Rice has suffered sadly all the summer with her teeth — has at last been obliged to have them out, which I hope relieves her. She is to be confined again in November and I believe I shall spend that month with her ... I expect her here in about a fortnight to accompany me to London to buy wedding clothes. Edward & William are at present at Chawton for some shooting — they got a few weeks' leave lately but returned last week to join their regiment in Norfolk — Charles returned lately to Winchester & my little Johnny is still with Mr Smith, though not at Eltham ... George is the only one of my brothers at home at present. We like Miss Dickinson, my sisters' new governess, very well, & I think she will remain with them. Marianne is rather young to be at the head of a family — only 19, but she is steady, & it is a great comfort to me to collect that I shall be within reach of rendering her much assistance, Hatch being only nine miles from this place.[38]

No doubt Fanny did mean to help Marianne, as she had Lizzy, but she could not have anticipated the extent to which not only Lizzy's concerns, but also those of her new family would occupy her mind and energy. Quietly and inexorably, Marianne was assumed into Fanny's position. In December 1820, Fanny wrote that after Lizzy 'was brought to bed the 7th November of a little girl ... Marianne came from Godmersham where she had been staying on Wednesday, & will remain till near Christmas, so that Lizzy will have a good succession of companions to assist her in regaining her strength'.[39] Her father echoed the sentiment in a letter to Edward Rice in 1821, following the birth of Lizzy's second son: 'Marianne is already as anxious to nurse her little Nephew as if it were the first she had ever had'.[40] Their praise for Marianne's goodness and steadiness was genuine, like the general praise of *Persuasion*'s Anne Elliot as the best possible person to nurse Louisa Musgrove after her fall at Lyme: there is no doubt that the party at Lyme did consider Anne the best nurse for Louisa, and equally, there is no doubt of the deep attachment of the Knights to Marianne. Yet, as with Anne Elliot, everyone had stopped thinking of her as a young woman with prospects of her own. This was true of Fanny, in particular. Perhaps because she herself had had to make duty her watchword, Fanny expected no less of Marianne, and Marianne was not accustomed to questioning her sister's judgement.

The perceptive Lizzy, whose own husband was ten years her senior had commented during Fanny's engagement to Sir Edward that their 'united ages amount to nearly seventy' and said she had thought of 'presenting [them] each with a gold-headed cane when [they were] married'. Fanny's reaction – 'it delights me that she can treat the subject in an amusing light' – suggests either that she could then shrug off the age discrepancy, or that her sense of humour, not in adulthood her most prominent characteristic, was already in decline.[41] Yet, it does not seem to have occurred to her that in appointing Marianne her successor as housekeeper she had severely limited her sister's chances of finding the same happiness she herself had sought. Her inability to give Marianne the opportunities she had allowed Lizzy may have been the result of indifferent health in the first few years of her marriage: Fanny spent five weeks in 1821 taking the waters at Leamington Spa, the resort made fashionable by the Prince Regent. While this might have been a chance for her sister to meet other young people, Marianne was not Fanny's chosen companion. Instead, she was accompanied by George, still considering his role in life, and Louisa.[42] 'All my family are in Hampshire except my sister

Louisa,' Fanny wrote to Miss Chapman in September 1821. '[She] has been dividing the summer between the houses of her ... friends & is at present here, but goes to Dane Court tomorrow. They are all pretty well except my father, who has lately been suffering from gout, quite a new complaint for him.'[43] Though only in his early fifties, Edward Knight seemed to be slipping into the clichéd role of elderly gouty gentleman while Louisa, not yet seventeen, was considered old enough to be at a spa for five weeks rather than in the schoolroom with her governess. If Louisa was now ready to be out in society, where did that place Marianne, not yet twenty? She seems not to have been much involved in social outings. She may have been much too occupied with her duties as mistress of Godmersham, or she may yet again have been with her sister Lizzy, who was expecting her third child at only twenty-one. A letter of family news from Fanny to Miss Chapman, dated 12 March 1822, sheds some light:

> [Charles] ... is now at Cambridge, and is intended for the law ... Wm took his degree at Oxford in November and is now studying for Orders, which I hope he will receive in June and he will I believe take a curacy in Hampshire immediately. My two eldest brothers are at present in town for a few days only, & Henry nominally at Canterbury with his regiment ... My little darling John is still at Mr Smith's but he will go to Winchester I believe at midsummer ... Mrs Edward Rice has just weaned her baby — it is unfortunate that her children never thrive till they are weaned. Marianne has been staying with her and has just returned home. Louisa is now grown & is a very nice girl — she has already been to several balls & will probably come out at the Races. Cassandra is with me. Their last governess, Miss Dickinson, left them in the summer ... and as we have a governess for Miss Knatchbull, it was arranged that their education be finished together — you may imagine what a pleasure it is to me to have the dear child always with me. She and Mary have several masters and go on very nicely with their studies.[44]

In other words, the brothers were fairly firmly on their career paths, and it was now Louisa, Cassandra and Mary Knatchbull – not Marianne, the 'dear, good girl' – whose futures concerned Fanny. Nonetheless, despite her relegation to the role of housekeeper and companion, Marianne was once more touched by romance. It happened in 1822, the same year in which the cousin who had been so struck by her was writing despondent verses about lost love. The gentleman was a Mr Billington, who had attended Winchester College with Marianne's brother, Edward, and in 1809 and 1810, while Marianne was still away at school with Lizzy, was one of the schoolfellows who dined with the Knights when Edward was returning to Winchester. Later, in 1813, he hunted with the young Knights at Godmersham, and once again joined the family at dinner. It seems most likely that he was Mr John Billington, who was born in 1798, and ordained in 1821, becoming Rector of Kennardington and Vicar of Kennington, two parishes near Ashford in Kent. This young clergyman, who dined on more than one occasion at Fanny's house in 1822, proposed to Marianne in November of that year. Fanny's diary records the event without comment: 'I heard that Mr Billington proposed to Marianne the other day and was refused'.[45]

Perhaps Marianne refused John Billington because she did not love him; perhaps, with her father to attend, two sisters of only eighteen and sixteen and a lively fourteen-year-old brother still in need of care and guidance, she felt she could not. To do so would have left Louisa or Cassandra in the same position as herself. She was only twenty-one, yet it was already too late. Her only real chance of marrying without abandoning her family had been between the weddings of Lizzy and Fanny, and her only chance of romance at that time was too slender to survive family disapproval. Now, whatever her feelings towards Mr Billington, it was once more irrelevant. Duty came first. There would be no more proposals for Marianne and gradually, as her sister's children were born, she began to become Aunt May – like Jane Austen before her, a lively, much-loved, but unmarried aunt in her early twenties. 'I am sorry I shall not be at your races, for all your sakes,' the witty Henry Knight wrote to his sister Lizzy from Brighton in June 1823. 'I daresay we should have had very good fun. Does not Marianne know yet, that she is not to go?'[46]

Henry at Brighton, and Lizzy, just returned from London, were having a busy summer between town and the seaside. Marianne was at Godmersham and not, apparently, going anywhere.

Fanny, meanwhile, was beginning to find that her stepchildren and her own brothers gave her more than enough anxiety to keep her occupied. At first, she was relieved and content that Cassandra could be placed with Mary Knatchbull's governess, Miss Verney. When a successor to Miss Verney, a Miss Atkinson, arrived in 1821 she too seemed, at first, a success. Sir Edward Knatchbull described her as 'tall — very well-looking — without being handsome — her manner — good and Ladylike ... very much the sort of Being I best like for a governess'.[47] If Fanny had to be absent from home, Miss Atkinson was entrusted with the care of the two young girls, and frequently met visiting members of the Knight family. One of these was William Knight, who had delighted his aunt Jane first as a child, working a footstool for her, and again in the last year of her life, when he stayed at Chawton Cottage. After taking his degree at Oxford and making the customary trip abroad, he had decided on the church. In the summer of 1823, he was ordained, and was to become rector at Jane's first home, Steventon. His future was clearly marked: Edward Knight had within his gift the living at Steventon, and Henry Austen's late vocation to the priesthood meant that he could hold the living until William was ready to take it over.[48] Meanwhile, William spent the summer of 1823 with the Knatchbulls in Kent, assisting the rector of Mersham in his duties. By August 1823, however, there was a problem: it emerged that he and the ladylike Miss Atkinson had, in the parlance of the day, 'formed an attachment'. Miss Atkinson was immediately dismissed.

Unsurprisingly, given the prevailing double standard for behaviour in men and women, there appears to have been no immediate consequence for William, who took up his position as planned and, two years later, married Miss Caroline Portal, a match which did not quite please his family socially, but was not actively discouraged.[49] His father had, after all, told Lizzy that, with the cost of levelling the old house at Steventon and remodelling it for William, he hoped his son would 'find a good rich wife to help furnish as well as fill his mansion', and his son had obligingly done his best.[50] As to his affair with the governess at Mersham, though the family kept it a secret 'from our friends', the matter leaked out later that year, and caused considerable embarrassment, if not to William, certainly to his brother-in-law Sir Edward Knatchbull, who was by then increasingly prominent in political life.[51] Once again, the incident lacks only the ironic assessment of Jane Austen, who had been so unimpressed when George and Henry Knight dallied in their teens with a servant at Godmersham; yet, in her early cautionary tales of George Wickham and John Willoughby, equally handsome and charming, just as capable of disappointing those who loved them and, in both cases, not only subsequently unreproved for their conduct, but actually enabled to make advantageous marriages, she had already made sufficient comment.

William's affair with the governess was not to be the only such embarrassment. By 1826, an even more serious situation took all of Fanny's attention, not least because it came from an unexpected source. Her eldest stepdaughter, Mary Dorothea, had made a favourable early impression. 'I never met a more promising child and one more thoroughly disposed and even anxious to do whatever she is told is right,' she wrote early in their acquaintance. In the first months of the marriage, Mary visited her stepmother each morning before she rose, and Fanny encouraged the 'dear child' in her needlework and her study of the piano. 'Her affection,' she wrote, 'I hope to gain in time. She shows ... much excellent feeling.'[52]

Her 'excellent feeling', unfortunately, was what would cause the next crisis. In the summer of 1824, Fanny wrote with emphasis in her journal, 'Mary *came out*, and went to her first ball at Ashford in August.'[53] By the end of the next year, she was writing that she had 'never known so much care and anxiety', some of which she attributed to her brother Edward's proposal to and refusal by a Lady Elizabeth Bligh.[54] Edward Knight, acting as caretaker for his father at Chawton House, was now in a position to marry and, at almost thirty-two, was apparently anxious to do so. The disappointment of a refusal was clearly a blow, yet he was so much recovered by the end of December 1825 that he asked Sir Edward Knatchbull for nineteen-year-old Mary's hand. If he hoped his near relation to the family would help his suit, he was much mistaken. Fanny wrote in January 1826: 'We are all under the disagreeable influence of the proposal ... which is now under discussion and deliberation.' She complained of 'care, anxiety, worry and uneasiness'.[55] Sir

Edward refused permission, and the matter was considered closed as far as Fanny was concerned. She described in her diary a pleasant evening in mid-May 1826 when, after her father and Cassandra Jane had left after a visit, and her husband had gone out to dine, she and Mary dined 'tête-à-tête'. Her entry for the next day, Sunday 14 May 1826, was very different. 'We were thrown into the greatest distress this morning by the discovery that Mary had left the house in the night; and a few lines from Edward soon after explained that she had eloped with him to Scotland!!! Alas for her father! God support him!'[56]

This was no exaggeration: on the night of Saturday 13 May 1826 Mary Dorothea Knatchbull and Edward Knight – like Jane Austen's fictional Lydia and Wickham – eloped. Unlike Lydia and Wickham, they were married at Gretna Green in Scotland on the following Monday. There was no question of keeping this a secret: it was fact. Yet, just as in *Pride and Prejudice*, because it was fact it had to be accepted. Edward Austen Knight, who was at the same time struggling to conclude his dealings with the claim made some years before on his estate, met the Knatchbulls on the following Wednesday, 17 May 1826. Fanny described it as 'a wretched meeting'.[57] Sir Edward Knatchbull did not blame Fanny. He simply expressed his wish 'to restore tranquillity with as much propriety as possible and to make the best of a bad business'.[58] The difficulty was in the degree of the relationship, as Edward Knight was step-uncle to Mary; for this reason Sir Edward Knatchbull's fury was directed first towards Edward and then Mary, whom he refused to see.[59] Not everyone shared his view. Letters flew among the various Knight, Austen and Knatchbull homes. Sharp-tongued Caroline Austen, James's younger daughter, reporting with relish some of the family's reactions – including those of the volatile Jane Leigh Perrot – blamed Sir Edward Knatchbull himself for the situation. Interestingly, Caroline had only limited sympathy for her cousin Fanny, whom she evidently thought somewhat overbearing:

> I sincerely wish he could take all the suffering on himself, as he is the sole cause of the mischief. He made no objection except the connection which was I think most childish. I am very sorry for my Uncle and Lady K., but it will teach her that people cannot

always be schooled and advised out of their feelings. Mama heard today from Mrs Leigh Perrot. She wrote full of the news. It had disturbed the party at Scarlets very much, and taken them away sooner than had been intended that Aunt Cassandra might be at Chawton to receive the fugitives. She was very much agitated. How soon do you think they will let the world have a peep at the Bride? I suppose not under two months as a runaway Bride must be twice as great a curiosity as any other.[60]

In a rather bitter twist, Edward Knight and Mary Dorothea Knatchbull were then married under English law, on 15 June, by the reformed scapegrace of the previous scandal, the Reverend William Knight. The whole episode cries out for the relief of Jane Austen's humour, sadly missing in the reactions of both families, except in Caroline's mischievous wish to have 'a peep at the Bride'. Caroline's comment on Fanny also shows how radically the eldest of the Knight girls had changed since her youth, when she was Jane Austen's favourite niece, and longed for love and romance. Nonetheless, whatever Fanny's feelings on the subject of Edward's marriage to her stepdaughter, he was her brother, and she was fearful that his attitude had caused a real rift, writing on 19 May 1826: 'Oh! That my dear husband would suffer Christian feelings to influence him!' Her summary for the year 1826 showed her very despondent:

> The events of this wretched year have been greatly influenced by the decided negative Sir E. gave to Edward's proposal for Mary, which after causing great discomfort between the families ended in her eloping with him on 14th May from London and being married at Gretna Green and afterwards at Steventon by my brother William. This deplorable step occasioned immediate estrangement between Hatch and Godmersham. Sir Edward's mind is so extremely alienated from his daughter, & disgusted at her conduct ... that I fear matters can never be set to rights.[61]

Fanny's prediction was accurate: strain, however well-disguised, entered the relationship of the Knight and Knatchbull families, and was never quite eased. Even worse, though all the Knights welcomed Mary after the initial scandal, Sir Edward Knatchbull was to see his daughter only once more in her lifetime.[62]

With all that was happening, it is perhaps not surprising that Marianne was left to deal with Godmersham, where even the youngest were now almost grown. By the time of Edward's elopement in 1826 their brother John, Fanny's 'little darling', was almost eighteen, about to leave Winchester and go into the army. Louisa was twenty-one and Cassandra Jane nineteen. After Edward and Mary's shocking breach of conduct, and their betrayal of Fanny's trust, the family intended to make sure that the two youngest sisters would not go the same way.

CHAPTER 3

'No Money – All Charms'

Pride, Prejudice and Persuasion
1827–1834

'The gentleman is in the army then?'
'Yes, ma'am.'
'Aye – there is nothing like your officers for captivating the ladies,
young or old. – There is no resisting a cockade, my dear.'

THE WATSONS

It is one of the oldest devices in literature, well-known to Jane Austen, to have a stranger – mysterious, handsome, or dangerous – arrive in the middle of a settled community, upsetting all previous assumptions. The introduction in 1827 to the Knight family circle of Lord George Hill would have great and far-reaching consequences, not just for Cassandra but also for Louisa, and even for Marianne. He was the catalyst that would change everything.

As 1827 began, the Austen and Knight families were still reeling from the shock of Mary Knatchbull's elopement with Edward Knight the previous spring, and it was beginning to become apparent that Edward's allegiance had shifted from Godmersham to Chawton.[1] More change was to follow. Charles Knight, who had been studying for the Ministry, was ordained, and the youngest brother, John, who had left Winchester College in October 1826 and become an Ensign in the 37th Regiment of Foot, went in the spring of 1827 to join his regiment in Ireland.[2] Mrs George Austen, Jane's mother and grandmother to the Godmersham family, died on 22 March of that year, aged seventy-two, and was buried at Chawton.

Major alterations were being made to the Knatchbull house at Mersham le Hatch in Kent and, in February 1827, Fanny and her family went to their

London house at 30 Great George's Street, accompanied by Louisa. At the end of March, shortly after their grandmother's funeral, Fanny brought Louisa home and took Cassandra Jane to stay in London until the end of June. Though Louisa did make a few short visits to her sisters in London that spring, Cassandra was essentially on her own with Fanny, who could not fail to be conscious that her sister might now feel the loss of her schoolroom companion; the former Mary Knatchbull remained so deeply in disgrace with her father that he would not see her, though she was shortly expecting her first child. Fanny undoubtedly did her best to ensure that, apart from the customary and probably painful visit to the dentist, her young sister enjoyed her days and evenings. They walked in the park, dined out or went to the opera. They attended musical evenings at the homes of their friends, where Cassandra, on at least one occasion, played on the harp and sang.[3] They wrote letters every day, including some to poor banished Mary and, like Jane and Cassandra before them, they loved to go out driving and shopping. They paid many social calls and received a great number of visitors, both family and old friends. There were also some new friends, carefully scrutinised by Fanny, one of whom was a young Irish nobleman named Lord George Hill.

His name first appears in Fanny's diary in the spring of 1827. On 8 May, she wrote: 'Lord George Hill ... accompanied Cass, Lou and me' on a shopping expedition.[4] Over the next two months his name would recur with increasing frequency. His place in society was unquestioned, Fanny noting that they had attended an evening gathering on 17 May at the home of Lady Salisbury, who was Lord George's aunt.[5] He joined them on their shopping trips twice in early June, and on 9 June, Fanny and Cassandra went to the opera, 'where,' Fanny wrote, 'Lord George Hill joined us'. Four days later, on 13 June, he called and accompanied Fanny, Cassandra and one of Fanny's little daughters on their walk to Kensington Gardens; two days after that he called and drove with them again on a shopping trip. On 25 June they went out shopping and visiting yet again and, as Fanny wrote, 'met Lord George Hill, who accompanied us a little way and afterwards dined here'. The next day, however, her diary records that 'Lord G. Hill left town early for Ireland to join his regiment.' Yet, the day after that, Fanny found to her great surprise that Cassandra had received a proposal from a 'Mr Boroughs'.

Mr Boroughs, or Burrows, was immediately refused.[6] It is difficult to avoid the impression that his offer was most ill-timed. If he was in London, he can hardly have been unaware of Lord George's attentions; perhaps it was that, combined with the fact that the family was just about to return to Kent, which precipitated his sudden proposal. Yet, there was clearly no contest. The diary account of Lord George's courtship reads almost uncannily like Jane Austen's description in *Persuasion* of Anne Elliot's fateful meetings in Bath with Captain Wentworth, echoing her sense of his growing interest and her desolation at his departure after the musical performance where they have tried, unsuccessfully, to spend a little time together.[7] There is in this part of the diary, though Fanny could not be said to have inherited her aunt's gift for narrative any more than for irony, the same charged sense of an unspoken affinity and a steadily developing attachment, and the same sense of frustration and anti-climax at the gentleman's sudden removal.

It is not clear whether Lord George signalled any intention of returning, or of proposing. Like Anne Elliot, however, Cassandra made her allegiance clear in her refusal of another suitor. Some days later, at the end of June 1827, the whole family party returned as planned to Kent for the summer. Then, on 11 August, a short entry in Fanny's diary gave welcome news: 'Wet morning, but it cleared before 3 when I set out with my 2 babes and 3 maids to dear Godmersham. G. H. W. & Ch. are here to my great delight. Cass told me of her proposal from Ld G. Hill from Ireland, which Papa answered yesterday'.[8] No exclamation marks were necessary. It is a calm entry, and the presence at the family home of George, Henry, William and Charles Knight seems to emphasise the sense of general delight over the proposal. Only John, who was still with his regiment; Lizzy, recovering from the birth of her latest child; and Edward, at Chawton, were missing from the gathering. Even Mr Billington, the neighbouring clergyman whom Marianne had, without rancour, turned down five years before, was among the happy party that evening.

On 27 August, Louisa and Cassandra called with Fanny on their way to visit their Deedes cousins at Sandling, no doubt to share the good news. The next day, everything changed. 'My dear excellent father,' Fanny wrote, 'rode over to see me & told me of Lady Downshire's disapprobation of Ld. G.H's marrying Cass, on acct. of not money enough.'[9] This terrible news, so much worse because unexpected, had now to be communicated to Cassandra, and it fell to Fanny to deliver the blow. As expected, Louisa and Cassandra called again on their way back from Sandling on 29 August, the day after Fanny had heard of Lord George's mother's veto, and her diary simply records, with the understatement of the inevitable, 'I told Cass of Lady D's letter.' She says nothing of her sister's reaction. There may not have been time: many visitors called that day, and a large party, including Fanny, went to the Ashford ball. It was 'a good ball', Fanny wrote, and the party 'came back to supper & all slept here except the officers'.[10] Fanny does not say whether Cassandra and Louisa were of the party; yet, it is hard to imagine which might have been worse – attending in misery the opening ball of the season, or going home. For the two sisters, close in age and temperament as Jane and Elizabeth Bennet, it would have been a dismal evening in either circumstance. In any case, whatever Cassandra's reaction, there was nothing to be done. 'No money – all charms,' was Lady Downshire's reported view of Cassandra, worthy of Lady Catherine de Bourgh at her most cutting.[11] It is clear by Fanny's summary written at the end of 1827, that she for one was certain that the affair was over. 'Ld G. Hill paid [Cassandra] great attention in London & proposed to her in August,' she wrote, 'but they could not make money enough and it all went off.'[12] As in her aunt's novels, financial considerations and the veto of a powerful matriarch had dictated the end of love.

When Cassandra first met him in 1827, Lord George was twenty-five years old, and a career soldier. A portrait by Richard James Lane shows him to have been dark-haired, lean and handsome, and he was also, as Jane Austen preferred a young man to be, courteous, clever and cultured.[13] To Cassandra, aged twenty, the young officer must have appeared quite as dashing as Captain Wentworth to the young Anne Elliot, or George Wickham to the Bennet sisters. Like Mr Darcy, he was of a noble family. Born on 9 December 1801, the youngest son of Arthur, 2nd Marquess of Downshire, and his wife, the former Mary Sandys, he had but one fault: like Cassandra, he had no money.

Lord Downshire had been the owner of extensive properties in both Ireland and England, his family's long service to the crown having been rewarded by the granting of extensive tracts of property. The Hill family motto, '*Per Deum et Ferrum Obtinui. Ne Tentes Aut Perfice*,' translates as

'Through God and my sword I have obtained. Attempt not, or accomplish.'[14] The first of his ancestors to take up land in Ireland had been Moyses Hill, a follower of the first Earl of Essex in his attempted settlement of Ireland in the 1570s, and later a participant in the campaigns by the second Earl of Essex against Hugh O'Neill.[15] The 2nd Marquess had died, aged only forty-eight, three months before Lord George's birth: partly because of debts inherited from the 1st Marquess and mainly because his political expenditure had left the estate in great financial difficulty, his youngest son was largely unprovided for, and could not expect to inherit any sum of consequence. A career was essential and, given the family's tradition of military service, the army was an obvious choice.

As a boy, Lord George studied at the Royal Academy at Woolwich; then in late 1818, at about the same time as Edward and George Knight, he travelled for a year through France, Belgium, Holland and Germany with his older brother, Lord Augustus, and their tutor. In addition to mathematics, Latin and German, they studied drawing, dancing, fencing and flute playing; their list of expenses included not only clothes, books, blotting paper and sealing wax but also the presumably essential brandy, magnesia water and salt for foot baths. This expensive forerunner of the modern gap year was still considered essential for a gentleman's son, even one without prospects, as 'a sales point in favour of young men who were seeking a wife'.[16] On his return from the continent, just following his eighteenth birthday, Lord George was gazetted a Cornet, and joined the Royal Horse Guards (the Blues). Over the next ten years, after transferring to the 8th King's Royal Irish Hussars, he reached the rank of Major.

His eldest brother, the heir to the title and considerable property, would not come of age until 1809. In the meantime, it was left to the Marchioness of Downshire to act as a kind of regent, trying to restabilise the finances of the estates while making provision for her five sons and two daughters. Her marriage articles of June 1786 and a post-nuptial settlement of July 1789 had made provision for a jointure of £5,000 per year, if she survived her husband. In addition, because of the property she had brought to the marriage she was in a position to ensure that she had enough security to raise portions for her younger children.[17] As it was left to his mother to decide how to divide the money, Lord George's financial future depended on her approval of his choices, political and personal.

Lady Downshire, able and formidable in the eighteenth-century female mould familiar to Jane Austen, was a lady of decided opinions. She was a figure of some note in her own right, having been politically active all through the later years of the eighteenth century. The brilliance of her marriage in 1786 to Arthur Hill had consolidated lands and power between their two families, and his inheritance of the title on the death in 1793 of his father, Wills Hill, the 1st Marquess, strengthened their political position even further. The 2nd Marquess, however, chose to live in England, visiting Ireland for only one week in the three years before the crucial debates over the proposed Act of Union between Great Britain and Ireland, which became law on 1 January 1801. When he did come, it was to make known his political opposition to the proposal, a stance which did not help him or his family after it was voted through. Robert Stewart, Viscount Castlereagh, who had promoted the cause of the Union, made sure that Downshire paid, in a series of humiliations, for this perceived disloyalty.[18] After her husband's death, undaunted by any of the vicissitudes of the previous few years, Lady Downshire managed to revive her grandfather's title so that, by the time Lord George was six months old, his mother had been created Baroness Sandys in her own right.[19]

Politically, she remained a Whig, and the sworn enemy of Castlereagh, whose earlier battle with her husband shortly after the marriage for control of County Down had cost both men a vast sum, and contributed in no small part to the Downshires' subsequent financial difficulties.[20] She undertook to raise money through skilful, if ultimately limiting decisions over the granting of leases to tenants. Subdivision of small land holdings on the estates had 'created a concealed class of occupiers, where it had not already added to the number of official tenants': this intrepid lady was given the power in 1802, under a private Act, to grant and renew leases.[21] This meant that after the enfranchisement of Roman Catholics in 1793 she could ensure that she had a greatly increased number of voters on her side, no small achievement, and vitally important to her conception of the role she was to play, for until her death in 1836, she remained a politically active force.[22] Yet, though her eldest son, the 3rd Marquess, would make peace with Castlereagh three years after he attained his majority, she was never prepared to do so. Lady Downshire did not change her mind easily.

Lord George was quickly reminded of this when he proposed marriage to Cassandra Knight, though it is unlikely that political and financial considerations dominated the minds of the two young people. Lord George and Cassandra wanted very much to marry: given their dependence on their families, however, without his mother's consent there was no chance that they could afford to do so and, predictably, Lady Downshire seemed immovable. It is hard to decide whether she bears a closer resemblance at this point to Lady Catherine de Bourgh, or *Persuasion*'s Lady Russell. Jane Austen was ever conscious of the hard fact that money and the entailment of property decided more marriages than love: Lady Downshire may be closer in her intransigence either to Frank Churchill's aunt who, holding the purse strings, indicated in *Emma* where Frank might or might not attach himself, or to *Sanditon*'s Lady Denham, 'a great lady beyond the common wants of society – for she had many thousands a year to bequeath, and three distinct sets of people to be courted by'.[23] Interestingly, while Jane Austen frequently satirises such an attitude, she never goes so far as to say that it is wrong, or unjustified. As Elizabeth Bennet asks her aunt, Mrs Gardiner, in *Pride and Prejudice*: 'What is the difference in matrimonial affairs between the mercenary and the prudent motive? Where does discretion end and avarice begin?'[24] It came to this: Lord George at twenty-five was not independent, and could not expect to be so if he opposed his mother. Cassandra, not yet twenty-one, the youngest girl of a large family in which only her eldest brother might – and did – decide his future for himself, could expect very little unless she married well. As the heads of both families required financial security in partners for their children, the match between Cassandra and Lord George was clearly impossible.

It seemed that Cassandra's chance of marrying for love had gone. She had not refused Lord George, as Marianne had John Billington. She had not eloped, like her eldest brother Edward and her former schoolmate Mary Dorothea. It had all been decided for her, and there was nothing she could do. Her last brother was gone from home, stationed far away in Ireland and, now, so was the man she had expected to marry. Fanny, nearly fourteen years older, was very much more her mother than her sister, and Marianne, though only five years Cassandra's senior, was by 1827 so much occupied with the care of their father and the running of the Great House at Godmersham that no one thought of her any more as a young woman. Where was Cassandra to find company of her own age? Fortunately, she still had her sister Louisa, only two years older and, like her, unmarried and unburdened by family responsibility.

Yet, not long after Lord George went away, it seemed that Louisa might be the next to marry. Like Cassandra, she received two proposals, refusing the first in June 1828 from a gentleman named Sir William Young.[25] Her next proposal, which came the following year, was from a family friend which, of itself, made it more difficult to address. George Chichester Oxenden was the gentleman's name, and his sister, Mary, had been, since 1811, one of Fanny's close friends.[26] George and Mary Oxenden were the children of Sir Henry Oxenden of Broome Place, Barham, near Canterbury and Mary, who had married shortly after recovering from a serious illness in 1814, had once been the subject of one of Jane Austen's acerbic asides: 'Instead of dieing [sic] [she] is going to marry Wm. Hammond.'[27] George Oxenden was well known not only to the Knights but also to the Rices. In 1825, he had accompanied Lizzy, her husband Edward and Edward's mother Mme Sarah Rice on a trip to Scotland, where they all stayed with the Duke of Montrose at Braehaven.[28] He was seven years older than Louisa, and they shared an interest in botany and natural science: later in life he would correspond with Charles Darwin on the subject of orchids. He had gained some fame through the publication of poetry.[29] It may or may not be coincidence that in a collection of his works, published at the time of his pursuit of Louisa, several love poems are included. One of these, dated 1829, is wistfully entitled 'Pourquoi Pas':

> Because I see thee young and bright,
> Yet lovelier, purer far
> Than glittering flash of Polar Light,
> I love thee — Pourquoi Pas?—

Because my life has waned away
In many a wayward scene,
And thou art like the spring of day,
Unsullied and serene,

By yonder stars — which seem
To bless the spot
Where thy soft glances gleam,
And grief is not,

And by that crested wave,
Struggling to lie
Where its white wreath might lave
Thy feet — and die,

By all of joy or love
That life can give,
By every hope above,
For thee — I live.[30]

Why not? Whatever his gifts and attractions, they were not enough for Louisa. Fanny recorded in 1829 that 'the affair remained unsettled' and by 1830 was writing, decisively: 'the affair between Mr G.C. Oxenden and my sister Louisa entirely put an end to this summer'.[31]

A silhouette which seems, judging from styles of hair and dress, to date from the late 1820s shows the three youngest Knight sisters against a pencilled sketch of a drawing-room in Godmersham.[32] Louisa and Cassandra sit upright, almost at attention, one holding needlework, the other a book or paper, their gaze intent upon Marianne who, standing with what may be a ruler, a pointer or a skein of wool in her hand, appears to be instructing them. In 1827, when Cassandra and Lord George met and parted, Marianne was still only twenty-five, Louisa twenty-two, and Cassandra twenty. Strangely, not one of the figures in this silhouette looks young, though they do seem entirely self-sufficient. In the late 1820s and early 1830s, the Knights of Godmersham did appear to be content with their own company. Once the excitement of regular proposals had passed, they settled into a comfortable pattern with their father and their brother Charles who, though ordained, still lived at home, assisting the Rector in his parish work. He also kept a diary. This account, in which Charles displays a gift for description and dramatic narrative not unworthy of a nephew of Jane Austen, gives a unique picture of the years when he, Marianne, Louisa and Cassandra were all together at Godmersham.[33] Charles was not a natural clergyman, as he would later concede: his real life seemed to begin when he spent time outdoors, shooting with his brothers or his neighbours, or walking and listening to birdsong with his father or sisters. 'I walked with Lou & Cass down the river to East Stowe & by Winnigates & Coneybro home,' he wrote at the end of January 1832, 'then with my father to Ripple. Saw many hen Chaffinches at Winnigates. Robins chirped. Saw a Yellow Wagtail on the banks of the River by the Church.'[34]

Charles's diaries show that, among themselves, they were once more May, Lou, Cass, Charley and, when he was home on leave, Johnny – the same little group who had sat, excluded, on the stairs while Jane Austen read to their older sisters behind a closed door. They looked after one another: John contracted a form of smallpox in 1835, and Charles sat with him over many nights until he recovered. Afterwards, John seems to have been less than robust, and to have spent longer periods at home.[35] Fanny and Lizzy visited when family commitments allowed, and Charles's diary indicates that at least one other brother, the unpredictable George, came home regularly when his varying attempts at a career permitted it. George had not changed. Charles expressed his frustration with his brother's continuing indolence in September 1832: 'George went away not having done anything but stay in the house during his whole visit.'[36]

Though Marianne, Louisa, Cassandra and even Charles were dependent on their father, their lives do not seem to have been unhappy. Charles and Marianne, now the eldest of those at home, maintained a quiet, unhurried companionship, visiting and caring for the poor of the parish. They found great satisfaction working in the garden, and identifying different kinds of birds and plants. 'Herons flew about at night calling,' Charles wrote on 18 March 1832. 'Marianne found a longtailed tit's nest by Crows.'[37] Sometimes they went riding together, or visited an art exhibition, as they did at Lee in 1833: 'We saw the pictures, a beautiful Herodias and daughter by Carlo Dole, and several others much inferior but very well.'[38] They went to town, indulged their usual pleasure in shopping and, yet again, visited the dentist, where Marianne 'agreed to give 35£ to Mallen for stopping and whitening her tooth'. Charles was appalled: 'Amazing price!' he wrote.[39] They shared, as a family, a love of reading, writing diaries or letters, walking and riding and sometimes they all went out at night to study the sky: 'Louisa & Cass'ra were out till very late stargazing,' Charles wrote on 15 May 1833. 'It is so lovely, so nobody likes to come in.'[40] The younger sisters had a busy programme of social engagements, always beginning with the races in the late summer: 'Louisa & Cassandra went to the ball at Canterbury,' Charles wrote on 23 August 1832, 'being the beginning of their race gaieties, & I follow'd in my gig'. He added, rather ungallantly: 'There were very few pretty women.'[41] Charles had not yet resigned himself to bachelorhood: his diary records not only his attempts to find a suitable, and preferably pretty, wife at these events, but also the barely concealed amusement of his three sisters at some of his less successful efforts.[42] One of their brothers, however, had more success, and they had the joy of a family wedding when Henry married their cousin, Sophia Cage, in May 1832. Less than a year later, they mourned together when Sophia died of what was thought to be influenza, leaving an infant son, Lewis.[43]

During the dead of winter, the Knights gathered at Godmersham, reviving the old tradition of the family Christmas. Like Jane and her siblings in the generation before, they enjoyed team games after dinner, often with the wider family:

> We acted charades, Lou, Cass & I, *Band Box*, A military band, a boxing match & a woman with lots of Bandboxes going by a coach. Cass, George & Edward — *Dial*. A dying scene, shoemaker & a sun dial. George, Gage & Lou. *Infancy*. A scene at an inn, a fancy ball & a number of Babies.[44]

This was a typical party of between twelve and seventeen people, all staying for days or weeks on end around Christmas. The group included Fanny's stepson, Norton Knatchbull, and his wife; the Cage cousins and Edward and Mary Knight for, though Mary remained unforgiven by her father, she and Edward were always made welcome at Godmersham, despite their scandalous elopement in 1826.

Charles and Louisa had been close since the days when they had said their prayers together as little children. They read, studied German and spent long hours examining and identifying wildlife, occasionally dissecting birds and animals whose remains they had found on their many walks. They shared a fascination with science and the new developments of technology. On Easter Monday of 1832, they ventured together on the new 'rail road', and Charles's account conveys a vivid sense of the excitement of the early days of railway. They travelled at a heady twenty miles per hour, finding it all quite thrilling, though Louisa came to regret wearing her white bonnet:

> Lou & I went to Canterbury & thence by the rail road to Whitstable & back. We found it very pleasant. The day was fine & bright, wind fresh but mild S.E. We went in an open car with the world, and being Easter there was a good deal of company, chiefly shopkeepers & children. We were 38 minutes going the distance which I believe is 8 miles. The spitting from the steam boiler stained Louisa's white satin bonnet, which was the only disaster which happened to us ... We stayed about 1 ½ hours & returned in an open car as before; but a better one for it had cushions to sit on & a backboard to lean against. We had to stop 4 miles from Whitstable for ½ an hour to wait for the returning train from Canterbury, that we might get the rope by which we were to be dragged up the next hill. This is badly managed. After we once started again we went very well into Canterbury, very fast thro' the tunnel about the rate of 20 miles an hour. We did not get to the Fountain till nearly 5 and home soon after 6. Entry into the tunnel at a tremendous pace from the hot sun into the cold dank atmosphere, & quite dark, was a

curious circumstance, & as the wind blew strait up it, it made the change more striking. The thing is not at all complete yet, but I have no doubt it will improve.[45]

Cassandra, whose patience and sweetness of temperament had endeared her to Jane Austen, was drawn more to water. During the summers, they often went as a family to Herne Bay, and enjoyed several weeks of sailing and, on occasion, sea-bathing. 'Too rough to sail or bathe,' Charles wrote on a mid-July day in 1833, adding without comment, 'Cass'ra bathed'.[46] Cassandra may have been gentle, but she did not lack spirit and, as subsequent events would prove, did not shirk a challenge. 'Fanny, Cass'ra, Henry & I in the Victoria soon after breakfast to the shallow by the South Fields Bridge. The wind was not fair for sailing but we managed it,' Charles wrote on 23 May 1833:

> After lunch, Lou, Marianne & I rested in the shrubbery & found several nice & pretty nests, particularly a nightingale with 5 eggs below the old iron gates — also a bullfinch near the house, a green linnet, white throat, gold crested wrens, common wrens, grey linnets, beside Blackbirds & thrushes ... After dinner Cass'ra took three young birds which she calls black caps & put them, nest & all into a cage to see what would come to them, as she wants to rear a blackcap on account of their fine singing...[47]

Unlike Louisa, Cassandra preferred to study and cherish living creatures rather than analyse the dead. Charles's vignettes of his youngest sister are both revealing and poignant: she is the only one to have left no fragment of letters or diaries and, apart from the single silhouette of May, Lou and Cass, no sketch or painting of her appears to have survived. In Charles's diaries, however, she emerges as a quick, intelligent and intrepid young woman of independent opinions.

In this family-centred life at Godmersham, however, the three sisters were not without admirers: on 25 February 1832, 'old Valentine's Day,' Charles noted, 'the 3 girls got 3 Valentines'.[48] Among Charles's friends and shooting companions, he included his neighbours Mr Plumptre and Mr Wildman of Chilham

Castle, both of whom had once been Fanny's suitors, though by then they were long married and unlikely to have sent the valentines. There were others among the family's acquaintance, however, who might have done so. Charles was in the habit of shooting with a Captain Stracey, one of his neighbours; at the end of 1833, Captain Stracey proposed to Louisa, and was refused. When the gentleman married not long afterwards, Charles expressed surprise: 'We met Stracey and his bride coming out of C[anterbur]y. I was much surprised as I had no idea he was to be married so soon. They both looked very happy, very smart & were full of smiles & good humour. They were on their way to Tunbridge Wells to spend the honey moon.' Charles's next remark could have come from the pages of one of his aunt Jane's novels: 'I pity the bride because she is sick, & if he married her for her money, she will be an unhappy woman, or I am much mistaken.'[49] It is a curiously cold observation, yet, whatever Captain Stracey had done to incur Charles's displeasure, he cannot have proposed to Louisa in hopes of gaining a rich wife. Nor could money have been the motive of another prospective suitor of one of his sisters. Charles occasionally shot with two of the Harris family, near relatives of Mr Wildman: one of these would shortly express more than a passing interest in Cassandra, and his interest would not be unreciprocated.

Yet, just as Cassandra, like Anne Elliot, picked up the threads of her life despite her great disappointment, so, like Captain Wentworth, did Lord George Hill. He continued, for the moment, in his military career, although he might just as easily have entered politics. The symbiotic connection between army and society in nineteenth-century Ireland was, in the words of the daughter of a serving army officer of a later generation, 'an order so unreal and preposterous as to be like theatricals in fancy dress'. A first-hand account by this lady, Nora Robertson, illustrates its nuances by dividing Irish society into imaginary rows, adding, in echo of the opinion which ended the hopes of Lord George and Cassandra, that 'though breeding was essential it still had to be buttressed by money':

Row A. Peers who were Lord or Deputy Lieutenants, High Sheriffs and Knights of St Patrick. If married adequately their

L'Aimable Jane, silhouette of Jane Austen, *c.*1810–1815,
thought to be by her nephew, James Edward Austen Leigh

Silhouette portrait of Rev. George Austen presenting his son Edward
to Mr and Mrs Thomas Knight

Family crest of the Knights of Godmersham

Edward Austen Knight as a young man on his Grand Tour of Europe, 1788

Elizabeth Austen (née Bridges),
wife of Edward Austen Knight

Elizabeth and Marianne Knight, *c.*1804

Godmersham Park, Kent

Chawton Great House, Hampshire

Family crest of the Knights of Chawton

Edward Knight, eldest son of Edward Austen Knight

Rev. Charles Bridges Knight, Rector of Chawton 1838–1867

Chawton Rectory, *c.*1803

entrenchment was secure and their sons joined the Guards, the 10th Hussars or the R.N.

Row B. Other peers with smaller seats, ditto baronets, solvent country gentry and young sons of Row A, (sons in Green Jackets, Highland Regiments, certain cavalry, gunners and R.N.). Row A used them for marrying their younger children.

Row C. Less solvent country gentry, who could only allow their sons about £100 a year. These joined the Irish Regiments which were cheap; or transferred to the Indian Army. They were recognised and respected by A and B and belonged to Kildare St. Club.

Row D. Loyal professional people, gentlemen professional farmers, trade, large retail or small wholesale, they could often afford more expensive Regiments than Row C managed. Such rarely cohabited with Rows A and B but formed useful cannon-fodder at Protestant Bazaars and could, if they were really liked, achieve Kildare Street.[50]

Lord George naturally belonged in Row A: he was, therefore expected to marry 'adequately', and was not without opportunity. An account of the Hillsborough House Twelfth Night Ball, held in January 1828, gives a long list of 'most of our resident Nobility and Gentry'. The Marquess and Marchioness of Donegal were there; as were Lord and Lady Dufferin, the Misses Blackwood and Colonel Ward of Bangor and his family; and an array of young ladies: 'the Misses Saurin, Batt, Greg, Moore, D'Arcy, Curteis, Trevor, Innes &C'. When 'the dancing was resumed, with increased spirit, after supper', Lord George was much in evidence for, as the contemporary account relates, in the absence of Lord Arthur Hill, 'prevented from attending the ball by an unlucky accident in dismounting from his horse ... the attentions of the Noble Host and Hostess were most ably assisted by his brother, Lord George Hill who, with several of the Officers of the 8th Royal Irish Hussars, added much to the brilliance of the scene'.[51] Had Lord George wanted to marry he had, like Captain Wentworth, no shortage of young ladies eager to accept him.

Instead, he concentrated on his career. In 1829, two years after his parting from Cassandra, he was stationed in Portobello Barracks in Dublin. Following the passing of the Catholic Relief Act, signalling the beginning of Catholic Emancipation, there was considerable disquiet in England. In her diary for 1829, Fanny records with agitation: 'The Bill for Catholic Emancipation [has] passed in spite of our opposition!'[52] In Ireland, a simmering unrest continued as a new movement began for the repeal of the Act of Union itself, led by the first Catholic to be allowed to take his seat in the House of Commons, Daniel O'Connell. Yet when, only three months later, Lord George wrote to his brother, Lord Downshire, of his imminent move from Dublin to the North of Ireland, he refrained from political opinion, confining himself to his life as a soldier:

> July 20, 1829
> We acquired orders last night to hold ourselves in readiness to march to the north on Monday. I suppose Enniskillen will be our direction; there is therefore no chance of my getting to the House. Don't let her Ladyship fag herself. The General and I arrived at noon on Friday evening, having seen the troops at Dundalk and Drougheda [sic] on our way, we were well lodged at Newry and we dined with McKay [?] of the 50th. My last purchase has been dying of inflammation but there are hopes as she is not *yet dead*. Tell Arthur that his Grey Mare is well. Yrs affecly [53]

He was evidently not estranged from his family, and he had not given way to misery. Stationed in Dublin, he busied himself with the discipline of military life. Increasingly, however, he showed himself willing to assist his brother in political matters: he was, after all, the son of a mother who took politics very seriously. Lady Downshire was prepared to spend money on political campaigns, though she held back in matters of the heart. In 1807, during the 3rd Marquess's minority, she had spent £13,000 in an election in County Down, and at the same time purchased an estate at Carrickfergus which, though a speculative investment, increased the family's political strength in

County Antrim.[54] Such support had become even more important with the gathering strength of agitation for Catholic Emancipation and, after 1829, for repeal of the Union of Great Britain and Ireland. Lord George, as his letters to his brother from 1828–1830 show, was fully prepared to support his family in whatever action they took.[55]

The world Jane Austen left in 1817 had almost disappeared. In June 1830, William IV succeeded George IV who, as Prince Regent, had caused Miss Austen to be made aware that a dedication of her new novel, *Emma*, would not be unwelcome. His death brought an end to the England Jane Austen understood, inherited from the eighteenth century. In Ireland, by contrast, it seemed the troubles, which had ended the eighteenth century with a rebellion, were likely to resurface at any moment. The implementation of the Act of Union of Great Britain and Ireland on 1 January 1801 had brought in its wake the hope, almost the expectation, that the last main legal restriction on Catholics, namely the right to sit in Parliament, would be lifted. That this process did not really begin until 1829, with the passing of the Catholic Relief Act, and then only after a long and often bitter struggle, occasioned continuing tension between Catholics and Protestants, in both England and Ireland.[56] The charismatic Irish Nationalist Daniel O'Connell, who had lobbied tirelessly for Catholic Emancipation, moved immediately to a new campaign for repeal of the Union itself. This growing movement, combined with widespread famine followed by cholera, ensured an unsettled political climate. Lord Anglesey who, during his previous tenure as Lord Lieutenant of Ireland, had urged 'earnest consideration of Catholic Emancipation', now, when re-appointed to the new government formed by Earl Grey in November 1830, declared himself opposed to O'Connell's demand for repeal of the Union. In 1833, Lord Downshire, commenting on the unavoidable interconnection of land value and politics, wrote:

> Mr O'C[onnell] threatens to have the Boro' [Carrickfergus] disenfranchised. If that be the case the Lyndon property [bought by Lady Downshire in 1807] will sink one half, but if the Solicitor comes in for it, the Boro' would be preserved … and if

the Franchise is raised as supposed, the value of the Votes and Estate would rise.[57]

The 'Solicitor' mentioned in the letter was Philip Crampton who, through Lord George, had requested Lord Downshire's support at Carrickfergus. Why approach the Marquess through his youngest brother? By a strange irony, shortly after the marriage with Cassandra was forbidden, Lord George's standing in the world had begun to improve. Having reached the rank of Major at twenty-eight, he retired from the army in 1830, shortly afterwards standing for Parliament and becoming MP for Carrickfergus, in County Antrim, a seat owned by his brother. Though this ensured a further strengthening of the political power of his family according to Lady Downshire's grand plan, it was costly, as Downshire had to provide Lord George with £300 per year as a property qualification to represent Carrickfergus. Lord Downshire's letters of this time lament the straitened circumstances of the family, and the unlikelihood of any improvement in the foreseeable future. In hard economic terms, it seems Lady Downshire's objection to her youngest son's choice of bride was not without basis so that, whatever Lord George's feelings may have been about his broken engagement to Cassandra, and however much his standing had improved, his financial position had not. It did not seem, in 1830–1831, that there was any possibility of his renewing his proposals.

He had his share of personal grief. Lord George had only two sisters, both of whom died unmarried, Lady Charlotte six years before he met Cassandra, in 1821, and Lady Mary in 1830. Then, on 10 July 1831, his brother, Lord Augustus Hill, died. He was the brother closest to Lord George in every way, only sixteen months his senior and his travelling companion on the Grand Tour in 1818–1819.[58] Yet, whatever his private grief, Lord George's star continued to rise in the political world. In 1833, he was appointed Comptroller of the Household of the Lord Lieutenant of Ireland and Viceroy, Lord Anglesey. He was consequently of considerable importance and, while Ireland's political world was certainly not an easy or comfortable place to be, he was by then quite at home in it. In 1834, in his capacity as Comptroller of the Household, he accompanied the Viceroy on a fact-finding visit to outlying poverty-stricken coastal districts in the west of Ireland. It proved to be a turning point in his life.

Their guide was Sir James Dombrain, Inspector General of the Coastguard, who had recently purchased a small estate in Dunlewey, Donegal, and would become a trusted friend to Lord George. 'I believe,' he later wrote, 'I was in some measure instrumental in inducing Lord G. Hill to settle here,' and went on to explain how it happened:

> The wretched ways he then saw and the bad management on many estates first suggested to his benevolent mind the idea of purchasing a property and working out his own views as to raising the People to a moral and social scale of civilisation. His Lordship eventually succeeded in purchasing the property he now holds on most of Gweedore, a worse selection in its then state he could not have made. In encountering the extreme difficulties incident to all Proprietors ... he may truly have been said to have 'taken the Bull by the Horns'.[59]

Lord George's interest in Ireland was not confined to politics: he was endlessly fascinated by its landscape, history, culture and especially its language, in which he had become a considerable scholar.[60] When he first visited Donegal, he knew this was an opportunity he could not forego. He was, however, no idle dreamer. Though deeply struck by the countryside and its people, and determined to try to buy property there if and when he was in a position to do so, he was not motivated solely by appreciation of the wild beauty of Donegal. Lord George was eminently practical and had, in addition, the zeal of the reformer. His plans were radical: he was fired by a desire to rid the country of a farming system he thought outdated, and to introduce new and efficient methods. It would be no small undertaking, as Dombrain's description of his own first sight of 'this rough-hewn land' shows:

> My first attempt to see Dunlaoey [sic] was made on Horseback. I left James Gallagher's at Bunbeg, made to Gortahork to where the road terminates ... I was then four miles from Dunlaoey with nothing but a dangerous Mountain track before me and as night was coming on I was compelled to return ... Some months

afterwards I was induced again to attempt it. I then walked from
Bunbeg and by the side of the River where the Hotel now stands
and by the margin of the Lake to Dunlaoey. I subsequently
succeeded in getting the line of Road made ... to Gweedore and
in effecting other slight improvements ... [M]y official duties ...
precluded the possibility of doing more for the improvement of
the people, whose habits of self-will and lawlessness ... required
... watchful care to check and amend.[61]

A similar spirit of improvement had fired Lord George's mind and by 1834
he knew that he wanted to own land, and that Donegal in Ireland was where he
wished that land to be. Since 1827 he had known that it was Cassandra Knight
with whom he desired to spend his life and, accordingly, he now planned
to renew his proposals. Cassandra, having apparently reconciled herself to
disappointment and to have settled back to life in Godmersham, suddenly
announced in July 1834, to the surprise of her entire acquaintance, that she was
engaged to be married. It was not, however, to Lord George Hill.

CHAPTER 4

'WINTERING IN ENGLAND'

Cassandra's Marriage
1834–1842

'Irish! Ah! I remember – and she is gone to settle in Ireland. – I do not
wonder that you should not wish to go with her into that country ... '

THE WATSONS

'Cass'ra looked uncommonly well, but with her chaplet of orange flowers &
white veil over it was rather like a victim.'[1] It was an unusual remark for a
brother to make of his sister on her wedding day; yet, this was in many ways
a unusual wedding. Because of Charles Knight's habit of recounting in his
diary the details of everyday events, a unique account exists of Cassandra
Jane's marriage on 21 October 1834. Charles could not have known how sadly
prescient his careful observations would prove. 'The people crowded round,'
he wrote, 'to see her get in & out of her carriage, & poked their faces quite
close to her, saying poor thing, how handsome, how very beautiful, generally
adding poor thing or some compassionate remark as if she was going to be
buried alive.'[2]

That summer, like her aunt Jane thirty-two years earlier, Cassandra had
suddenly and most unexpectedly become engaged to a gentleman from a
neighbouring family.[3] In Jane's case, the engagement to Harris Bigg-Wither of
Manydown lasted less than twenty-four hours; in Cassandra's, wedding plans
were made. In temperament, the two suitors were not dissimilar. Like Harris
Bigg-Wither, Musgrave Alured Henry Harris was a youngest son, awkward
and shy, much indulged by his parents and older siblings. His father, George,
1st Baron Harris of Seringapatam and Mysore, lived in Belmont House, near
Faversham in Kent, and had a distinguished military record, not only in India,

but also in the War of American Independence. Musgrave, 'Mus' to his family, had been a source of continuing concern to his parents, showing no interest in a military life and preferring to enter the Church. His academic qualifications however, rather precluded this at first, his father remarking that he was not 'one of the *illumine*', and he went to India in 1822, aged twenty-one, to join the Bombay Civil Service. A notoriously poor correspondent, he did not tell his parents of the severe damage caused to his health by his contracting cholera soon after he arrived; as a consequence, he gave up India after six years and returned to England, this time realising his early ambition to enter the Church. In 1833 he became Vicar of St Peter's, Southborough, Tonbridge in Kent, a mission church, not very far from Godmersham. His appointment left him far from wealthy, and cholera had damaged his constitution. No one could understand why Cassandra had accepted him.[4]

Her sister Fanny, the only mother she had really known, was appalled. 'A letter from Cassandra with the astounding announcement of her having accepted Musgrave Harris!!' she wrote on 10 July 1834, with the characteristic exclamation marks she reserved for shocking news. 'I am afraid she is mad!' The entire family was in agreement, and Fanny went to Godmersham as soon as possible. 'We all talked over & lamented dearest Cass's infatuation. Oh that it could by any means be stopped!' By 12 July, she had written to her father and Louisa 'in hopes of suggesting some means of stopping her odious match!' After a week in which no one could talk about anything else, a letter came from Louisa 'to say Cass's horrible engagement is put off for at least 6 months, & that she is to go today into Hants with Papa'. Fanny wrote at once to her aunt Cassandra Austen to tell her what was happening, and was rewarded some weeks later by a letter from Chawton on 1 August, 'with the delightful intelligence that Cass has given up her horrible engagement with Mr Musgrave Harris!!!'[5]

A query by her cousin, Caroline Austen, worthy of Elizabeth Bennet at her most acerbic, may give a clue to what happened. 'We depend upon your being able to tell us,' Caroline demanded in August 1834 of her sister-in-law Emma, James Edward's wife, 'why Cassandra Knight's marriage is to come to nothing — was she afraid of Mr Harris' poverty, or did he become less agreeable on further acquaintance?'[6] Her barbed afterthought, while almost an echo of George Wickham's discourteous comment on Georgiana Darcy, gives a less than flattering view of Cassandra, and her family: 'I dare say she is much improved — I used to like her the least of my cousins. I thought she had the family faults without their redeeming good humour, but she was scarcely grown up when I saw her.'[7] Caroline does not list the family faults of which she found Cassandra guilty. A letter from Jane to Cassandra, however, written during Caroline's last visit to Godmersham in 1808, when she was three and Cassandra not yet two, may give some explanation of her antipathy: 'Little Caroline looks very plain among her cousins,' she wrote, '& tho' she is not so headstrong or humoursome as they are, I do not think her at all more engaging'.[8] Cassandra may well have been headstrong: she had, just the summer before, gone bathing in rough seas at Herne Bay when her brother Charles would not attempt it. Caroline's judgement, however, may not have been without bias: she does not seem to have been overly fond of her Knight cousins, and had once made strenuous attempts to dissuade her brother James Edward from an attachment to Marianne.

It may have been, in Fanny's words, a horrible and odious infatuation, or as she described it in calmer mood at the end of the year, a 'short-lived and absurd engagement', but the whole family took it very seriously indeed.[9] Yet, it is difficult to see why they were so much opposed to Mr Harris, who seems to have been a well-meaning, if slightly dull and rather delicate clergyman. He was also one of Charles's shooting companions and had been on several occasions a dinner guest at Godmersham, so he was not socially unacceptable. It is possible that Fanny may have been prejudiced against Mr Harris by the fact that his eldest sister's daughter had married the same James Wildman who was, in her youth, one of Fanny's own unsatisfactory suitors, and was considered by Jane Austen not properly in love.[10] Whatever Fanny's argument, it did not move the gentle, patient and possibly headstrong Cassandra. It was only after her father brought her to Chawton, where her aunt Cassandra Austen may have added further weight to the case against Mr Harris, that she was persuaded against the engagement. Whether Cassandra Austen reminded her namesake, in the place so much associated with Jane, of her warning to Fanny in 1817 that she must not marry a man she did not love or, worse, suffer the torture of being married to one man while loving another, what is certain is that this visit to Chawton had a strange, and rather wonderful consequence.

Shortly after Cassandra left Kent, Fanny received a visit on 19 August 1834: 'Aunt Louisa and Louisa arrived to my extreme joy and astonishment to announce the astounding fact of *Lord George Hill*'s having actually been to Chawton, & dearest Cass being engaged to marry him! I was mad with delight all day.' A 'delicious long letter from Chawton' then came from Lizzy 'with the whole acc't of Ld G's arrival &c&c which I answered and enveloped to Louisa' and at last, on 21 August, 'a charming happy letter from Cass'.[11] Lord George Hill, like young Lochinvar, had come out of the West. He had gone in person to Chawton, found that Cassandra's love was still his after almost eight years, and all was settled. Even Lady Downshire ceased to object. 'Lord George Hill is to be married immediately to a Miss Knight ...' wrote one contemporary in Ireland, 'an old courtship of eight years' standing. Old Lady Downshire has been opposing it all along, but has at last consented.'[12]

So it came about, finally, that on 21 October 1834, Edward Knight's youngest daughter Cassandra Jane, in a white satin gown, with a grey satin pelisse about her shoulders, and a pink satin bonnet on her head, was married to Lord George Hill at St George's, Hanover Square in London. It was the church famously favoured by the fashionable set, the *bon ton* of the Regency, such a choice representing in itself a statement by the Hills, and a departure for the Austens. Surviving accounts of the weddings of Lizzy, Fanny and their cousin Anna Austen lay emphasis on the family tradition of simple morning affairs at the local church, with a breakfast at home and, usually, the groom going shooting with a brother-in-law or two, and the bride, relaxed and happy, spending a last little while with her family.

The celebration of this marriage could not have been more different. From the outset, Charles's account makes it clear that Cassandra was a very nervous bride. In fact, nearly everything about the wedding spoke of anxiety for, though the resolution was a most happy one, everyone seemed on the day to be conscious of how very nearly it had not come about. The couple had had to wait as long as Anne Elliot and Captain Wentworth and, in another curious reminder of *Persuasion*, Cassandra had nearly married someone else, so that an echo of the uneasy feeling at the very end of *Persuasion*, the sensation that the opportunity to reunite had almost been missed, seems to have pervaded the atmosphere of the day. Moreover, the account Charles gives of the wild autumnal days leading up to the wedding strengthens the impression of a family on tenterhooks, preceding by over a decade the romantic fervour of the Brontës. Indeed, Charles's account anticipates something of Jane Eyre's frenetic engagement to Mr Rochester.

Preparations for the long and arduous journey to London began several days before when Lord George's older brother Lord Arthur came to stay with the Knights. The next evening, 17 October 1834, at the end of a 'cold blustery squally day ... Cassa's maid came & said that the House of Lords and Commons were burnt down'.[13] This strange and unsettling national disaster, which had happened just the night before, recurs in Charles's account: the next day, he commented that 'the papers were full of the fire'.[14] It was a shocking event, symbolically burning away hundreds of years of England's history and, with the winds and storms of autumn which continued all over the weekend, a less than happy omen for a wedding. 'Blowing up for rain,' Charles wrote on Sunday 19 October. '... I am afraid it will be a thorough wet day for our journey tomorrow.'[15] Nonetheless, the large party – brothers, sisters, father, aunts, and several servants, though not Cakey, the Knights' old nursemaid, Susanna Sackree, who was by now elderly and unwell – set out on what turned out to be 'a cool fresh morning, looking rather as if it wd blow up for rain'.[16] Their travelling arrangements alone provide a strangely apt snapshot of the relative positions of the family members:

> We sent off Mr Ross the painter in a chaise by himself to Ashford to meet the coach, & soon after, about 9 o'clock we all set off in 3 carriages and a gig. The gig went only to Charing, where the rest of the party disposed themselves in the 3 carriages & on we went. Lizzy, Fanny Rice and May in the chariot with Shilton Goodworth on the box; Lou and Cass in her new carriage with her two servants behind, Aunt Louisa, my father and I in the Barouche, with Joseph and Pilcher on the box.[17]

The portrait painter, like the servants, was of secondary importance in the entourage: only Louisa, who would follow Cassandra in every way, joined her sister in the excitement of the new carriage, appropriate to the station of

Lady George Hill. Their father and Louisa Bridges, their late mother's sister, occupied the stylish but relatively solidly built barouche and Marianne, rather displaced, sat with her slightly older but long-married sister Lizzy and her young niece in the chariot, lighter, less substantial, and certainly lesser in consequence than the other conveyances.[18] That evening, almost certainly as a result of motion sickness, Marianne withdrew. 'All the travellers in our ride had bad headaches,' Charles noted, '& Marianne was unable to attend the dinner, but otherwise they all bore it very well.' Everyone else – twenty of them – sat down to a celebratory dinner in Albemarle Street. Cassandra's father Edward, her sisters Fanny, Lizzy and Louisa were there, several of her late mother's family, and Cassandra Austen, Jane's sister. Four of the Knight brothers, Edward, Henry, Charles and John came, as did the groom, Lord George, and his brothers Lords Arthur and Marcus Hill. Later, they were joined not only by the redoubtable Lady Downshire, but also by Lord George's aunt, Lady Salisbury, grandmother of a future Prime Minister, who would not have been outranked even by Lady Catherine de Bourgh. Indeed, Lord George's position in society was not dissimilar to that of Mr Darcy, and his marrying for love a young woman of a good but unmoneyed family, almost equally remarkable. For the Knights, even without the new relationship to the extremely well-connected Lady Salisbury, this match had social *cachet*. 'Altogether,' Charles wrote, with Austenian understatement, 'the day was very satisfactory.'[19]

The next day, Tuesday 21 October, was the wedding day itself. 'It was a beautiful bright morning when I woke,' Charles wrote, 'but clouded over and got cold & inclined to rain very soon.' Soon, however 'it blew off & it was a famous marrying morning.'[20] The party reassembled: Charles at 7 Suffolk Place, Henry and John a little further down at number 16. The whole party breakfasted together, then Lord George arrived at half-past eleven to collect the clergymen. Carriages came for the ladies, while the gentlemen took advantage of the clear weather and walked, and everyone arrived in good order at St George's. It is at this point in his narrative, just as everything seemed set for a wonderfully happy conclusion to a love story, that Charles suddenly and inexplicably perceived his sister as a sacrificial victim, watching the crowd press in on her with as much pity as admiration 'as if she was going to be buried alive'. The impression did not recede: even inside, as the wedding party waited in an anteroom, his sense of unease continued:

> We got to the resting room off St George's Church, before morning prayers were over, and had to wait a long while, at least 20 minutes before we could begin. It was a very trying time for Cass; for before she came in we had all been talking together & chatting, when as soon as she and my father entered the room there was a dead silence, & everybody was whispering, O here is the bride, here she comes, & were standing on tiptoe to look at her, & the party was so large that the room was thoroughly and very hot.[21]

It reads as though, instead of rejoicing with her, those fortunate enough to be present had sensed and echoed the behaviour of the mob outside. With the commencement of the ceremony, however, Charles's account became more resolutely optimistic:

> It came at last to our turn, & in we all went, & I never saw a better wedding; everything was done with the most proper solemnity, Uncle Henry read it exceedingly well, & all behaved most beautifully. Poor dear Cass could hardly speak at first, but got better as she went on. It was a very prettily dressed and pretty party, & as few tears shed as could be at any wedding. Then as soon as ever we got back to the vestry room there was great fun in distributing favours, & signing names, & kissing the bride, & chatting & laughing & making observations for a long while, till we could get the carriages and be off.[22]

Yet, he never quite dispelled or dismissed as fanciful his sense of Cassandra as victim, and the feeling of wellbeing seems to have been short-lived. As soon as they were outside, the sense of foreboding returned. 'There was an immense crowd to see her go,' Charles wrote, '& as soon as she got in she pulled the blinds down, or she thought were down, but George Hill immediately pulled them up that his bonny bride might be seen, which pleased the mob very much & they cheered them off heartily.'[23] The disturbing picture of Cassandra shrinking from the crowd while her husband encouraged their attention seems to anticipate the relatively recent image of the fragile Lady Diana Spencer, struggling on her wedding day with a newly public role.

Charles's narrative then moved to more cheerful thoughts on the celebrations following the wedding, with speeches by Lord Downshire and Edward Knight, and the further social embellishment of 'the chief fashionables added to our party' including Lord Westmeath, Lady Rosa Nugent, Col. Hill, Col. de Roos, and Charles Gore, all solidly part of the Anglo-Irish ruling class of which Lord George was a member. Yet, they must have served as reminders to her family of the fact that Cassandra was leaving England for what was, effectively, a foreign land. No one appears to have said so: Cassandra's parting from her family in mid-afternoon 'of course was sad,' Charles thought, 'but still very well sustained, though there were a good many tears shed as we have since heard when they were fairly off'.[24] Charles did not say who shed the tears, but went on to record that 'a good many of us went to Lady Salisbury's to spend the evening, where we had music & dancing & playing with Hill girls & came hme [sic] & went to bed'.[25] It may well have been a very merry gathering: Lady Salisbury was famous, or notorious, for her enthusiastic enjoyment of society.[26]

However entertaining the evening, Charles made one telling allusion at the end of his description of the day, to Cassandra's incomprehensible engagement to Musgrave Harris. 'The more we know of [Lord George],' he reflected, 'the more we feel sure that he will make her happy, and the more we know of all his family the more we have reason to be satisfied with the match.' 'And,' he continued, 'when we think of what would have been her misery had the other event taken place, how wretched not only she but every one of her family would have been, we cannot but be most thankful that such a shocking thing was averted, and that the only person she has ever loved & who is in every way worthy of her should have got her at last.'[27] His relief is palpable, and his joy in her having married the man she loved genuine: no novel could have a happier ending, and yet that sense of unease persists, all through his account. In real life, of course, the story does not end at the wedding. Even in *Persuasion*, the novel the romance so closely mirrors, Jane Austen adds a sombre, autumnal note at the last, reminding the reader that in this world, even the happiest couple cannot be guaranteed lifelong felicity. For Lord George and Cassandra, as for Anne Elliot and Frederick Wentworth, this was very much an autumnal wedding.

The next day, the party broke up. Henry, Edward and Charles 'had a lunch of turtle to eat Cass & George's health & champagne to wash it down, at the London coffee house, Ludgate Hill'.[28] The last thing Charles did was to go with his brother John and Lord George's brother Lord Marcus Hill to view the remains of the fire. They were, he says, 'glad to go over it all & see the destruction'.[29] The troubling image of the terrible fire beginning and closing his description of Cassandra's wedding seems to echo the general unease underlying Charles's account. It is not dispelled by one other peripheral image which is, if not as unsettling, certainly a reminder of something, or someone forgotten; those who left early on the day after the wedding were Cassandra's elderly father and aunt, the married Knight sisters Fanny and Lizzy, Lizzy's young daughter – and Marianne, once more excluded from the continuing celebration. Barely thirty-three, like Jane Austen before her she was the maiden aunt, Aunt May, relegated in society to the company of the elderly, the young and the married. At dinner at Godmersham that night Charles, looking about him at the depleted company, commented that May and Lou were 'the only two Miss Knights now'.[30]

The autumn settled in towards winter: 'the leaves have turned amazingly in the last few days & the high winds have stripped off great numbers', Charles wrote, as the family began to feel Cassandra's loss.[31] It had been sixteen years since Lizzy's wedding, and fourteen years since Fanny had married; now Cassandra, who had seemed a permanent part of the rhythm of life at Godmersham, was suddenly absent, and the loneliness of the remaining unmarried siblings and their father was acute. By Christmas, however, to their joy, Lord George and the new Lady George Hill were back with the family, in a pattern of 'wintering in England' which they were to follow for the next seven years. They stayed for seven weeks, and were joined for a week in January by Lord George's brother Lord Downshire and his family, so that their January house party, with its shooting and walking by day and charades in the evening, was even larger than usual. Lord George quickly became part of the family.

He went out shooting with Charles, establishing an enduring friendship with him. Over time, they cut down trees on the estate together, walked and rode on two favourite horses, wonderfully named Kildare and The Painter; discussed and exchanged dogs and guns, and, after such merry activities as improvised gymnastics, during which they attempted to walk along a pole (normally used for rolling up carpets) balanced between two chairs, they relaxed in the evenings over cigars and the occasional treat of punch.

The Hills returned to Godmersham again at the end of August 1835, once more part of all the family activities, including their musical evenings, Lord George practising his singing with Henry and Charles early in the day to be at his best. He was with Charles when he heard of the terrible death by fire of Lady Salisbury in November 1835, and again in early 1836 when news came of Lady Downshire's final illness; Lord George immediately galloping away on Charles's horse, The Painter, to catch the coach. In quieter moments, Lord George was able to persuade Charles to undertake some reading on Irish language and history: 'I read some more of G. Hill's old book on the ancient history of the Irish, which is full of absurdities,' Charles wrote in November 1835, 'but he thinks it is all founded on fact, & I daresay it is.'[32]

Cassandra, happy at last, settled back into the old patterns, and it may have seemed to her and to the family that her life would not change a great deal. At first, this was the case and her sisters, especially Fanny, who had helped her choose her trousseau, clearly anticipated a life in Ireland not materially different, if rather more grand, from that which she he had known in England. An inventory of her wardrobe at the time of her marriage shows comfortable provision of clothing suitable for all occasions – morning calls, walking and riding in the afternoon and attendance at evening soirées:

> 24 Day Shifts; 10 Night Shifts; 24 Prs of Drawers; 9 Night Caps; 40 Napkins; 4 Flannel Petticoats; 2 Prs of Stays; 12 Prs Morn. Silk Stockings; 12 Prs Evening ditto; 4 Prs Brown Cotton; 6 Prs Socks; 4 White Dressing Gowns; 1 Short White Ditto; 2 Flannel ditto; 37 Cambric Pocket Handkerchiefs; 12 Morning Petticoats; 6 Evening ditto; 4 Riding Habit Shirts; 4 Prs Riding Drawers; 5 Prs Under Sleeves; 12 Swiss Muslin Handkerchiefs; 4 Smocked

Cambric Pelisses; 8 Smocked Muslin ditto; 1 Cambric Chemisette; 6 Dimity Petticoats; 6 Toilette Pincushions.[33]

That was simply her underwear. Her morning gowns included '1 Lilac Merino' and '1 Lavender Silk'; her evening Gowns '1 White Satin, worn on the Wedding Day; 1 Green Velvet; 1 Piqued Blue Satin; 1 Apricot Merino; 1 Moiré Silk'. She had evening shawls in blue, white, cloud and '1 *mousseline de laine*' which, the list practically reminds, 'would do for morning as well'. In addition she had a cloak of black satin; a yellow shawl and another of plaid; a hat and habit for riding, and a travelling cap of green velvet. As well as the pink bonnet 'worn on the Wedding Day with the Grey pelisse' and the 'White Blond Veil', she also had another veil of black Chantilly lace, a bonnet of yellow silk and another of green gauge ribbon. There were bags, thinner shawls, handkerchiefs, mittens of black silk and white thread; morning caps; a 'Blond Bonnet Cap'; and gloves, both long and short, in white and gold. The list ends with 'Shoes of all Sorts'.[34] Cassandra's list would have been appropriate for the married life of a gentlewoman in England, and was entirely appropriate for a member of the great Downshire family, accustomed to high society at Hillsborough and Dublin Castle. Indeed, for the first four years of Cassandra's marriage, her extensive wardrobe was essential, given Lord George's prominent position.

Wintering in England for the second year of her marriage, she was at home in Godmersham for the birth of their first child, Norah Mary Elizabeth, on 12 December 1835. Charles's diary gives a vivid account of the night Norah was born. He had known since breakfast the day before that his sister was in labour. All that day it continued, 'and now at night,' he wrote on the evening of Friday 11 December 1835, 'she has made but slow progress'. Unable to be of any practical assistance, he went to bed, and his diary tells of the long and anxious night that followed:

> I woke at 4, & it froze as if it was never going to leave off. I could not get to sleep again for thinking of Cass, for I kept hearing moving going on in her room below. At last I got up & crept down to the clock but no one was stirring, so when I was very nearly starved, I came back to bed, & lay waking till 6 when I

read ... with no better success. At last old Mag came to light my fire ... & brought the joyful news of d[ea]r Cass's safety & the birth of a little girl which took place about 2 in the morning. Then I did not sleep much for joy, but still dozed until past 8, when I got dressed & came down to breakfast.[35]

Once Cassandra was known to be safe, the new father and his wife's brother went out shooting, as was usual for them in the morning. It was part of life at Godmersham, and it was a comfort to Cassandra to be at home and have such familiar rituals about her. When Lizzy began her large family, it was natural for first Fanny, then Marianne, then Louisa to go and be with her during her confinements. They did not travel to Ireland to Cassandra, as it was equally natural for her to come home to have her children. Moreover, given the memory of her mother's sudden death in 1808, she shared her sisters' apprehension about childbirth. She had reason to be glad of her family, for she was far from well following Norah's birth. 'I have not seen Cass for 2 days,' Charles wrote in his diary at the end of December 1835, adding delicately, 'She is not well. The babe & she don't agree exactly. I suppose it will end in a wet nurse.'[36] Cassandra did not join the family in the evening until 10 January, and neither she nor the baby ventured out until the end of January. When they did, they did not go out together: 'It was a beautiful morning,' Charles noted, 'and Cass & Norah both took advantage of it, one for the first out of doors airing along the stones by the Portico in the nurse's arms, the other for the first drive, in the closed carriage, with her husband by her side.'[37]

A pattern of dividing their time between the two countries was soon established, and a second child, Arthur Blundell George, was born in England on 13 May 1837. By then, however, Lady Downshire had died, and life had begun to change for Lord and Lady George. Because of a settlement in 1811, the portions due to Lady Downshire's younger children became due in 1837. Her title and property having gone to her second son, now Baron Sandys, his portion was reduced to £1,000: this meant the two remaining younger brothers, Lord Marcus and Lord George, each received £24,500.[38] The immediate impact of this inheritance may not have been appreciated by the Knights, including Cassandra: it was quite sufficient to allow Lord George to leave the military and political path he had been following, and achieve his ambition of owning land in Donegal. As geographer Estyn Evans explains, in his introduction to the only twentieth-century edition of *Facts from Gweedore*: 'It seems his family provided him with enough capital to leave Hillsborough and to purchase, from 1838 onwards, some 23, 000 acres of land in the parish of Tullaghobegly West, in the barony of Kilmacrenan, extending northwards along the coast from the Gweedore River.'[39] The result was that, by 1838, although her regular visits home continued, Cassandra found herself not the centre of society in Dublin and London, but the wife of a landowner in remote, barely accessible Donegal.

By then, in England, the world was changing again. In 1837, the young Victoria ascended the throne and, as a new age began, the Knight family faced a number of new concerns. Jane Austen had been dead for twenty years, and now it was her ageing sister and brothers who needed attention. Edward Austen Knight, though in good health, turned seventy in 1837: in January 1838 his brother George Austen, who had been in care since he was a child, died of dropsy at the age of seventy-two, and Cassandra Austen was becoming increasingly frail.[40] At Godmersham, too, there were changes. In that same year, 1837, the still unsettled George Knight, Jane's 'itty Dordy', finally met and married a lady of a famous name, Hilaire, Countess Nelson, widow of Lord Nelson's brother.[41] John Knight, now a Captain on half pay, took to spending more time at Godmersham while Charles, who had been so happy at home, began to feel that he should learn to live independently. In 1837, he left to take over the living at Chawton from Mr Papillon, whom Jane had often, teasingly, told her family she would marry.[42]

Meanwhile, the rift between Fanny's husband, Sir Edward Knatchbull, and his daughter continued to widen. It was no nearer resolution when, in 1838, Mary became dangerously ill. Sir Edward showed no sign of relenting, but when Mary wrote to him in desperation, begging him to see her, he did visit her, just once. He had little choice: she was gravely ill of fever following the difficult birth of her seventh child, William Brodnax Knight, on 3 February 1838. Edward Knight wrote to his father-in-law telling him that her fever had returned and then, nineteen days after the birth, to inform him of her death. It was a frightening repetition of the death of Elizabeth Austen in 1808. Just as then, the whole family was deeply shocked: Edward Knight, like his father before him, was plunged into grief. The body was brought to Chawton, and Mary was buried in the family vault. Sir Edward Knatchbull called, for one day, at Chawton Great House on 18 March, a visit as distressing to himself as to Edward Knight. In a strange irony, he was received in Mary's sitting-room: it was the same Oak Room in which Jane Austen had read to his wife Fanny from *Pride and Prejudice*, almost exactly twenty-five years before.[43]

It was a tumultuous time for the Knights and Knatchbulls, so that Cassandra's own changing situation in Ireland may not have been uppermost in their minds. In reality, however, from 1838 onward Cassandra's main home would be in a country of which she and her family knew little. Jane Austen had been so conscious of the cultural differences between the two countries that when her niece Anna, engaged on a novel of her own, had been on the point of sending her fictional family, the Portmans, to Ireland, she had advised her that she 'had better not leave England ... Let the Portmans go to Ireland,' she wrote, 'but as you know nothing of the Manners there, you had better not go with them. You will be in danger of giving false representations.'[44] For Cassandra, in marrying the youngest brother of the Marquess of Downshire, there seemed no option but to leave England, though it may not have seemed at first to be a permanent move. The Downshires had considerable properties in England as well as Ireland and, while Lady Salisbury and Lady Downshire lived, additional political influence. It may well have appeared that anything could happen to change Cassandra's circumstances, and bring her back home to England. The sudden and tragic death of Lady Salisbury in 1835, followed by that of Lady Downshire in 1836 had, however, removed the potential influence of those two formidable women; and the inheritance of more money than he might have had, if his older brother Augustus had not unexpectedly died, made quite a difference to Lord George's prospects. He had already demonstrated his capacity for patience, and dogged determination. He had carried out his plan of marrying Cassandra Knight after waiting nearly eight years, and now, against the odds, he made his dream of land ownership in Ireland come true. With this money he was at last able, four years after his marriage to Cassandra, to set about his project in Donegal.

From Lord George's perspective, all the signs were good. To begin with, he was personable, unassuming in his manners and generally well liked. His decision to visit each tenant personally, and to live on his property as much as possible from the outset, was well, if cautiously received. His knowledge of the Irish language was an advantage, and came as a pleasant surprise to most of his new tenants: 'It was pleasing and attractive to the people, and brought about an intercourse to which they were unaccustomed, and they asserted he could not be a lord at all, particularly as *he spoke Irish.*'[45] He needed to gain the confidence of his tenants, for his determination to remove the habit of illegal whisky distillation created suspicion, as did his building of a grain store and harbour at the port of Bunbeg. Some saw these enterprises as improvements, while others feared the loss of established sources of income, whether legal or illegal. The prevalence of illicit distilling of whisky, or *poitín,* was a problem: it paid, whereas the transport of corn involved a journey of fifty miles to a market, without the prospect of much return. While a police force existed to deal with the problem of illicit distillation, it was less than effective. Lord George's guide in Gweedore, Sir James Dombrain, considered that the revenue police lacked discipline, as a consequence of the temptations to which they were subject. The establishment of the coastguard in 1821, with Dombrain at its head, was intended to address this, but the officers' initially aggressive approach proved counter-productive and, in the case of one *poitín* maker in 1823, fatal. In addition, Dombrain made it clear he did not wish to have his coastguard officers, who were at the time all naval lieutenants, associated with the Revenue: 'We have no connection with the Revenue Police,' he stated, 'and I should be extremely sorry that we should have.'[46]

In such a volatile environment, it was an act of either extreme courage or extreme foolhardiness on the part of Lord George to attempt to address the problem by building in the little port of Bunbeg a store for grain, with the capacity to hold up to four hundred tons of oats, and a small quay where ships of up to two hundred tons could load or unload.[47] In addition, he intended to do no less than reorganise the farming system which had been in use for generations, and to replace it with modern, efficient methods. His tenants lived mostly in clusters of dwellings, or *cláchans,* between the sea and the hills. They supplemented the basic resources of the land by catching fish, including shellfish, and collected seaweed, not only as a foodstuff, but also as a valuable source of manure. When their main farming base was under crop, they practised transhumance, or 'booleying': they drove their livestock to the mountains for grazing in summer, and sometimes in autumn to the islands, one of which was Gola, part of Lord George's estate.[48] In a sense, Donegal farmers had their own version of 'wintering in England' and were as attached to their established custom as the landlords were to theirs. As Estyn Evans has pointed out, 'such nomadic habits – the ease with which the cattle could be taken to the safety of the mountains – help to explain the effective resistance of the area to landlordism until the early nineteenth century, and the strength of the opposition to Lord George's improvements.'[49]

For Lord George, having grown up between England and Ireland, the ambivalence of his tenants and the intricate politics of such an ambitious enterprise in Ireland were no surprise. For Cassandra, however, it cannot have been a pleasant discovery. By 1838, she was the mother of two very young children, with a third to come the following March. Nineteenth-century Donegal was quite beyond her experience: it could not have been more different from the countryside to which she was accustomed in Kent and Hampshire. Even if she had been familiar with the politics and the ambiguities of landlord–tenant relations, the geography must have come as a great shock. The roads in north-west Ireland were rough and almost impassable, and it would be some years before the railway would find its way there.[50] A letter to his brother Marcus, sent from Dublin in the year following the purchase of his Donegal estate, shows Lord George's awareness of such issues and obstacles as the ever-present danger of famine and distress, and the consequent dependence of his new tenantry on the caprices of the weather:

> Beautiful weather, which is fortunate. I hear from Donegal that provisions are getting up very much. No doubt there will be great distress if the dry weather continues — for I see in the papers that they are suffering in Mayo and by this misfortune I shall get plenty of hands for my work, and be able to give the people some assistance in their distress.[51]

This letter displays the shrewd mixture of the philanthropic and the pragmatic which characterised Lord George's dealings with his tenants; the work he refers to here is the building of a hotel to attract tourists, the next part of his long-term plan. The distress to which he refers was indeed very great: famine and want were regular occurrences. When he published the results of his work in Gweedore, in 1845, Lord George quoted at length from a pamphlet written in 1837 to the Lord Lieutenant of Ireland by the Gweedore National School teacher, Patrick McKye, setting out the extreme poverty of the people of the area:

> They have no means of harrowing their land but with meadow rakes. Their farms are so small that from four to ten farms can be harrowed in one day with a rake. Their beds are straw, green and dried rushes, or mountain bent; their bed clothes are either coarse sheets or no sheets, and ragged, filthy blankets. And more than all that I have mentioned, there is a general prospect of starvation at the present prevailing among them, and that originating from various causes, but the principal cause is a rot or failure of seed in the last year's crop, together with a scarcity of winter forage, in consequence of a long continuation of storms since October last in this part of the country. So that they, the people, were under the necessity of cutting down their potatoes, and give [sic] them to the cattle to keep them alive. All these circumstances connected together have brought hunger to reign among them, to that degree that the generality of the peasantry are on the small allowance of one meal a day, and many sometimes one meal in three days ... I will venture to challenge the world to produce one single person to contradict any part of my statement.[52]

This was the situation Lord George was determined to address as, with excitement and determination, he embarked on the enterprise of his life, a vast project which would occupy him for the rest of his career and earn him as many enemies as friends. Yet, if Lord George was about to set out on this enormous task, so too, whether it was at first obvious to her or not, was Cassandra. The same steely resolution which had prompted him, on his wedding day, to raise the blinds which his nervous bride had drawn down to shield her from the gaze of the mob, now enabled Lord George to look beyond the immediate and disconcerting upheaval which his family might expect. His commitment to them was, however, no less great than his determination to see his project through. Although resolved to live as much as possible on his estate, he did not at first require it of his wife and children. Until he found a house which he judged fit for them to live in, he made the long journey overland and by sea from Kent to Ireland every week, staying in Gweedore in a small house known as Heath Cottage.[53] For Cassandra, staying in England could be only a temporary solution. Before long, she could expect to live for at least half the year in Ireland. There, the clothes listed in her wedding inventory would contrast embarrassingly with the pitiful collection of garments possessed by the entire population, at least 4,000 people, of the estate over which she would be mistress. In a very different inventory, Patrick McKye had listed the clothes of the tenantry as part of his 1837 appeal to the Lord Lieutenant:

> None of their either married or unmarried women can afford more than one shift, and the fewest number cannot afford any, and more than one half of both men and women cannot afford shoes to their feet, nor can many of them afford a second bed, but whole families of sons and daughters of mature age are indiscriminately lieing [sic] together with their parents, and all in the bare buff...[54]

With such contrasts, Cassandra's move to Donegal could not be other than a great change, requiring considerable adjustment. Cassandra, however, had demonstrated throughout her life a remarkable capacity for patience, and a considerable degree of courage in facing challenges. Moreover, there was always the prospect of wintering in England. She was not alone in regarding this as her refuge. When Fanny wrote to Miss Chapman in October 1838 of all the family's whereabouts, she made it clear that she wanted Cassandra and her family to spend more time away from Ireland:

My dear father is 71 and delightfully well. He and Mne and L are now in Hants for a few weeks. George and Lady Nelson are travelling in Germany for his health which is not strong. Charles is settled in the living at Chawton, which is a great comfort to Edwd, & John is at present a Captain on half pay, but soon hoping to get a Commission again. Ld and Ldy George Hill with 2 little children are in Ireland but we hope will return to winter in England ... [55]

They did so. Their third child, Augustus Charles Edward, was born at Godmersham on 9 March 1839. The family stayed again at Godmersham in the winter of 1840–41, Charles Knight in his diary recording for that winter shooting and riding expeditions with Lord George and walks with Cassandra.

They were still there in early March 1841, and then went back to Ireland to spend the summer, according to their new custom.[56] In Charles's diary for late 1841 and early 1842, however, there is no record of the Hill family's arriving to winter in England. Another child was expected in March 1842 and Cassandra, for the first and only time, stayed in Ireland for her delivery. Her second daughter and fourth child, Cassandra Jane Louisa Hill, was born at Gartlee, Letterkenny, on 12 March 1842 and Lord George, in great joy and considerable relief, thought his wife 'wonderfully well' after the birth.[57] Three days later, in a shocking and wholly unexpected repetition of her mother's fate, Cassandra Knight, of the dark eyes and sweet temper, the little stargazer who longed to stay out all night, was dead, at thirty-five, of puerperal fever.

CHAPTER 5

'THE MANNERS THERE'

Louisa and Lord George
1842–1849

'... I believe you capable of everything great and good in your married lives.
I believe you equal to every important exertion, and to every domestic
forbearance, so long as — if I may be allowed the expression, so long as you
have an object. I mean, while the woman you love lives, and lives for you.'

P E R S U A S I O N

Suppose that Captain Wentworth, having finally regained Anne Elliot, had
found himself a widower less than eight years later; that not war, but the perils
of childbirth had separated them. Would he have remarried? *Persuasion* leaves
the question open; Frederick Wentworth insistent on the impossibility of such
an event, Anne Elliot less certain.[1] Yet, if one may suppose Captain Wentworth
to have been left with four young children to bring up alone, and suppose
him further to be in a foreign land, a pioneer in a barely-tamed wilderness,
what then? This was the situation in which Lord George Hill found himself
in March 1842. Like Wentworth, he had waited almost eight years for the
woman he wanted to marry, had learned almost too late that she was engaged
to another man and had finally married her in her twenty-eighth year with
the blessing of both families and all their friends. Within another eight years,
he had watched her die in childbirth.

Lord George was a man of action: in an earlier time he might have been an
adventurer, like his ancestor Moyses Hill. In the years before his wife's death
he had found his life's purpose almost by accident in the bleak but beautiful
Gweedore. He had then committed himself to the overhaul not only of a
place but of an entire way of life, thinking nothing of commuting weekly

from England while his dream was in the process of creation, or of living in a
cottage while he sought a family home. He found it not in Gweedore, where
he had purchased his estate, but at Ballyare, six miles from Letterkenny, outside
the village of Ramelton.[2] He knew the task he had set himself in Donegal was
difficult: yet, it was the challenge which most attracted him. 'The district
extends for some miles along the N.W. Coast or corner of Ireland,' he wrote
with enthusiasm, describing his work, 'and the scenery is of the very wildest
description; the Atlantic dashing along those shores in all its magnificent
freshness, whilst the harsh screeching of the sea-fowl is its continual and
suitable accompaniment.'[3] At the outset of the 1840s, right in the vanguard of the
Victorian age of philanthropic improvement, he adopted a scientific approach
and had a complete survey made of the property, then spent three years, from
1841 to 1843, reapportioning the holdings on his twenty-three thousand acres.
As Estyn Evans explains:

> Having visited the houses of all his tenants, he gave them
> 'notice to quit' and persuaded them to appoint a committee to
> assist him in laying out the new farms, though he admits the
> opposition was 'vexatious and harrowing'. As an encouragement
> he instituted a system of premiums for improvements in crops,
> livestock and housing.[4]

He had to compromise: he could not persuade all his tenants to have
square or rectangular holdings, and had to settle for long, narrow strip farms
to balance out the demand for fair sharing of the varying quality of Gweedore's
land. In addition, by the beginning of 1842, he was on the point of opening a
commodious tourist hotel, confident that he could rival or surpass the best
he had seen in the Highlands of Scotland. He was forty-one years old, and life
could not have been better.

Then, on 15 March, his wife died, leaving him a widower with four children
under seven. He had loved Cassandra deeply, and his shock and grief were
very great. Yet, he did not sink into depression, and the letter he wrote to
his brother, Lord Downshire, within hours of his bereavement, speaks to his
dignified composure:

I had only time this melancholy morning to inform you of my sad loss — my dearest wife was wonderfully well until Sunday eve — when she got a chill — after that, inflammation set in, which the most vigorous measures could not subdue, & the poor dear creature breathed her last this morning at 11 — The Lord knows what is best for us — & nothing happens but with his permission. It remains for me to submit humbly to his holy will — he has helped me for some years with a most affectionate and faithful wife, & my regret at her being taken from me, is much diminished by the knowledge of the hope that was in her, & I trust she is now happy for ever. I know all your kindness to us & my dearest Cassandra was ever sensible of the affection showed to her by my dear sister and nieces who I know will share my grief — [5]

On the back of this letter is a short but telling note written in Lord George's hand, reading: 'Poor Cassandra: Death'. It was the only time Cassandra had not been in England for her confinement. She died, not at Godmersham, with her sisters in attendance and her father and brothers close by, but far away in Donegal. There was no Charles to tiptoe down in the night to check on her welfare, no Louisa or Marianne to comfort her in her distress. Lord George knew what a shock her sudden passing would be for the Knights and Austens, and that there would be, in addition, a terrible familiarity in the news. The uncanny similarity between Cassandra's death and that of her mother in 1808 would be a severe blow. Thirty-four years later, a chill following childbirth could still mask puerperal fever, and the recent death of Mary Knatchbull Knight could serve only to underline the fact that childbirth remained highly dangerous. Worse still, Cassandra's family, having received Lord George's letter with its welcome news of the safety of mother and child, did not know for two days that Cassandra was dead. The first time it is mentioned is in Fanny's entry for 17 March 1842: 'On this wretched day we rec'd the account of the death of our beloved Cassandra at Gartlee 15th, 3 days after her confinement! God's Will be done!'[6] She sent an express to Chawton: Edward, George, Charles and Louisa came at once. In what Fanny described as 'great misery', they set about making plans. Cassandra had died on Tuesday. On Wednesday, the news arrived, and on Thursday Charles, George and Louisa set off early to take the mail train to Ireland, while Edward went back to Chawton. In a poignant reversion to another time, Fanny's diary and the letters she forwarded from Lizzy speak of their brother John, though he was thirty-three years old and a Captain in the 6th Dragoon Guards (the Carabiniers) stationed in Newbridge, Kildare, as 'poor dearest Johnny', as if he were once again the child in the nursery, even younger and more vulnerable than Cassandra. No account of the funeral, or of Cassandra's burial in Letterkenny, has survived.[7]

Louisa, however, did write to her sisters from Ireland and, though the letters have not been preserved, Fanny's diary indicates the extent of the grief the family felt. 'A letter from Mne,' she wrote on 28 March 1842, 'enclosing another heartbreaking letter from Louisa at Gortlee [sic].'[8] Two days later, another came, followed by a letter from Lizzy 'enclosing a miserable letter to her from poor dearest Johnny'.[9] Fanny continued to receive letters throughout April, including one from Charles. On 7 April, she wrote, 'Charles arrived from Ireland and spent a miserable evening with me.'[10] Charles could not bring himself to mention his youngest sister's death in his diary, confining himself to one brief, formal entry on Monday 11 April 1842, some days after his return: 'I have been to Ireland. There is no use writing about that journey of wretchedness. God grant that it may be to my spiritual good and that of all interested in the sad event that occasioned it.'[11]

Lord George himself was nothing if not stoic. He had two immediate tasks to complete: to consider how best to bring up his four motherless children, and to launch the Gweedore Hotel. He had help and support, not only from his own family, but also, crucially, from the Knights, both at Chawton and Godmersham. For all but one of the children of Edward Austen Knight, the great house of Godmersham in Kent was still home. Their eldest brother Edward, heir to the whole estate, preferred to live in Chawton House, in Hampshire; yet, though a certain coolness had existed between Fanny's and Edward's families following his elopement in 1826 with Mary Knatchbull, the Knight and Austen families had not been split by the scandal. In good times and bad, they gathered at Godmersham. It was natural that Lord George, by then so much a part of the Knight family, should go there with his children. By the end of April, Fanny recorded that 'Lord George and Louisa & the four dear children' had arrived in London, where she and her husband went to meet them at the Grosvenor Hotel.[12] Marianne and her father received the grieving family at the beginning of May, and Fanny had 'a long miserable letter from poor dear Louisa with an acct of their sad arrival at Godmersham'.[13] George Knight arrived in London at Fanny's house on 10 May, and within a few days he was followed by Lord George, without the children, who stayed with their aunts and grandfather at Godmersham. By 13 May, Fanny wrote, Lord George had 'called and sat some time with me'.[14] When Fanny returned to her home at Mersham le Hatch in Kent, George Knight and Lord George came together to visit.[15]

By July 1842, Fanny was able to report that 'Lord G Hill took Updown and settled there with Louisa & his 4 dear children, the baby Cassandra Jane Louisa being my God-daughter'.[16] Updown, close to Lizzy's home at Dane Court, was also within driving distance of Godmersham, where Fanny met 'the dear little Hill children' in August.[17] As there was no question of bringing in a stranger to help him with the children, or of entrusting them to the care of servants in Ireland, it gradually emerged that Louisa would assist. It was a practical solution: Fanny had her own children and stepchildren, Lizzy had fifteen children of her own, and Marianne was still fully occupied with the tasks which had devolved to her twenty years earlier, the care of her father and the running of Godmersham. Lord George needed someone who could be in charge of his household. As well as the new baby, the older children – Norah, at six and a half, Arthur, almost five, and Augustus, three – were still very young. They were distressed and bewildered, just as the young Knights had been when their mother died. Louisa simply stayed on: she was still with them at Updown in October 1842, when she rode with Lord George to Mersham le Hatch, and at Christmas, when the Hills joined the Knights at Godmersham.[18] It does not appear that the children returned to Ireland during the first year following their mother's death, though Lord George certainly did. At the time of the first anniversary of Cassandra's death in March 1843, he visited Fanny in London. He was suddenly and inexplicably taken ill, so that he was unable to travel back to Ireland for some days. By September 1843, Louisa had travelled to Brighton with the children and their father, and they were all still there at the beginning of November.[19] Eighteen months later, in May 1845, following the sudden death of Lord George's brother Lord Downshire after a fall from his horse, the whole family left Godmersham to return to Ireland, and Louisa went with them.[20] They stayed that year at Ballyare until December 1845, when they all went to Godmersham to join the Knights.[21]

Grief, however, did not cloud Lord George's business sense, any more than it affected his analysis of the best available childcare. In those years between the death of his wife and the return with Louisa to Ballyare, he worked hard to realise his plans for Donegal. In May 1842, shortly after his arrival at Godmersham, he wrote to his brother Lord Downshire to instruct him on the deposit of monies owing: he had to be sure of his finances, as the hotel, an imposing square white building round a courtyard, overlooking the mountain of Errigal and tranquil lake waters, was within months of opening: a landlord and other staff had to be appointed and furnishings supplied.[22] Despite the family tragedy, and despite the fact that the building was not quite complete, the Gweedore Hotel opened for business in the year of Cassandra's death. Photographs taken later in the century show the hotel when fully developed, but *Facts from Gweedore* provides a description of it as it appeared in those early days of its first opening:

> The plan of the hotel is well adapted to an exposed situation. The traveller on arriving drives into a courtyard at the back of the house: in one corner is the entrance door, sheltered by a long porch; by this arrangement the three sitting rooms, which occupy the front of the house, are free from draughts, and have the benefit of all the sunshine. There are six bedrooms. The whole of the establishment (including the stables) is fitted up, and furnished with every attention to comfort and convenience. The River Claudy in its course from the Dunluighy Lakes to the sea, flows at the foot of the Hotel Garden, where a boat is provided for the use of visitors who may wish to go to the lake by water, or amuse themselves fishing. A post car is also kept, and mountain ponies can be obtained to assist ramblers in their excursions.[23]

On 19 September 1842, an entry in the visitors' book, known as the *Gweedore Hotel Book,* comments that though 'the house is not yet finished and consequently cannot be expected to possess all the advantages of an old established inn ... it is very comfortable — the beds are excellent.'[24] The *Hotel Book,* of which two volumes have survived, provides a remarkable record of the world to which first Cassandra and later Louisa had to adjust. Visitors to 'the wild Gwydore', as one early hotel guest termed it, recorded and occasionally illustrated their often colourful experiences, frequently adding their opinions of the state of Ireland in general, and Lord George's enterprise in particular.[25] It is quite unedited and, while largely complimentary, its quota of candid, even blunt remarks provide a useful counterbalance to the uncritical assessment of the enterprise given in Lord George's own account. As Jane Austen's Mr Parker points out in *Sanditon:* 'Those who tell their own story ... must be listened to with caution.' Yet, the record of the hotel, though it gives other sides to the story, seems to bear out Lord George's own belief in the importance of his work in Donegal. One of his first and most supportive visitors, for example, his eldest brother, Lord Downshire, visiting in May 1842, gave weight to his brother's philanthropic mission in an entry in the *Hotel Book:*

> I dined and slept last night in this ... inn built by my brother Lord George and have found everything in it, the bed, entertainment very comfortable and I have no doubt the landlord and his wife will continue to deserve the good opinion of their customers and the support and favour of their employer as they are both of them county of Donegal people. I feel an interest in their welfare which must depend on their own merit — this inn has been extremely well-built and is well suited to its situation and I hope that Lord George's excellent object, that of improving the mountainous district, possessed as it is of many natural advantages, will ere long be crowned with well merited success.[26]

Undoubtedly, the hotel made a difference to the district from the outset. One visitor, a naval man who had cause to be grateful for his navigational skills, wrote in 1843 of having been one of a group 'benighted and nearly lost' in the area in the early 1830s, when there was neither inn nor road. 'The night was dark,' he wrote, 'their only guide a star, and through forgetting to make allowance for its northing, as it declined, they had deviated from their proper course (being without chart or compass), and had nearly foundered in a sharskin (a shaking bog). What a charming contrast now presents itself to the view!'[27]

Lord George put great efforts into making the district accessible. Though a bridge had been built at county expense across the Gweedore River in 1840, no road had been made to enable travellers to make their way to such towns as Dungloe and Bunbeg. Lord George had several miles of bridle roads made through his property, so that visitors were able to reach previously inaccessible areas.[28] For him, this was a crusade, a civilising mission.[29] Lord George saw it as his duty to care for his tenants, just as his brother Downshire, who visited again in 1844 and commended the 'mutual exertions' of landlord and tenant, saw it as his duty to care for his own tenants.[30] A Royal Commission, set up by Sir Robert Peel in 1843 under the chairmanship of Lord Devon to 'inquire into the state of the law and practice with regard to the occupation of land in Ireland', declared in its report of 1845 that it was 'impossible to describe adequately the privations which [cottiers and labourers] and their families patiently endure.'[31] Lord George declared himself willing to tackle whatever problem he encountered. 'I will perform my duty as a landlord,' he said. 'I will persevere against all difficulties, I will not be deterred by any opposition I may encounter from my tenants and neighbours, but I will persevere in my attempts to improve the conditions of the people.'[32] He had grown up with a paternalistic ethic and, when she found herself based in Donegal, Louisa, who understood such an ethic from her own experience of life on the Godmersham estate, threw herself into the moral improvement of the tenants quite as thoroughly as she did into the care of her sister's children.

Nonetheless, the cultural shock of her removal to Ireland may have been even greater than it was for Cassandra, who had gone there with all the expectations of a bride. Louisa, already in her thirty-eighth year when her sister died, was ten years older than Cassandra had been when she went to Ireland and, unlike her younger sister, who had spent some time early in her marriage in the relatively familiar society world of Dublin, had no time to ease herself into life in Donegal. Yet, she understood that she would be based there until the children were grown, and did not question it: this was her duty, just as it had been first Fanny's, then Marianne's duty to make a commitment to the care of their father and the younger children. Jane Austen had expressed a similar view in *Persuasion*: 'If I mistake not,' Anne Elliot tells Captain Wentworth, 'a strong sense of duty is no bad part of a woman's portion.'[33] Louisa's new commitment meant that for at least half the year, during the spring and summer which she had always enjoyed with her family in Kent and London, she would now be exiled in Ireland. Unlike Marianne and Fanny who were obliged, while still very young, to become accustomed to the running of a large household, Louisa had comparatively little experience, yet was suddenly mistress of a vast estate, staffed by servants and surrounded by tenants in a foreign country. Moreover, that foreign country was in turmoil.

As agrarian unrest and political protest had increased rather than diminished in Ireland following Catholic Emancipation in 1829, Sir Robert Peel's government concluded that it must begin to work towards extra measures, including an education act and the establishment of a system of poor relief. In 1838, just when Lord George bought his property in Gweedore, the Poor Relief (Ireland) Act meant that the English system established in 1836 was – despite the advice of an earlier Commission of Enquiry against it – extended to Ireland. Taking no account of the difference in culture, custom and conditions in Ireland, the extension of the system led to overcrowding which, exacerbated by recurring famine, encouraged the spread of infectious disease.[34] Daniel O'Connell's Repeal Association was established in 1840. Mass or 'monster' meetings were held and over the first five years of the decade the movement for repeal attracted young men inspired by the wave of revolutionary spirit sweeping Europe. William Smith O'Brien, himself a landlord, whose name would recur in the lives of Louisa and her family many years later, was one of these. Others included John Mitchel, a gifted orator of a more militant disposition than the increasingly weary O'Connell, and the idealistic poet Thomas Davis. Davis was one of the founders with Charles Gavan Duffy and John Blake Dillon of *The Nation* newspaper which, inspired by the writings of Thomas Carlyle, called for a non-sectarian, cultural nationalism, including a revival of the Irish language.

After the prohibition of the latest in a series of mass meetings to demand repeal, planned for Clontarf in October 1843, and the arrest and imprisonment of the nearly seventy-year-old O'Connell, the young men became increasingly militant. Davis's untimely death in 1845 deprived the movement of a moderate voice, one consequence of which was that a number of those left broke with O'Connell to form Young Ireland and, in 1848, to make an unsuccessful bid to mount their own revolution.[35]

Louisa was familiar with the debate over Catholic Emancipation, for her brother Charles considered it a moral issue and discussed it within the family, while her brother-in-law Sir Edward Knatchbull and her sister Fanny were utterly opposed to it. Comprehending the debate as it applied to Ireland, however, with its extra layers of political complication was another matter: Jane Austen had warned Louisa's cousin Anna as far back as 1814 of the difference in 'the manners there' when Anna had proposed sending her fictional family to Ireland. By 1834, the year of Cassandra's wedding, Maria Edgeworth, the Irish novelist whose work Jane Austen greatly admired, considered it 'impossible to draw Ireland as she now is in a book of fiction'. 'We are in too perilous a case to laugh,' she wrote, 'humour would be out of season, worse than bad taste.'[36] If it had been difficult to understand Ireland in 1814, the intervening years had made it no easier and, however conversant Louisa might have been with existing political issues in England, nothing could have readied her for what she found in Ireland in the middle years of the 1840s.

Landlords had become accustomed to dealing with the recurring nightmare of famine, to which Ireland had for many years been subject.[37] Though Lord George was aware that this could happen in any year if the crop failed sufficiently, neither he nor anyone else was adequately prepared when the autumn of 1845 signalled the beginning of the latest and most devastating famine yet, with the spread of a new fungal disease of the potato, *phytophthora infestans*. About half of the population of eight million people subsisted largely on potatoes: if the crop failed through bad weather or disease, famine ensued, as had happened in the terrible winter of 1816–17, when the harvest failure had been followed not only by famine, but also by the rapid spread of disease amongst an already weakened population. The novelist William Carleton, from Donegal's neighbouring county of Tyrone, had lived through several such famines since his birth in 1794. Witnessing the partial failure of the potato crop in the autumn of 1845, he wrote graphically and urgently of the effects of the 1817 famine in his novel, *The Black Prophet*, in the hope that it might serve as a warning, 'to awaken those who legislate for us into a humane perception of a calamity that has been almost perennial in the country':[38]

> Famine, in all cases the source and origin of contagion, had done, and was still doing, its work. The early potato crop, so far as it had come in, was a pitiable failure — the quantity being small and the quality watery and bad. The oats, too, and all early grain of the season's growth, were still more deleterious of food, for they had fermented and become sour, so that the use of them, and of the bad potatoes, too, was the most certain means of propagating the pestilence which was sweeping away the people in such multitudes.[39]

Like Maria Edgeworth, Carleton was despairingly conscious that unless he could convey his message to a British readership, nothing whatsoever might be done. 'Alas,' he wrote, 'little do our English neighbours know or dream of the horrors which attend a year of severe famine in this unhappy country.'[40] Carleton did not exaggerate, yet, though all the signs of imminent acute distress were present, and though he dedicated his preface to the then Prime Minister, Lord John Russell, little was done in the first year, when further disaster might have been averted. Russell was not sympathetic. 'The common delusion,' he wrote to Lord Lansdowne in October 1846, 'that government can convert a period of scarcity into a period of abundance is one of the most mischievous that can be entertained. But, alas! The Irish have been taught many bad lessons and few good ones.'[41] Therefore, although the blight was, if anything, worse in 1846, Russell's administration took the view that responsibility towards the famine-stricken belonged not to government but to the wealthy of Ireland.[42] This meant that it was, in real terms, the responsibility of the Irish landlords to address the problem, an attitude which accorded not only with that of Louisa Knight but also with that of her family and the great majority of their acquaintance.

For Louisa, the need to comprehend Ireland's distress came in the wake of a series of personal losses. In the year following Cassandra's death, Henry Knight, the charming, affectionate older brother who had left in his teens to join the 6th Light Dragoons and risen to become a Major in the 9th Lancers, died at the age of forty-six. He had been suffering from 'attacks in the head', later discovered to be epileptic fits, one of which was to be the cause of his premature death.[43] His visits home had always been a source of joy to his family, and despite the fact that he and his volatile brother George had briefly shocked their aunt Jane by dallying in their teens with a servant, she liked him 'to the utmost, to the very top of his class, quite brimful', and he had sorely missed her after her death.[44] Henry had grown up to be a kind and good husband, first to his cousin, Sophia Cage and, three years after her death in 1833, to Charlotte Northey. Charles was deeply distraught over his brother's last illness and death. He was almost unable to describe it, as with his sister Cassandra's funeral, and his uncharacteristically illegible diary entries on the subject speak to the depth of his distress. This time it was he, Marianne, William and their father who 'on the wettest night almost ever known' got the sudden call. 'An express came in the night', Charles wrote on 5 May 1843, 'with a bad acc't of Henry, whereon William and I went in the middle of the night to B[asing]-stoke in his four carriage to meet the next train.' They were joined the next day by their father and Marianne. 'May & I saw Henry & talked to him', Charles entered in his diary; yet, though Henry survived the crisis which caused their emergency dash to his side, he did not improve. He died on 31 May 1843 with Charles at his side.[45]

Two of the Godmersham children Jane Austen had known were now dead, and other losses followed that year, with the death, in August, of James and Francis Austen's second wives, the former Mary and Martha Lloyd. The two sisters had been dear friends of both Jane and Cassandra Austen. Mary had helped nurse Jane in her last illness at Winchester in 1817 and Martha had been, for a time, a member of the Austen household. With so many companions gone, Cassandra Austen too had become very frail. On 23 March 1845, Easter Day, Charles wrote: 'We heard today the sad news we had been expecting of poor At. Cassandra's death, which took place yesterday at 4 in the morning at Portsdown Lodge.'[46] She had been staying at her brother Francis's house in Portsmouth, tended by her brothers Henry and Charles Austen, and her niece, James's daughter Caroline. By strange coincidence, she died at about the same hour in the morning as her sister Jane. The old order had passed, but there was no room for sentimentality among the Austens. By the beginning of April, Edward Knight Jr had cleared the cottage where Jane had lived the last eight years of her life. 'After Cassandra Austen died it was used for labourers' tenements,' her great-nephews wrote in 1911, by which time it had become a village club. Edward's decision ended his family's link with Chawton Cottage, and its memories of Jane Austen, for over a century, until the efforts of the Jane Austen Society and Jane Austen Memorial Trust ensured its survival.[47]

Louisa's new commitment to her sister's children meant she could not always choose to be with her family. In the summer of 1845, Fanny, whose own daughter Fanny Elizabeth was dying, wrote to Miss Chapman: 'Marianne and my youngest brother are going to Brighton, and my sister Louisa has been all the summer in Ireland with Ld George Hill and his children.'[48] Lord George's family was already in mourning for the 3rd Marquess of Downshire, who had died on 12 April 1845 as the result of a fall from a horse, 'whilst he was riding over his Blessington Estate in the company of his agent'.[49] In her new circumstances, Louisa could not easily return to comfort her sister. As with the Austens and Knights, so with the Hills: the sentimental had no place. Lord George, determined to be known as a landlord who did not leave the care of his estate, or his business, to others, threw himself into his work. The hotel provided the perfect opportunity. It had begun the year 1845 with a reputation for such hospitality that prospective guests could knock on the door at any hour of the day or night and expect to be admitted.[50] Just a month after his brother's death, Lord George was attending to his hotel guests personally, and explaining his mission to them. 'We had the pleasure,' wrote one, 'of meeting Lord George Hill who kindly accompanied us, and pointed out the various improvements made in that part of his Lordship's property — a most gigantic undertaking, in this wild but highly interesting district affording a bright example — how much may be effected by judicious management by a Landlord residing upon his estates & attending to the moral and social condition of his Tenantry.'[51]

In that last summer before the onset of the Great Famine, visitors continued in a stream, writing of the sights to be seen and the good care taken of them by Lord George. They included the Young Irelanders John Mitchel and John O'Hagan, who wrote that they had been 'much pleased with the accommodation afforded in this hotel and the attention of the servants'.[52] Mitchel, with Duffy and O'Hagan, had travelled to Donegal, armed with a copy of Carlyle's *Sartor Resartus*: they experienced no sense of foreboding about the famine to come, and went away cheered by all they saw in Gweedore. 'And here I once for all, remark what I observed in the South as well as in the North,' John O'Hagan wrote in his account of that journey, 'that the Irish-speaking population, who generally live in the mountains, never present the same aspect of destitution as we see in the English-speaking townlands. I suppose they are not ground down by high rents, or eaten up by too large a population.'[53] O'Hagan's diary of that trip especially commended Lord George's work in expanding the port of Bunbeg: 'Lovely little quay, most convenient for Lord George to land his goods ... Immense business done at the store, considering the bareness of the country.'[54]

Despite the personal stress of 1845, by the year's end Lord George had published his detailed pamphlet, *Facts from Gweedore*, an account of the work he had begun in 1838 on his estate.[55] At the same time, Louisa began to find her own mission. Though she had originally come to Ireland to care for the motherless Hill children, she found herself becoming increasingly involved with their father's cause. It became a matter of vital importance to Louisa to publicise her brother-in-law's efforts to improve the lot of his tenants, and she enlisted the willing assistance of Fanny who, in her turn, wrote to her old friend Miss Chapman, asking her to make the work known. This early marketing was quite concentrated: the sisters were determined to raise money through the sale of the book and of hand-knitted garments, mostly socks and stockings, in order to bring Anglicanism to Gweedore. The fact that it did not seem to be particularly welcomed by the majority of the tenants seemed irrelevant: good was to be done to them whether they wished it or not. When the impact of the famine began to be felt in Gweedore, and Lord George started to put all his efforts into relieving the distress of his tenants, Louisa simply added this concern to the work of improvement. Famine did not take precedence over missionary zeal and nothing would persuade her, or Fanny in her letters to Miss Chapman, that one issue might be separate from the other.

Because neither Louisa nor any member of her family had lived in an area stricken by famine and, crucially, because she did not, in Jane Austen's phrase, 'know the manners there', she failed to comprehend some unalterable aspects of life in Ireland. Louisa did not see that a change in religion was not acceptable to the Catholic tenants of Gweedore. She was as determined as Lord George to see the establishment of an Anglican Church at Bunbeg for the approximately seventy tenants on the estate who were Protestant, with the additional plan at the outset of a glebe house for the Minister and his family. She may also have been in need of a project, finding herself so far from all that was familiar. Whatever her reasons, Louisa concentrated her energies into the selling of Lord George's book, and her influential oldest sister gladly took up the cause, as Fanny's letters of the mid-1840s to Miss Chapman show:

> I want to ask you ... to patronize a little work just published ... called 'Facts from Gweedore' compiled from notes made by my brother-in-law Lord George Hill ... Lord G. Hill has bought of late years some property in this almost isolated part of the North of Donegal and he & his children & my sister Louisa have been passing the summer near the spot — they are now at Godmersham House and I have heard so much of interest from them about these poor people that I feel anxious to assist in promoting their welfare. The proceeds of the sale of 'Facts from Gweedore' are intended to assist in establishing a clergyman and if possible building a place of worship, for they are 10 miles from the nearest place of protestant [worship] ... It is only 7s 6d & I think you would find it interesting & well worth the money.[56]

Miss Chapman responded immediately, and Fanny offered to send her a copy of an ' "Appeal" for subscriptions for a Church & etc'.[57] The appeal was 'made on behalf of a district on the north-west coast of Donegal ... where there are upwards of seventy souls, including children, without any permanent provision for the supply of their spiritual wants'. The expense of providing teachers and a schoolhouse, which had to double as a place of worship, had fallen, the appeal explained, on Lord George Hill: if money were forthcoming, he was prepared to give ten acres 'as a glebe' and, if further subscriptions should be made available, would add a church to the glebe house. Yet, despite the appeal, by February 1846 there had been only a limited response and Fanny's next letter to Miss Chapman indicates a certain distancing from the concerns of the Irish:

> There has not yet been much collected, but Lord G. is determined to begin the clergyman's house. I trust to providence for being enabled to do more. I am trying to assist by spreading the fame of the book as far as I can, & my contributions whether by way of selling the book, or by friends offering subscriptions (all of which tell in the long run) will of course be thankfully rc'd. You are so kind in really thinking about it, that I am tempted thus to enter into details, but you are by no means to think it necessary to *torment* yourself or your friends on the subject. In Ireland it is particularly desirable to have the 'Appeal' circulated ... [58]

In other words, the problem was for the Irish to solve; and the attitude that Ireland's wider difficulties were Ireland's problem followed on from that perception.[59] Lord George, however, did not distance himself from his tenants' sufferings, any more than from their spiritual welfare. As the famine worsened, soup kitchens were established at Stranacorcragh and Dunlewey and, as Chairman of the Relief Committee in Donegal, Lord George made urgent requests for help in setting up a soup station at Bunbeg during 1846 and into 1847. Having heard from Sir James Dombrain that a ship was shortly to sail to Sligo in the west of Ireland, he set out to try to relieve his tenants' immediate anxiety that they would run out of food before relief came. In September 1846, he wrote to the Relief Commission:

> I trouble you with these few lines to request that you will have the goodness to order a cargo with as little delay as possible

to Bunbeg Store at Gweedore, as the wants of the people are daily increasing & their fears — that their provision, which is but small, will run out before a supply is sent in — are great.[60]

During that year, Lord George divided his time between Ireland and England in his efforts to relieve the distress of his tenants.[61] 'I will … send you another paper about the present distress in Ireland which Ld. George Hill has been an eyewitness to,' Fanny wrote to Miss Chapman at the end of November 1846. 'You will see he is on the Committee of Relief & he has sent over £500 worth of meal to be stored at Gweedore *on trust* as the necessity is too pressing to wait. We have collected a little, & I believe much has been given, but every trifle is of assistance.'[62] By mid-January 1847, this second appeal for funds, this time not for the building of a schoolhouse, but for simple famine relief, was in circulation:

Distress at Gweedore

In soliciting aid on behalf of the famishing Poor of the Gweedore district, the population of which exceeds 3,000 souls, those benevolent persons who have contributed to this object are requested to accept the most grateful and heartfelt acknowledgements for the aid already offered, and which has been husbanded with the most rigid economy, attention is now directed to the following *facts*:

The people are all of them in a starving condition, few having more than one scanty meal in the twenty-four hours. On this account, together with the very unwholesome nature of the food, severe Dysentery has broken out, and is daily hurrying numbers into eternity.

There are, as yet, no Public Works going on, and when they are proceeded with, only a limited number of hands will be employed.

These are trying circumstances; and it is well worthy of observation, that while in some parts of Ireland the most alarming outrages are daily being perpetrated, here, under hardships and sufferings of no common kind, the greatest patience is exhibited. The poor people have already — at a great disadvantage — disposed of the few sheep they possessed; numbers have, long since, sold their Cows; but now, from the unhealthy and weak condition of those remaining, caused by want of food, no purchasers are to be found. The prospect wears a gloomy and dismal aspect, and what adds to it is the certainty that next winter will, if possible, be much worse than the present, unless some means for tilling and sowing this ground be afforded.

LORD GEORGE A. HILL who possesses property here to a considerable extent has, ever since he purchased the Estate, been in the habit of spending yearly, double, or more than double, the amount of his Rents in promoting the happiness and welfare of the tenantry, but this year it would be utterly impossible for one individual to meet the wants of so large a population without some assistance; hitherto, provisions have been brought in by his Lordship and sold to all around, without exception, at a considerable sacrifice; but the stock is at an end. This appeal, then, is made to the sympathies of a kind and benevolent Public, to enable the people to purchase Indian Meal at the Government stores, at a reduced price.

Subscriptions will be most thankfully received and acknow-ledged by LORD GEORGE A. HILL, Gweedore, Dunfanaghy, Ireland; or by the Rev. Samuel O'Neill Cox. January 11 1847.[63]

This appeal was in keeping with government policy in the early part of the famine, whereby public works would ensure that the needy could earn money to buy food: the government's unwillingness to take direct responsibility for maintaining these public works, already voiced by the Prime Minister, Lord John Russell, placed a great responsibility on voluntary organisations and on voluntary subscription. It was not until January 1847 that this policy was altered;

by the spring of that year, public works had been replaced by direct outdoor relief, and with the introduction of soup kitchens, some three million people were subsisting by mid-1847 on what was provided by public expense.[64]

A revealing fragment of a letter from Louisa to Fanny in the winter of that year, describing the misery of the Gweedore tenants, demonstrates her genuine compassion for their sufferings. Unfortunately, it also shows her utter inability to comprehend their unwillingness to go to the workhouse, the last resort for the poor.[65] It was not simply that the Poor Law Unions had much larger units than in Great Britain: there was, to make matters worse, horrific overcrowding. Ironically, because the Poor Law Extension Act of 1847 refused relief to anyone owning more than quarter of an acre, to qualify for the poorhouse meant destitution, and almost certainly, death:

> Ld George did not get sufficient [funds] ... to build a Glebe House and Church & and the latter is obliged to be given up — the Glebe House is nearly completed & the Cleggmore rector and his wife & 3 children hope to leave their present makeshift house at Bunbeg for their new mansion. The school house in which there is service every Sunday is being enlarged 14 feet to accommodate the enlarged congregation — the utter wretchedness of the poor children about here is miserable to see — but as all need clothing in the same degree and it is impossible to clothe three thousand we are obliged to do nothing in that way — added to this it would do very little good — for they will neither [dress] the children in the clothes or [sic] mend them & had rather go about in dirt & filth than go to the Poor House & be fed & clothed & have the children educated — there are of course a few exceptions, some who really strive to learn & do better — but this last year of bad suffering & privation has destroyed their energies & produced a kind of torpor which comprehends nothing.[66]

Louisa's resistance to the tenants' point of view was not unique to her. As J.C. Beckett points out, 'the widespread sympathy with the sufferings of the Irish poor was not unmingled with impatience, and sometimes with contempt'.[67]

A sense of this is conveyed in an entry written in the *Gweedore Hotel Book* by Louisa's brother, John Knight, during September 1847:

> The comfort and interior economy of this inn is equal to its outward appearance which in my experience is high praise, for a more substantial well built or commodious house with stable byre & etc it would be difficult to find anywhere, & impossible I should imagine in any other part of Ireland of so wild a character as this. It is, in fact, a fair sample of the Lord George Hill's doings in Donegal, which have effected such an extraordinary revolution in the space of a few years in the habits of the people & the appearance of the Country, substituting cleanliness & industry for sloth & dirt — & changing bogs, rocks & heather into cornfields & potatoes farmland, that one scarcely knows whether most to admire or wonder at the transformations we behold ... [68]

John seems fairly dismissive, if not outright contemptuous of the tenantry in Gweedore. Yet, this bears out Jane Austen's observation of 1814: her family did not, and could not, comprehend the cultural differences between the two countries. Fanny's view, unsurprisingly, was that famine had simply interrupted the good work of conversion, as she wrote to Miss Chapman at the height of the distress in 1847:

> With regard to the Gweedore affairs, I am sorry to say the dreadful famine of last winter obliged Ld. G. Hill to apply all his resources to keeping the people alive, & while the work has continued to progress slowly it has not gone on as it had done, had not this sad state of things occurred. I will ask him to tell me for your information exactly what progress has been made, & what there is yet to do.[69]

Lord George had indeed put every effort into relief, commuting at a frenetic pace from England back to Ireland, even while his family were settled at Godmersham. In the middle of the crisis, however, he had another, very pressing matter which required his full attention.

On 11 May 1847, Lord George Hill was married to Miss Louisa Knight of Godmersham, Kent. It was no whirlwind romance, yet, though their decision to marry came as no surprise to Fanny, the union had been almost as difficult to achieve as Lord George's marriage to Cassandra. 'My sister Louisa's marriage was a great joy to us,' Fanny wrote to Miss Chapman, 'when it was found possible to accomplish it.' The difficulty centred on an Act of Parliament, passed several years before, making it illegal on grounds of consanguinity for a man to marry in England the sister of his deceased wife. As a consequence, Lord George and Louisa had to be married abroad, as Fanny went on to explain to Miss Chapman:

> She had been devoted to those 4 dear little children & had never left them since their own dear Mother's death & it was not surprising that an attachment had grown up between Lord George and herself, but until the last year it had been believed impossible that a marriage should take place with a wife's sister since the passing of Lord Lyndhurst's Act ... — the question however was brought forward again amongst Lawyers, & as you probably know the Queen's Commissioner now issued ... to try it — meanwhile as my Father & most of our family (including Ld G and Ld D) felt convinced that there is no Divine or Moral Law against it, & as England is the only country in which it is not legal, it was determined that they should go to Denmark where no doubt exists, & there the marriage was celebrated. My Aunt Louisa & brother John accompanied them & they staid a few weeks at Godmersham after their return home & then went with the children to Ireland, where they have been ever since the middle of June at Ballyare House near Rathmelton in the County of Donegal, which is Lord George's place & is about 18 or 20 miles from Gweedore, the seat of his labours, & where he goes constantly for a few days at a time to superintend the prosecution of his benevolent plans.[70]

This wedding was a very different occasion from the grand affair of 1834 at St George's, Hanover Square: Charles, who had written in such precise detail of that wedding, was not even present when Louisa married. His diary for May 1847 records only a brief, unembellished entry, written a full week after the marriage, following a dinner with his brother Edward in Chawton House: 'Heard of G. Hill & Lou being married.'[71] He expressed no joy, and no opinion. Yet, he had been very close to Louisa all his life, and especially so when they both lived at Godmersham: she cut his hair, read German and dissected wildlife with him, rode with him on the railway, partnered him in charades and once, to his considerable mortification, presented him with a baffling birthday present of three bars of soap. 'I daresay I am not of a clean habit,' Charles had written at the time, with more than a suggestion of injured pride, 'or else I can't imagine why anybody should give me 3 bars of soap.'[72] Louisa once knew him well enough to suggest an improvement in his personal hygiene: yet, he was not informed of her wedding until a week after it had occurred, and then only through Edward, at once the most detached of their brothers and the one most likely to understand, through early and bitter experience, what it was to be in an unconventional marriage in that family. One possible explanation for Charles's cool reaction is that he, unlike Fanny and most of the family, did not approve of the marriage.[73] Apart from his many scruples over details of doctrine and morality, a source of continuing unease to him, he was not in favour of second marriages, and had been far from enthusiastic when his widowed brother Henry married Charlotte Northey in 1836. 'Not a first wife – not the wife of his heart,' he had written then, 'for she is gone, but only one that will do.'[74] If that was his view about Henry's wife, it is entirely possible that Charles felt the same about his friend Lord George's second marriage, despite the fact that the new bride was his own dear sister, Lou.[75]

Whatever the opinion of the brother to whom she had always been closest, or of the Houses of Parliament, Louisa was now Lady George Hill. There was no prolonged honeymoon, however – there was too much work to do. 'I hear of course from my sister constantly,' wrote Fanny to Miss Chapman, 'and am happy to say that accounts are good as to the crops & the condition of the people at present & now that relief committees & soup kitchens are established in every district, we may hope that no such misery as existed last winter will occur again.' Fanny, too, continued on her mission to promote the sale of *Facts from Gweedore*: 'I am now negotiating the sale of 6000 pair of Gweedore socks & stockings, which [Lord George] has on hand, knit by his own people, all of which he buys from them & disposes of as he can.'[76]

For the Knights, the wedding of Lord George and Louisa signalled a significant change. Edward Austen Knight was not far from eighty years old, and felt keenly the loss of another daughter to the unknown country of Ireland for, after 1847, committed to her husband and the nieces and nephews who were now her stepchildren, she was no longer a Knight of Godmersham. 'My dear Father felt parting with Louisa very much,' Fanny wrote, '& so did we all, but it was impossible for Lord George to remain longer away from his property & people & of course his wife & children must accompany him.'[77]

In political terms, the marriage caused something of a unwelcome stir, and within five years it would be the subject of discussion in the House of Lords, to establish the position of such controversially married couples in society, and to discuss the legal position of any children who might be born to them.[78] In the mid-1840s however, Lord George was being commended in the House of Commons for his work in Gweedore.[79] It was on the strength of this fame that the celebrated author Thomas Carlyle, former hero of the young idealists who had founded *The Nation*, made a visit to Gweedore during his journey to Ireland in 1849.

'Ireland really is my problem,' he wrote in his journal for May of that year, 'the breaking point of the huge suppuration which all British and all European society is.'[80] For the Irish people themselves, he had as little regard as John Knight: 'Beggars, beggars; only industry really followed by the Irish people,' he wrote in August 1849.[81] On his way from John Hamilton's estate to his appointment with Lord George, he commented without enthusiasm on the 'bare miserable country – moor, moor, brown heather, and peat-pots, here and there a speck reclaimed into bright green'. He transferred to hired transport for the road to Letterkenny, and began his journey to Lord George's house at Ballyare, outside Ramelton, recording his impressions in his own inimitable and idiosyncratic style:

Fourteen miles; a tilled country mostly, not deficient here and there in wood; ragged still, tho' greatly superior to late wont; recognize the *Ulster* dialect of carman, Ulster practice of the population generally. Talk — burdensome, had there been much of it? Mountains about Gweedore, details (eulogistic, enthusiastic) of Lord George Hill; three men (officialities, of some kind) — excise or other with dish-hats, before us in their car; road now rapidly winding downwards: pass them at last; can bethink of no other road-fellow whatever. Country greenish for most part, with gnarled crags; I should have expected ferns in the ditches, but don't remember them. Millpond at the bottom of our descent, then long slow ascent up Letterkenny Street, broad, sometimes rather ragged-looking, always idle-looking, — busy only on market days, with corn and cattle, I suppose. Hotel at last; and carman satisfied, a grateful change into Lord George's car. To Ballyarr [sic] then! Now towards 6 or 7 o'clock. Long, mile-long straight steep ascent; then complex cross roads 'to Rathmelton' … country commonplace, hill-and-dale, not quite bare; at length Ballyarr [sic], clump of wood; high rough hedges, gates, farm-looking place; and round the corner of some offices we come to an open smooth kind of back court, with low piazza at the further side ...[82]

Suddenly, he beheld Lord George and had a first glimpse of Louisa, his descriptions giving a rare insight into their family life at Ballyare. His picture of Louisa may be all the more revealing because he did not know, and never realised, that the quiet lady whose name he could neither retain nor recall, was the niece of Jane Austen. Lord George was, in August 1849, only forty-seven years old, and Louisa three years his junior; yet Carlyle saw a rather elderly, if elegant couple:

From below piazza, — then at the back entrance, (the only handy one to his mansion) Lord George himself politely steps

out to welcome us. Handsome, grave-smiling man of 50 or
more; thick, grizzled hair, elegant club nose, low cooing voice,
military composure and absence of loquacity; a man you love at
first sight. Glimpse of Lady (Georgina?) Hill, a nun-like elderly
lady, and of one or two nice silent children; silent small elegant
drawing-room; a singular silent politeness of element reigns; at
length refection in a little dining room, (tea, I suppose?) — and,
in a bare but clean and comfortable room, presided over by the
Great Silences, one sinks gratefully asleep.[83]

It is a strange, almost ghostly scene: the only vibrant character in it is Lord
George himself, while Louisa and the children seem like pale ghosts, and the
'Great Silences' sound not tranquil, but unnatural. The eldest of Cassandra's
four children, thirteen-year-old Norah, whose birth in the middle of a winter
night had caused Charles such anxiety in 1835, would spend the spring and
summer of the following year at Godmersham; accounts of her there show a
lively, sociable child.[84] Arthur, her next eldest brother, was twelve, his brother
Augustus ten and the youngest, Cassandra Jane Louisa, was six years old.
Moreover, there was that year a new addition to the family: Louisa, at forty-
four, had been fortunate to be safely delivered of a son. A delicate child, he had
his father's name, George, and his middle name, Wandsbeck, commemorated
the place of his parents' marriage. It seems odd that not one of the children
disturbed the pervading silence. It makes a strange, unsettling contrast with
the charades and music of Godmersham, in which Lord George and Louisa
had once played so enthusiastic a part. Carlyle, however, appreciated the quiet,
and enjoyed the next day:

Gweedore ... like an unopened scroll lying before — I bethink
me, we walked out too, that evening, Lord George ... and I, with
pleasant familiar talk; and for supper after our return, he ordered
me Irish stirabout, a frightful parody of 'Scotch porridge,' (like
hot dough) which I would not eat and even durst not except in
semblance.[85]

He was glad the following morning not to have to face any more of it. Louisa was not present at breakfast, Carlyle wrote, struggling once more to remember what she was called, and making a gallant attempt to attribute to her Lord George's middle name: 'Dim, moist morning, pleasant breakfast (Lady Augusta (?) who has a baby, not there), paternal wit of Lord G. with his nice little modest boys and girls in English, German, French.'[86] It comes as a relief to see that the children talked at breakfast, and in several languages. Carlyle then went from Ballyare with Lord George to see Gweedore. He admired the hotel, the mill and quay, despised the 'ghastly staring new Catholic chapel' and, though he was mightily disapproving of the 'dark barbarians', Lord George's tenants, he was greatly impressed with his host's care of them: 'Lord George knows all these people; speaks kindly, some words in Irish or otherwise, to everyone of them.'[87]

Lord George did care for his tenants and, Gaelic scholar as he was, understood their customs and working practices. As far back as the winter of 1835, full of his newfound enthusiasm for Donegal, and encouraging his reluctant brother-in-law Charles to read some Irish history, he had recounted a story from Gweedore, which Charles recorded in his diary:

> In the west of Donegal a proprietor wanted a ditch made a year or two ago, & instead of taking 2 or 3 fellows as we should in Kent to employ them for the winter, they got a hundred men & a fiddler & finished it in 9 hours. About 30 worked at a time, then rested, eat [sic] and drank whiskey, & danced to the fiddler whilst the others were working, & so on to the end. That is the way they do things in Ireland.[88]

Lord George understood the Gweedore way of living so well, that he could recreate the sense of it for the phlegmatic and cautious Charles Knight. In the spirit of Sir Walter Scott, who had expressed the belief in 1825 that the Irish 'natural condition is turned toward gaiety and happiness', and of the Census Commissioners who had noted 'the proverbial gaiety and lightheartedness of the peasant people', Lord George left another, similar account of the removal of a cabin from one site to another:

The custom on such occasions is for the person who has the work to be done to hire a fiddle, upon which engagement all the neighbours joyously assemble and carry in an incredibly short time the stones and timber upon their backs to the new site; men, women and children alternately dancing and working while daylight lasts, at the termination of which they adjourn to some dwelling where they finish the night, often prolonging the dance to dawn of day.[89]

The corollary of this seems to be that Lord George, despite his philanthropic commitment to bettering the condition of his tenants, understood more than almost every other landlord the cost to the people of Gweedore of the enormous changes he instituted. He built good roads, and ensured that travellers could traverse previously unnavigable territory; yet, this meant that his tenants were separated from the neighbours who were as close to them as family. 'Lord George Hill,' Cecil Woodham-Smith observed, 'found his tenants in Donegal unwilling to accept a new and better house if it meant separation from their neighbours'.[90] Louisa and Fanny may have been baffled at the refusal of the Donegal tenants to accept the changes made to their way of life – whether it was the squaring of farms, the prohibition of illegal distillation, or the Big House monopoly on the grain produced at Bunbeg Mill – but Lord George understood his tenants very well.

After Carlyle's guided tour through Gweedore in 1849, he and Lord George returned on that chilly August evening to the house at Ballyare. 'All were glad enough to get within doors to a late cup of Christian tea,' Carlyle recalled, 'Lord G. lights fire, too, by a match; very welcome blaze: presents me two pairs of his Gweedore socks. Bed soon and sleep.' On the next day, before leaving, he visited and despaired of yet another 'rough peasant farmer ... *sluttish, sluttish*', then went back for the last time to Ballyare. One final attempt to remember Louisa's name reduced Carlyle to attempting an approximation of 'Augusta': 'Lady A. with the children in the garden: a delicate, pious, high and simple lady; sister of Lord G's former wife.'[91] Then, though he had barely noticed Jane Austen's niece and god-daughter, Carlyle went away with the highest opinion of Lord George Hill: 'In all Ireland, lately in any other land, I saw no such beautiful soul.'[92] Fanny Knight, critical of so many who fell below her standards, had, three years before, unknowingly anticipated Carlyle's words: 'I wish all the Irish landlords would follow his example,' she wrote to Miss Chapman, '& the famine wd be more easily met.'[93]

Fifteen years earlier, Charles Knight had looked at his sister Cassandra on her wedding day and had seen her suddenly, chillingly, as a victim about to be buried alive. In Carlyle's portrait, it is Louisa who appears buried alive: a distant, pale wraith, scarcely noticeable behind her dynamic husband. Jane Austen's Captain Wentworth had said a man who loves deeply 'does not recover from such a devotion of the heart to such a woman! – He ought not – he does not.'[94] Lord George, unlike Captain Wentworth, had risen above his grief and made a new life. For Louisa, his second wife, far from home and all that was familiar – her marriage almost unmarked by her favourite brother, her name unmemorable to the distinguished visitor – life was now lived on the periphery of those of her husband and five children. From the time of her marriage onwards, she could go back to England only as a visitor; and, as a visitor, she would see, but be powerless to prevent, the cataclysmic changes about to take place in her old family home.

CHAPTER 6

'OUR LOST HOME'

Marianne and Her Brothers
1849–1860

'Dear, dear Norland,' said Marianne, as she wandered alone before the house, on the last evening of their being there, 'when shall I cease to regret you, when learn to feel a home elsewhere?'

SENSE AND SENSIBILITY

> My dearest Fanny
> Nothing — but I must write once more in my life to you at 'Mersham Hatch' [sic] So, here I am, beginning — I won't keep you long, so never mind; and I won't make you cry, if I can help it, tho' my heart is crying for you, and has been for a long while. I cannot bear your leaving Hatch, and I want to hide somewhere and see your gd bye tomorrow but I don't know where or when.[1]

With these words, Marianne Knight began a compassionate letter to her sister Fanny in July 1849. Fanny had recently been widowed: Sir Edward Knatchbull, having failed, after repeated efforts, to find a cure for his 'severe bronchial affliction', had died on 24 May. One daughter, Fanny Elizabeth, had died in February of tuberculosis; another, Alice, had lost her own struggle with the disease as her father entered his last illness.[2] Now, as the dowager making way for her stepson and his wife, Fanny was compelled to leave the home she had known for almost thirty years.[3] Marianne's heart was, indeed, breaking for her sister. She felt able to write it for, of all the sisters, Marianne – once rather grudgingly acknowledged by her cousin Caroline to be 'very like poor Aunt

Jane' – showed herself to be possessed of the most expressive voice in her letters. She was also, unlike either Fanny or Louisa, gifted with a dry sense of humour, and the fortunate ability to remain optimistic in adversity. 'Well, well, my dear', she continued to Fanny, 'this is the world and t'other's the country!! and if we were to get there, we shan't have to turn out, but whoever will come there will be room for all!' Like Jane Austen, Marianne had attained what her aunt had described as 'the true art of letter-writing, which we are always told, is to express on paper exactly what one would say to the same person by word of mouth'.[4] Marianne's letters display that same sense of lively immediacy: 'Tomorrow Johnny sets off', she concluded in her letter of commiseration to Fanny:

> ... and I am very glad of it, tho' I shall miss him sadly — it will do him good I think, and be a pleasant change for him. He joins his friend Mr Hill in London tomorrow, and the next day they steam off for Dundee. I hope the wind won't blow as it does now. Papa is having a rest before luncheon. It rains a little every now and then. I hope it won't be a bad afternoon. Aunt Louisa goes tomorrow to Goodnestone & comes back on the 11th August. Louisa Rice takes her place here tomorrow, so with both the girls, I hope I shall get our pretty peace & if papa is comf. and nicely, he will not mind being awry for 2 weeks.[5]

Aunt Louisa was Louisa Bridges, their late mother's sister, and Louisa Rice, Lizzy's daughter, was now aged twenty-five, and about to join her younger sister Marianne Sophia at Godmersham for the summer. Lizzy's early marriage in 1818 meant that by 1849 many of her fifteen children were already adults, and it is clear that the Knight sisters had begun to assume the roles once taken by their aunts Cassandra and Jane, providers of refuge and advice to their nieces and nephews. Marianne Sophia would soon reject the unwelcome advances of Fanny's eldest son, Edward, and Lizzy's daughter, Fanny Margaretta, would shortly marry the much older George Finch-Hatton, 10th Earl of Winchilsea, who had been a friend of her father.[6]

The letters exchanged among the Knight siblings also served to provide, for themselves as often as for their children, much-needed help and comfort.

Three of William Knight's little daughters, aged only five, four and three, died in one day of scarlet fever in 1848, and in the same year Lizzy's second son Henry Rice, just twenty-seven, died of cholera while serving with the army at Barbados. His brother Cecil Rice, at eighteen, had just joined the same regiment, the 72nd Regiment of Foot (the Duke of Albany's own Highlanders), as an Ensign. At home, meanwhile, as the generations moved up, the young began to assume their share of responsibility, while the remaining great-uncles and aunts of Jane Austen's family grew more frail. Henry Austen would die of gastritis in 1850, and Jane's youngest brother Charles, serving on the Irawaddy River, would die, like Henry Rice, of cholera in 1852. Of Jane Austen's siblings, only Francis Austen and Edward Knight were left, and Edward, who had turned eighty in 1847, was far from well. He suffered badly from gout, and had grown almost totally dependent on Marianne. Though John Knight, the ever-indulged Johnny, had time and leisure enough to be helpful, he lacked the patience his father's age and illness required, as Louisa Rice observed:

> Morny went to Godmersham to take Uncle Charles's place with Grandpapa who is well as usual but always getting weaker. Uncle John does not do well for him — he is not good or gentle and next to Uncle Charles he likes to have Morland better than anyone.[7]

'Morny' was John Morland Rice, Lizzy's son, a quiet, clever young clergyman – with a quick and sometimes acerbic wit – who had assisted his uncle Charles Knight in his parish duties at Chawton and now helped Marianne look after his grandfather.

What no one said, but everyone knew, was that the ultimate fate of the Godmersham household was entirely in the hands of Marianne's eldest brother, Edward. As early as 1822 his father, feeling himself at only forty-five to be failing in health and likely to die, had made it clear that he expected Edward Jr to look after not just the estate, but also any of his brothers and sisters who needed his help. He hoped and trusted that all his children 'would find in [Edward] a second Father as well as an affectionate Brother and Friend'. He urged prudence and economy, failing which Edward might find himself without 'the means of giving that occasional assistance to [his] Brothers and Sisters, which both Affection and Inclination, would otherwise naturally lead [him] to'.[8] Edward's scandalous elopement less than five years later, and his subsequent attachment to Chawton rather than Godmersham, did not shake his father's faith. Edward Austen Knight made this clear in a careful postscript, added thirteen years after the letter had been written:

> Although you are placed in a different situation to that which you were then in, I am unwilling to destroy what I have written, it will show you what my feelings then were and I am not aware that a lapse of a dozen years has made any difference in them, I am sure it has not in any affection for you and those most dear to you, or in my Anxiety to promote and secure as much as may be in my Power the Comfort and happiness of you all, may it long continue.[9]

Edward Austen Knight, a diplomat at heart, had avoided unpleasantness throughout his long and fortunate life. He was resolute in his refusal to think ill of his son. The question, however, of the younger Edward's interpretation of his commitment to the house and his siblings remained unaired and unresolved. If his own father's understanding of the duty to family were to be his example, Edward Jr need not do more than provide a cottage formerly belonging to a servant – a point of view thoroughly and satirically anticipated in Jane Austen's *Sense and Sensibility* many years earlier. In the meantime, as Edward Austen Knight's health genuinely declined with advancing age, it fell to Marianne to maintain the appearance of stability within the family.

Fortunately for her, and for the large establishment which she was required to run, Marianne was able for the task. She was clearly very bright and capable, qualities her mother had remarked upon before she was six years old. In addition, she was possessed of an essential pragmatism which, with a quick wit untainted by bitterness or resentment, enabled her to overlook, or at least to decline to question the unfairness of the assumption that she would devote her life to the best interests of everyone else. In this, she followed the example of her famous aunt, who left no comment on the unfairness of her brother's leaving his mother and sisters to live without permanent accommodation for several years, despite his being in possession of two extensive estates. Marianne's readiness to rise to any occasion, however, endeared her not only to her family but also to their many friends. She maintained so equable a relationship with her rejected suitor of 1822, the Reverend John Billington, that he continued throughout the years to be a regular and welcome visitor at Godmersham; and Louisa's former suitor, George Oxenden, kept up so fond a correspondence with Marianne during the 1830s, writing not only letters but also poems in her praise, that it seems he may have transferred his affections for a time to this least demanding, yet most open-hearted of the family.[10] Her replies have not survived, but it is unlikely that she would by then have contemplated leaving her father, and the responsibilities she had so selflessly undertaken.

When their little group of siblings – the long-ago children left outside on the stairs – May, Charley, Lou, Cass and, sometimes, Johnny, all lived at Godmersham in the late 1820s and early 1830s, it was Marianne who was the still point of the family's turning wheel. She ran the household quietly in the background, occasionally enlisting the help of the amenable Charles to help her prepare rooms for the visits of the those brothers and sisters who had married and left, more often accompanying her father on activities too old for her or coming home early from celebrations to look after him. In one sense, she was what Emma Woodhouse might have become if Mr Knightley had not realised his love for her; unlike the rich and independent Emma, however, she had no security of tenure. Yet, she was happy in the company of her father, Charles, and the unsettled Johnny, becoming the family's 'dearest Aunt May'. They all relied on her, and Charles, in particular, thought her essential to his work.

Once Charles had resigned himself to bachelorhood, sometime in his early thirties, Marianne was his chosen companion. He was close to Louisa, who shared his interest in the scientific, yet as both Louisa and Cassandra spent much of their twenties at once encouraging and fending off suitors, it was to the home-based May that Charles turned when he needed help. When his friend and brother-in-law Lord George Hill accidentally gave away a walking stick Charles had intended for a present to his aunt Louisa Bridges, Charles did not know what to do. It was Marianne who, with Lord George, brought about the practical solution. 'Marianne and Aunt Louisa went to Canterbury,'

Charles wrote in October 1835. 'They brought back Aunt Louisa's stick, which I am to consider as my gift to her from abroad, the original being given by mistake by G. Hill to Crawley, & this being a facsimile made by order of G. Hill to make up for his mistake.'[11] Charles, in his own world of scruple, moral debate and the beauties of nature, had not thought of that himself.

Charles's parish duties, while he lived at Godmersham, involved assisting the incumbent with such outlying parishes as the nearby village of Molash. He took these duties very seriously, however, insisting on battling through unusually deep snow and a freakish storm to take the Christmas morning service, and attending most assiduously to the welfare, both spiritual and physical, of the needy of the parishes under his care. It was here that he turned most often to Marianne, already proven as a calm and capable organiser. She ran the Penny Club, ensuring that the poor received adequate clothing, which she often made herself. There was a custom that the daughters of parishioners who were going into service should be provided with clothes: 'Mrs Wright of the parsonage and Mrs James Ruck came to Marianne for things for their daughters who are going out to service,' Charles wrote in October 1835. They were not from a local parish, and Charles, who felt strongly that only those from the parishes to which he ministered should be granted this service, was put out; Marianne, however, though quite aware that they did not have the right to ask this of her, nonetheless looked after them. Her action recalls Jane Austen's last, uncompleted work of 1815, *Sanditon*, where the officious, interfering Diana Parker tries to prevail upon her good-hearted sister-in-law to apply to the mean and overbearing Lady Denham for charitable offerings to parishes far distant from Sanditon:

> If you find her in a giving mood, you might as well speak in favour of another charity which I and a few more, have very much at heart — the establishment of a charitable repository at Burton on Trent.— And then, — there is the family of the poor man who was hung last assizes at York, though we really have raised the sum we wanted for putting them all out, yet if you can get a guinea from her on their account, it may as well be done. —[12]

An important difference, of course, is that Marianne was no proud, cold Lady Denham, but a quiet, graceful and compassionate gentlewoman. Diana Parker, on the other hand, in her overbearing determination to do good, anticipates some of the correspondence between Louisa and Fanny during the Irish famine of the 1840s.

Through all her years in England, Marianne's nature generally predisposed her to see the point of view of others, even if she did not agree with it. A curious story, from Charles's diary of October 1835, demonstrates Marianne's steady, uncondescending common sense:

> Old Dame Partridge asked Marianne today whether it was true that an army of soldiers had been seen fighting in the sky. All the old crones seem much struck by this report, which someone has put into a newspaper — they were all attention as Marianne told them it was not true, & then proceeded to explain that the newspapers had nothing to put in to fill their columns & employed people called wonder workers to invent extraordinary stories for them.[13]

It shows, too, what a good teacher Marianne might have been or, in the present age, what an intelligent and sensible commentator on the continuing media habit of employing such 'wonder workers'. It is a strange anecdote, oddly and unsettlingly anticipating the time eight decades ahead when armies of soldiers would indeed be seen fighting in the sky. Nonetheless, the trusting innocence of Dame Partridge and the other old ladies of the parish is touching testament to Marianne's ability to bridge the generations, to comprehend and explain, to those who were young with Jane Austen, the rapidly changing face of the world.

As the new decade of the 1850s began, Marianne's own world was about to change equally radically. Charles was not in residence to help as her father fell into his last illness. Since 1838, he had been rector of Chawton and though, like John, and the kind Morland Rice, he came and did his best for a while, Charles then resumed his own life. Godmersham was Marianne's life and, in 1850, despite her father's illness, she was content. Louisa and Lord George, with all five children, were with her for the summer, as were her aunt, Louisa Bridges, and some of Lizzy's children. Their old ways, lessons and walks, trips to the river and excursions to neighbouring towns went on as before. Morland Rice who, though kind to his grandfather, does not seem to have been overly attached to the rest of the household, took a hard look at the Godmersham gathering that summer, and sent it to his brother, Edward Rice:

> At Godmersham all is much as usual — the German tutor — or hog as you view him in his physical or intellectual capacity — and Aunt May still make violent love to one another — Uncle John has still got more or less gout — All the Hills are still there — my Grandfather is still going on just as usual (perhaps better) — and Aunt Louisa still utters goodnatured societisms and bitter politicals.[14]

Marianne had not, of course, launched herself into a torrid affair as Morland's nineteenth-century expression might suggest to a twenty-first century mind; what his barbed comment does show is the attractiveness of Marianne's personality at fifty years old, and her lively intellectual interest in the work the Hill children were pursuing with their tutor.

By 1850, Cassandra's children, under the care of Louisa, were growing up rapidly. Her eldest daughter, Norah, was particularly striking, as her cousin Louisa Rice noticed that summer. 'About a month ago,' Louisa wrote, 'Uncle George Hill brought Norah over from Ireland to Godmersham … she is the prettiest as well as the nicest girl of 14 I ever saw … she always looks pretty and never thinks an instant about it.'[15] Norah, like Lord George himself, was a general favourite. Cassandra's daughter had inherited not just her mother's looks but also her passion for the Godmersham hobby of 'nesting', searching for birds' nests in the forest and hedgerows. 'I have just been nesting with Norah,' Lizzy wrote to her daughter Caroline Cassandra Rice in May 1850:

> … we only went about the Piece and the Lime Walk and we carried the little ladder out of the Orange House with us … we found a good many and she found the most beautiful Golden Cresteds I

ever saw, hanging at the end of a branch of a yew tree, down by the Piece — she is longing to come to Dane Court and I hope she will soon after you get home — she is taller than Charlotte and just like what she used to be — she likes nesting and reading better than anything — her hair is immensely thick and long — she wears it plaited in front like Louisa's and then joined to the back hair ... The Park and Woods are more perfectly lovely than I can describe, the Cuckoo is cuckooing over the thatched seat and yesterday I heard it by the Tower when I was walking in the Park with Uncle George Hill ...[16]

That seemingly perfect summer of 1850 was to be one of the last the family would enjoy. Though Morland thought his grandfather's health improved a little, Edward was not really getting better and, by 1852, at eighty-five, was clearly deteriorating. His death, however, came suddenly, as another grandson, Montagu Knight, recorded years later:

The squire himself lived on at Godmersham until his death, which took place 19th November 1852. He had been able to take his usual drive on the preceding day; early in the morning of the 19th he desired his servant to leave him, as he felt comfortable and should go to sleep. He seemed to be asleep when the servant returned, but it was the sleep of death. 'It strikes me,' wrote one of his relations soon afterwards, 'as a characteristic end of his prosperous and placid life, and he will certainly leave on the minds of all who knew him an image of Gentleness and quiet Cheerfulness of no ordinary degree.'[17]

He was certainly gentle, cheerful and placid, and remained to the end of his life in no doubt that his eldest son would carry out the wishes he had expressed thirty years before, and share his good fortune with the others. Yet, Edward Knight Jr had never expressed any intention of moving back from his home at Chawton. His roots were there: his first wife Mary lay buried within sight of Chawton House beside their eldest son, Edward Lewkenor, who had died at school soon after his mother's passing. It seemed at first, however, that Edward was undecided about Godmersham, as Fanny wrote to Miss Chapman in March 1853: 'I do not think Edward has determined yet what to do with the place. He has had an architect down and talked of alterations — he cannot afford to keep up both places, but which he will sell he does not know.'[18]

Edward did not rush to make up his mind, but the family knew that only he had the right to live there, and that he was unlikely to ask any of his unmarried siblings to stay on. The rest of the family, almost all with their own homes, accepted the necessity to hand over the decision to the heir. They were all, however, concerned about John: at forty-four, he had never known any home but Godmersham and, while he could view with equanimity the need to remodel the lives and homes of his brother-in-law's tenants in Gweedore, he had never had to consider until now that a similar restructuring at Godmersham could affect him. Yet soon, he too had other plans, for he had met a lady, Margaret Pearson, whom he would marry three months after his father's death. 'We are very glad,' Fanny told Miss Chapman, 'that he should have met with a person, who promises to make him amends for the home he has lost.'[19] Who, if anyone, was to make amends to Marianne was not clear. When it emerged, as it very soon did, that Edward wanted vacant possession of the house in order to renovate it, she was the only one left utterly bereft: having given her late girlhood and all her adult years to the care of her father and the estate, and having lived nowhere in her life but Godmersham, she would now, in her fifty-second year, have to find a new home. No longer Miss Woodhouse, she had suddenly become poor Miss Bates.

The loss of Godmersham, though perhaps predictable, seems to have thrown the family into a regressive confusion. Even Fanny, accustomed to command and prepared to overlook some of the most pressing demands of other people's lives, seemed to need extra support: 'My poor sister Lady G. Hill came over after my father's death,' she told Miss Chapman, 'but she could not leave the children for long — I wish they could sell their Irish property & come & live in England.'[20] Though Fanny described the misery of 'the packing up, the division of everybody's things, parting with servants & ... the expense!', it was Marianne and her elderly aunt Louisa Bridges who carried out the real, heartbreaking work of emptying the family home, staying on until everything was gone in January 1853.[21] Jane Austen, of course, had known such misery years before – first the painful uprooting from Steventon, then the departure from Bath and Southampton without regret but with endless, repeated disruption and distress. Her removal from Steventon all but silenced Jane, and it may be significant that the most fluent and expressive of the Knight letter-writers, Marianne, either left no record of her feelings about this terrible loss, or left a record which no one thought to keep.

Fanny did record that difficult period, telling Miss Chapman that her aunt Louisa Bridges was to go to Goodnestone, the old Bridges home and, assigning to Marianne her usual role of family support, took refuge in the thought that 'my sister for the present [goes] to Dane Court, where she is a great comfort to Mrs Rice'.[22] Lizzy Rice had herself come to give some help with the packing up. She brought her daughter Marianne Sophia, who wrote from Godmersham to her sister Louisa Rice describing the distress and confusion of the upheaval:

> I want to go back because if I do not go home with Mama (which I *hate*) I shall only see her for a night, but they all want me to stay, & if it will be the last time in my life — *dr Louisa* — if you could see the view from the windows — just how *dearest* At Louisa [Bridges] (who I think cares more for Grandpapa than anybody) suddenly burst out crying, when At. May & At. Lou [Hill] were gone out of the room ... I *wish* I was going home — but mama says she had rather I would not ...[23]

Her sister Caroline Cassandra had also given some help in packing up the house, and wrote to the reluctant Louisa of her experiences with her aunts, uncles, and the very elderly aunt Louisa Bridges, as they all tried to clear a house that had been a family home for over half a century. In this time of crisis, their characters displayed themselves. Louisa's open affections, revealed to her family but unseen by, for example, Thomas Carlyle when he visited Ballyare, were here given full expression as she revisited the room she had shared with her sister Cassandra; Charles gave quiet support for the niece who wanted to go walking round the old haunts. Marianne simply withdrew, for the last time, to the room that had been hers:

I am here. I came back with At. Lou Saturday to dine & sleep — I only thought of it just before At. Lou came away— When we got here I went up directly to At. May who was in her room on her sofa reading over old letters. I sat with her till dressing time — she is much more cheerful than expected — I believe she has cried out all the tears — & she really seems to me […] nearly the same as usual — so they all are — at least you know they talk & laugh, dearest At. Lou is so nice & lovely, nicer than anybody nearly— she talked & cried all the way here yesterday — after dinner we all sat & talked all the evening — they were all very glad I came, as they are missing At. K & Mama horridly — This morning I had the Hall Chamber & did not go to sleep till between 4 & 5, thinking how different I felt from *our old* visits & directly after breakfast I asked uncle Charles to come out, & he & I walked to Bentigh, till past 11 — then I came in & went up to At. Lou's room, helping her take away & dispose of some of her dearest darling *old* things, that she could not bear to leave, & she did not know what to do with — she gave me some dear old […] books, to divide between us … with dearest At. Cass's name written in them —Oh Louisa the sadness of it is too great —At. Lou is in her *own* dear darling old room … full of relics of her & At. Cass — now it is after luncheon and everybody is somewhere except me & At. Louisa. She is not well, & Aunts May & Lou have asked me to stay in & take care of her whilst they go out walking — when they come in I daresay I shall go out with one or 2 uncles — I *wish* I could go alone — [24]

By June 1853, the house was 'uninhabited', as Fanny told Miss Chapman. Marianne had left Lizzy's house at Dane Court in May and gone to Louisa in Ballyare, 'where I daresay', Fanny wrote, 'she will stay till the summer', adding, 'I expect that eventually she will live at Chawton Rectory with my brother Charles, who is the only unmarried one.'[25] Marianne tidily deposited, all the old bitterness from Edward's elopement with Fanny's stepdaughter emerged once more:

MAY, LOU & CASS

My brother & his wife fancy without extensive alterations [Godmersham] cannot be lived in, tho' I cannot see any fault, or want of accommodation in it, & were I sure of being able to remain there the rest of my life I should be too happy to go into it, with all its 'defects' (if it has any), but Edward has had an Architect in to look over it & I believe it depends upon his estimate whether they will live there (after spoiling it) or let it alone & continue to reside at Chawton.[26]

Then, in the summer, Edward made up his mind. All his siblings' worst fears were confirmed: Godmersham was to be let out.[27] It fell to John Knight, whose birth had occasioned the first great break in the family, to describe the final heartbreak in a letter to Charles. Marianne, still strangely silent at this worst moment in her life, kept the letter. When it was found among her papers after her death, the envelope bore an inscription in her hand: 'Letter from John Knight when he went to Godmersham after his Father died':

We started out at abt 9.30 this morning to come home — Most unfortunately it is a thorough wet day: I shall not be able to visit half the dear old places outside which I had intended — in the first plce we drove up to the servts' hall door, *that* did not look natural. Mrs Gibson met us in the lobby—I have been all over the house — your room — my room— May's, Lou's, study — *nursery* — every where every where — & now I am sitting at the same table (under Grandmama's picture) & on the same stool where we all, but May especially, have so often sat & wrote — I pulled the table from the wall into it's [sic] old place, put the stool in it's [sic], and here I am, & when I look up (as I so often have done, it is a habit I have when writing or thinking) & look straight before me out of the window which looks to the ice house — I can imagine that 'the gone days' have returned, & that our misery is but a dream — everything looks so beautiful & calm & old in the Park, & *unchanged* too — but when I look inside & see the desolation which surrounds me — the horrid change *there!* — the silence — the perfect silence — it is but too evident that the misery is the reality — and the happiness the dream — I have seen Gibson & Wills & John Hoskin & several others — some of them asked me how I was, or hoped I had been well, but others did as you say, touched their hats and said nothing longer ... I could go on a great deal abt all the things which tug at one's heart strings here — but what is the use? — I would give much to have a Brother or a Sister with me. Yes! It is the silence the state of desolation which affects me most — it jars upon my very heart — I keep contrasting it's [sic] present state with that of the last 45 years — outside it is the same — nature is unaffected — the woods —walks — lawn etc, are as in times gone — but inside! oh how changed!

> 'Tis Greece but living Greece no more
> So calmly sweet — so coldly fair.
> We start! for *soul* is wanting there!

Those beautiful lines of Byron's convey to my mind an exact picture of our lost Home — 'soul' is indeed 'wanting here' — the soul of him who made it an earthly paradise for us — but surely we have a right to believe that he has but exchanged an earthly for a heavenly Paradise — & in that believe [sic] is of course our comfort ... Please to send this to May. How much you will be sorry for her hither coming back! What will you give me to go in your place?[28]

John, an unsentimental soldier, became on losing Godmersham a lost child, just as he had done when his sister Cassandra died. Leaving very few of his thoughts or feelings in writing, he nevertheless conveyed in this long and impassioned letter the part played by Godmersham in the lives of all the Knight children. He was correct, of course, in knowing that it would be worst for Marianne: now it would fall to the faithful Charles to be her companion.

When Marianne came back from Ireland she moved to the rectory at Chawton, and together she and Charles began a quiet version of the life they had lived at Godmersham, caring for their garden, seeing to the poor, and putting to one side, just as Jane Austen had done when she moved to that village, their desolation at the loss of their home. Marianne, within the means of a small annuity of £200, left by her father, gave up her status as Miss Knight of the Great House, and took on the role of the parson's spinster sister.[29] Where once she had listed the expenditure of a large estate, she now undertook the economies of a comfortable but modest rectory in the village where her Austen aunts had lived: instead of the supervision of the care of many acres, she now looked after the small rectory garden, just at the end of the driveway to her brother's great house. Yet, within two years of moving there, she had begun listing the details of her roses, her hyacinths and geraniums, as the garden became her refuge.[30] Gradually, the care of Charles, the rectory and its garden, and the relief of the poor became her life. As Aunt May, she took over where Jane and Cassandra had left off, the maiden aunt keeping an open door for any of the nieces and nephews who visited, wrote to her, or brought her to their grander homes: and neither the new generation nor the old remembered or considered that she had once been the 'bewitching beautiful' Marianne, with hopes and ambitions of her own.

The extended family soon faced another great consideration, even more pressing than the settling of their children's marriages and fortunes. The nephews who had been too young to enter the navy or army now became old enough to fight – just as another major conflict began. The Crimean conflict was the first major confrontation since the Napoleonic Wars. The Crimean prefigured the Great War of 1914–18 in its use of gas, exploding shells, and trench warfare. In its widespread and horrific loss of life, with three quarters of a million soldiers dead through battle or illness, it established the pattern of later engagements. While the older nephews, like Henry Rice, had been subject to such mortal dangers as cholera, they were unlikely to be mown down in a full-scale battle. The Crimea was different: battle lines were drawn up surprisingly quickly as the great powers of the British and Russian Empires saw the weakness of the once magnificent Ottoman Empire. Russia closed in to secure the strategic port of Constantinople, and Britain and France became anxious for the survival of their access to the Mediterranean through the Bosphorus.[31] Before long the dispute had moved from Turkey and the Balkans to include Jerusalem, and a wider debate over religion.[32] As one recent commentator remarked, 'it was the first war to be brought about by the power of the press and public opinion, and the first to be reported in real time via the telegraph.'[33] As had been seen during the famine in Ireland, the press had a very powerful effect for good or ill; indeed it is doubtful that without the publicity given to his efforts, Lord George could have brought about his wish to bring extra food to his tenants at Gweedore. Now, in time of war, the press promoted a jingoistic spirit, in contrast to Queen Victoria's initial reluctance to engage with the Czar, with whom she retained a strong bond. 'What he did,' she is reported to have said, 'was from a mistaken, obstinate notion of what was right and of what he thought he had a right to do and to have.'[34] Once the Queen's scruples were overcome, the press had no further need to hold back. When the Crimea became the field of operations, the young men of Jane Austen's family were ready to fight, just as their great-uncle Henry Austen had been prepared to fight in Ireland under General Cornwallis during the rising of 1798, or their great-aunt's fictional Captain Wentworth in defence of the Empire. What no one could have known was that their training left them ill-prepared for this first, deadly modern war.

Lizzy's son, Cecil Rice, who had already been a serving soldier for seven years, could hardly wait to get out to the Crimea: trapped in Ireland, as he thought, he was delighted to be sent at last when reinforcements arrived from Dublin. His brother Edward Rice was in the navy during the siege of Balaclava; Lewis Knight, Henry's only son by his first wife and cousin Sophia Cage, served in the 17th Lancers, and was fortunate not to be in the doomed Charge of the Light Brigade. 'Lewis was well out of that blundering, mad charge,' Cecil wrote to his sister Louisa in November 1854.[35] Their friend and neighbour George Billington, son of the Reverend John Billington who had sought Marianne's hand in 1822, told his father that he was afraid he would be sent home before he had the opportunity 'to have one go in at the Ruski.'[36] He got his chance, however, and wrote vividly from the camp outside Sebastopol of the former beauty and present devastation of the town: he was hoping that he would soon see Cecil Rice, who was stationed fifteen miles away. Lord George, too old to go into battle himself, sent consignments of the hand-knitted socks which his Donegal tenants had made in their homes, and George Billington appears to have been one of the recipients. His letter from the camp shows how necessary such apparently simple gifts were: in an attempt to keep their packs light and their progress swift, the men had been ordered ashore without tents, ambulances or sufficient protection against the Russian weather: 'I don't know what I would have done without those Irish socks you gave me the last time I was at home,' George Billington wrote. 'Those and the mittens Miss Rice gave me have been of more use than anything I have. I believe they saved me from being frostbitten the other night.'[37] Before long, Cecil Rice did arrive at Sebastopol: the Army List of 1861 shows that he 'served in the Crimea from 16th July 1855, including the Siege and Fall of Sebastopol', where he was decorated for bravery.[38] In the same regiment was a Chawton cousin, Edward Jr's son Ernest Knight, who would shortly die of cholera, and a young Irishman named Somerset Ward.

The Hon. Somerset Richard Hamilton Augusta Ward, youngest son of Edward Southwell Ward, 3rd Viscount Bangor, was twenty-two years old in 1855. He had joined the 72nd Regiment of Foot at seventeen, in 1850, just as the fourteen-year-old Norah Hill was charming her cousins at Godmersham. Before long, she would begin to charm Somerset Ward, too. First, however, not only Captain Ward but many of Norah's family, including her eldest brother Arthur, would have to fight in another war, this time in India.

As David Murphy has observed, while Ireland was both deeply interested and actively involved in the Crimean War, the news of such atrocities as the massacre at Cawnpore and the siege of Lucknow shifted the focus of public attention, and 'the Crimean war simply became old news in Ireland'.[39] The young Arthur Hill, aged eighteen, joined the Rifle Brigade (the Prince Consort's Own) as an Ensign in October 1855. Though two battalions were raised for the Crimean war, he was not sent there. He was, however, at the Battle of Cawnpore, and the siege and capture of Lucknow, serving in Oude and Central India with the Camel Corps under Sir Colin Campbell, who had been his cousin Cecil Rice's commanding officer in the Crimea.[40] From distant Donegal, where bitter struggles over land were once more causing anxiety, Louisa Hill gave news of Arthur to Fanny in January 1858:

> The last letter we had from Arthur was dated December 1st from an entrenched Tank about 3 miles from the rim of Tuttelpore, which is 50 from Cawnpore — they had been within 20 miles of C'pore but had been ordered to fall back and entrench themselves strongly in case of an attack from the Rebels who were in gt. force & very strong in artillery. Sir C. Campbell has since destroyed their force ... & dispersed it — he was very well & wrote in good spirits.[41]

Arthur's sister Norah had received her own letter from him, telling of his lucky escape from a planned ambush, as she told their cousin Louisa Rice:

> Yes, we have heard from Arthur several times lately — thank you, & are very anxious abt him. He was on his way to Cawnpore & had had a very narrow escape. They rec'd a message to advance to where Genl Windham was & if they had, would have fallen into the middle of the rebels who were there with a very [ruffianly?] force, but it was providentially discovered in time that he was a spy — & soon after a real messenger came with orders to retire — dearest Boy, we are longing to hear again from him. I am afraid there is a great deal to be done.[42]

Though Arthur Hill did survive, such experiences undoubtedly left their mark on him and his cousins. Cecil Rice, following his Crimean service, was sent to India during the Mutiny, as were two of Edward Knight's sons by his first marriage, Philip and Brodnax. The two wars were not unconnected, for although the Mutiny may in the end have been triggered by a incident offending the religious beliefs of the Sepoys in Bengal, there had been many indications of dissatisfaction for some time before. As Orlando Figes has observed in his recent study, Russia had considered organising attacks in the vicinity of India, in order to divert British troops from the Crimea. Though these plans were not executed, Figes maintains that rumours of an imminent Russian invasion in India encouraged both Hindus and Muslims to use the opportunity of British exhaustion in the Crimea to organise rebellion.[43] Both the Mutiny, and the acts of reprisal which followed it, marked it out as a terrible war and Jane Austen's great-nephews were infected by the general spirit of vengeful scorn against those whom they had termed 'the natives'. It was an attitude which Arthur Hill and Somerset Ward would retain and remember years later during the Land War, when Arthur had become the owner of Gweedore and Somerset Ward his agent. 'We didn't kill half or even a quarter so many of the brutes,' wrote Cecil Rice in December 1856,

> as we should have done if it had been an open plain. That sounds sanguinary you think, I daresay, but upon my word, without being, I believe, a more than ordinarily bloodthirsty party, I rejoice at the death of every regular Sepoy mutineer, as in spite of what people choose to say and write, the atrocities they have committed are perfectly frightful to think about.[44]

Like Louisa in Ireland during the famine, baffled by the refusal of the starving tenants to go to the workhouse, Lizzy's son could not fathom why the Sepoys were prepared to die rather than accept the shame of surrender: 'why the stupid idiots can't give themselves up I can't imagine, full pardon has been offered to them all'.[45]

In Ireland, meanwhile, Louisa had had her own battle to fight. In 1851, her marriage to Lord George had been examined and discussed in the House of Lords. The purpose of this was to ascertain the legitimacy or otherwise of children born to marriages contravening Lord Lyndhurst's Act of 1835. Lord St Germans referred to evidence given to the Marriage Commissioners by Lord Marcus Hill, Lord George's brother, giving examples of the degree of social acceptance enjoyed by Lord and Lady George following their marriage:

> The work of that evidence deserves attention, but I will only read the following passages from it. He is asked — 'Have they been

received in society on the same footing since their marriage as before?' Lord Marcus replies — 'I have no reason to doubt it. As soon as they returned from the Continent, they came to London and went over to Ireland. In regard to the reception generally given to my brother and sister on their return from Altona, I may add that Lord Winchilsea, who is Mr Knight's neighbour, near Godmersham, invited them to East Well Park, and that other neighbours called on her. Since their return to Ireland, everyone, high and low, has been to see her, and many have expressed their strong approbation of their union, such as Lady Bangor, Mr and Lady Helena Stewart, Sir James and Lady Stewart, Rev. Dr. and Mrs Kingsmill, Rev. Mr. Atkins, Rev. Dr. and Lady Anne Hastings, Mr Ball, Mrs Otway, and many others, the common people approving highly, and some saying how wise Lord George had been not to bring a stranger into his family.' Does anyone believe that the noble Earl here referred to, would have invited to his house a couple whom he believed to have contracted an incestuous marriage, or to be living in a state of concubinage? Does anyone believe that the other highly respectable and estimable persons whose names I have read would have called on Lord and Lady George Hill if they looked on their marriage as incestuous? Would they have expressed approbation of their union? Surely, my Lords, this sufficiently proves that persons who contract these marriages do not lose their position in society.[46]

It was then barely two years since Carlyle had seen Louisa in Ireland, and commented on her nun-like reserve and gentleness. For a reticent woman, public discussion of her private life, and the interrogation of their neighbours and the same society friends who had been so prominent at Lord George's first marriage to her sister, can have been nothing short of an ordeal. Yet, it had to be endured, not just for the sake of their son George, who would otherwise be rendered illegitimate, but also for the success in society of Norah and little

Cassandra. If the good opinion of society had been desirable in the time of Jane Austen, it was essential in the censorious Victorian age.

Social success, however, was not denied the Hill girls. Apart from their membership of the Downshire family, they had the advantage of Louisa's acquaintance with Pamela, Lady Campbell, wife of Sir Guy Campbell and an old friend of Lord Carlisle, who became Lord Lieutenant of Ireland in 1855. By an ironic twist, Lady Campbell's background could easily have barred her from society, for she was the daughter of Lord Edward Fitzgerald, the romantic, tragic young nobleman who had been a leader of the United Irishmen, rising against the crown in 1798. He was also, however, the younger brother of the Duke of Leinster, so very powerful and respected a figure in English and Irish society that no one thought any less of him for having had a rebel in the family. Lady Campbell was very much part of society, and had married further into the political world: her friendship was a very useful one for the shy Louisa and her stepdaughters.[47] Indeed, Lady Campbell's knowledge of and admiration for the work of Jane Austen may have led her to take a special interest in the Hill family, as Louisa wrote to Fanny in the spring of 1856:

> Lady Campbell is ... a most ardent admirer of Aunt Jane's works. Aunt Cassandra herself would be satisfied at her appreciation of them — nothing ever like them before or since. When she heard I was her niece she was in extasies. 'My dear, is it possible you are Jane Austen's niece? That I should never have known that before! — come and tell me all about her — do you remember her? Was she pretty? Wasn't she pretty? Oh, if I could but have seen her — Macaulay says she is second to Shakespeare. I was at Bowood when Lord Lansdowne heard of her death — you cannot think how grieved and affected he was —' I told her you were her great friend and used to correspond with her. 'Oh! Write and ask her if she can only send me one of her own real letters, and tell me any and every particular she may know about her life, self, everything, I should be so delighted! Pray do write and ask her. The Archbishop of Dublin is another of her

staunch admirers, and we have such long conversations about her.' Then off she went, talking over and repeating parts of every one of the books, & c.—[48]

The picture of Pamela, Lady Campbell given by Louisa shows a rare moment of humour on her part: it is not impossible to imagine Jane Austen's enjoyment of the great lady's 'extasies', as she repeated 'parts of every one of the books &c', for excess of any kind, though she invariably distrusted it, tended to amuse her. Louisa's account accords with the lively, enthusiastic style of Lady Campbell's address in her general correspondence. Yet, while it is heartening to see that the memory of Jane Austen was so much cherished, Lady Campbell was by no means typical, and was herself much more a product of Jane Austen's Georgian world than of the Victorian age. Lady Campbell's own letter to Lord Carlisle on the subject shows that she fully expected to have long and intimate discussions with Louisa, and possibly Fanny, on the subject of her favourite author:

> Only fancy the discovery we have made, dear Lord Carlyle [sic]! Lady George Hill is own niece to Jane Austen the authoress and she can tell us so much about her! She had large dark eyes and a brilliant complexion, and long, long black hair down to her knees. She was very absent indeed. She would sit silent awhile, then rub her hands, laugh to herself and run up to her room. The impression her books give one, is that she herself must have been so perfectly charming. I always fancied her Anne in *Persuasion* was autobiography of herself, except that the real Captain Wentworth had not been fortunate enough to marry her.[49]

Lady Campbell then went on to recount Louisa's revelation that Cassandra and Jane had discussed the ending of *Mansfield Park*, that Cassandra had tried to persuade Jane to allow Henry Crawford to marry Fanny Price, and reported in amazement that 'Miss Austen stood firmly and would not allow the change.'[50] Any hope of information from Fanny, however, in was vain: Fanny did not look at the box of letters for six months after the exchange and, having done so, she noted the fact in her diary, but gave no indication that she had responded or intended to respond to Lady Campbell's request.[51]

This incident may have marked the beginning of a strange divergence of opinion where it might least have been expected. Interest in Jane Austen from the outside world was growing in the 1850s, yet the family – with the exception of James Edward, who began to consider the writing of a memoir – felt less and less inclined to discuss her. The leader in this obfuscation was the niece to whom Jane Austen had felt closest, Fanny herself. Yet, there is another consideration: Fanny's letters and behaviour do indicate that for the last twenty years of her life she suffered from increasing memory loss, and it is possible that her reluctance to comply with the request from Lady Campbell may have indicated the beginning of that sad withdrawal.

Louisa, meanwhile, had two stepdaughters to launch, and Norah was by the middle 1850s her priority. Whatever her anxieties about her husband, stepsons, her own little delicate son George, Godmersham, or her sisters and brothers, Louisa had to follow the prescribed route for the two girls, so that they would not become what George Moore would famously term 'muslin martyrs', the leftover spinsters on the Dublin social circuit.[52] In the same letter of January 1858 where she told Fanny of Arthur's dangerous posting in India, Louisa wrote news of her other charges:

> George and the two girls went to Castle Ward about three weeks ago — to come back in ten days — they are there still & enjoying it very much — I hope they will come back the end of this or beginning of next week — Lady B is such a nice and excellent friend of them, particularly of Norah.[53]

'Lady B' was Lady Bangor, the former Hon. Harriette Margaret Maxwell, and mother of Somerset Ward. The Bangors were quite as important in society as the Hillsboroughs, and this was an excellent connection. Norah was indeed enjoying herself. It was from Castle Ward that she had written to Louisa Rice with news of Arthur's escape from the rebel plot, and Somerset's movements in India, managing to fit in between these accounts some of the delights of their visit to the Wards. She did not include sailing as one of those joys, having failed, it would seem, to inherit her mother's love of the sea:

> Cass & I are here by ourselves. Papa went back to Dawson Ct. yesterday morning & we are to stay until next week I believe. It is such a beautiful place even now — we like being here very much. Lady Bangor is kind and fond of us — we have been out in Ld. B's boat several times, but I was more wretched each time so now I have given up trying to like it — we have had most beautiful weather, today it is colder & stormy … Lady B. had a letter from Somerset from Bombay the other day — they did not know whether they were to stay there or be sent up the country …[54]

Not all the extended family were making such fortunate connections. Fanny's son Astley had just married an Irish girl whose background was not acceptable, and letters flew about concerning the desirability of his living somewhere far away. Canada was chosen, and a great sigh of relief sounded round the family. William Knight, still rector of Steventon, and clearly prepared to overlook his own youthful indiscretions, was quite blunt in his letter to his sister: 'No doubt you are disappointed at Astley's marriage, though with his peculiar habits, nothing was more likely, & now he has adopted a colonial life, his Lucy and her family will not interfere in any way with this.'[55] Louisa was one of the kinder commentators: 'I hope Lucy is good-tempered — where did he meet her — in *darling aristocratic Ireland* or mercantile England — Is she pretty or what caught him — did not the sisters ever see her — has she no father or mother or Uncles or Aunts or cousins —'[56] 'Darling aristocratic Ireland', however, as Louisa well knew, would be no more forgiving than her own family if the daughters of Lord and Lady George made unsuitable marriages: if she had had any doubt, the demeaning examination of her own marriage in the House of Lords would have brought it home to her. By March 1858, she was enduring the rigours of the Dublin season, with its round of balls and teas and dances and drawing-rooms, where the débutantes had to be not only

MAY, LOU & CASS

seen but also openly displayed on the marriage market. Despite her position and her friendships with the Lord Lieutenant and Lady Campbell, Louisa did not enjoy it, and wanted nothing more than to escape with the girls and her nine-year-old son:

> We went to the drawingroom & dinner at the Castle afterward, & that is the amount of our gaieties — & we shall prob. have nothing or little more to do with them. We are all well and little George better — the delicacy is his portion & will be I fear for some years — stomach not head is the weak point. We shall be so glad to get out of this — as we are squeezed to death & have no Piano. The girls practise daily at a friend's, whose house we have had for two months during their absence in England.[57]

She was very miserable: hoping Fanny and her family felt well she added, sadly, 'but nobody can in March'.

Unfortunately for Louisa, she was about to be 'squeezed to death' again in her own house at Ballyare, largely due to the fame of her husband's work in Gweedore. In June 1858, she had an unexpected visit from the Lord Lieutenant and his retinue. Ballyare, though a fine house, was not a large one and, as he wrote to Lady Campbell, Lord Carlisle was embarrassed to find that, in undertaking what he described as 'Hilliad', he had placed a strain on the accommodation. He was not too embarrassed, however, to give a critical assessment of the young ladies' musical abilities:

> I wished to have found time to write to you on Hilliad. The aggregate result of my visit is great liking and admiration, so I do not mind letting a few flings escape me. My conscience rather smote me on arriving at Ballyare — on foot, as they did not trust the four horse to drive up so limited a space, and there is the further peculiarity of there being no door to the house; we got in by bending much under a very low window. It struck me as cruelty to have imposed ourselves on so small a precinct, but I

was reconciled when I found that the Wards only got leave to come to them in consequence of my visit. I like him — Norah and Cassandra sang to us: they are near being Muses, Sybills, Sirens, but stop just a little short of any of these. The next night we spent in Gweedore, and there indeed was space, comfort, luxury, good cheer, good waiting, to our hearts' content. The drawback was 9 continuous hours in a perfectly open carriage in fierce rain. However it quite answered to us: he has done marvels, and the scenery is superb. My reception throughout has been a marvel to me.[58]

Quite apart from the fact that he was just as oblivious of Louisa's presence as Thomas Carlyle had been nine years before, one other fact in that glowing report, casually dropped, deserves attention. The fact that the Wards were staying there in June 1858 is significant for, less than a year later, Norah was to marry Somerset Ward. His family's presence in the house suggests an engagement, perhaps the reason that Louisa seemed so certain in her letter to Fanny in the spring that she had almost done with the round of the season.

Somerset Ward had not, however, been the first to seek Norah's hand. The vivacious, pretty fourteen-year-old who had so delighted her aunts and cousins in 1850 had gone on to win the heart, as Marianne had done forty years earlier, of one of her own cousins. Edward Bridges Rice, Lizzy's eldest son, had courted Norah despite a considerable disparity in their ages. He was sixteen years older; yet, he was captivated by her and, though later to make a happy marriage to Cecilia Harcourt in 1864, he was still vulnerable on the subject of Norah in the early 1860s, as his sister Marianne Sophia noticed: 'Poor fellow,' she wrote, 'I hope Norah will not sadden him, he said rather bitterly that he daresayed he could do without her — somebody else that is nice is what to turn his thoughts.'[59] Norah, however, had made her choice, and married Captain the Hon. Somerset Ward, two and a half years her senior, on 28 April 1859. The couple went to live at Isle O'Valla House, outside the picturesque coastal town of Strangford, County Down, only a few miles from the great house of Castle Ward.[60]

Norah's wedding was the first of many; the young Knights of Godmersham, whom Jane Austen knew, had grown middle-aged and given place to their children. Godmersham would never be home again: a letter from Edward Knight to his sister Fanny on New Year's day 1858 shows, despite its charm and kindness, how very far from thinking of making it his base he was. 'Instead of a merry party in the Drawing room,' he wrote, 'smells of smoke in the Passages & Cakey's stories of the goings on in "the room", here am I ... alone in my father's Study, thinking of old times, & almost beginning to be sentimental in my old age.' He was not, however, going to give into sentimentality: he had come to support his brother George, Jane's 'itty Dordy', at the funeral of his wife, Hilaire, and just as his own father had checked regularly on draughty, uninhabited Chawton, he now made the reverse journey to the house at Godmersham. 'I go home tomorrow,' he wrote towards the end of his letter, 'and have no plan of leaving it again just at present.'[61]

Edward's children, too, were well-grown. Montagu, his eldest son by his second marriage, to Adela Portal, had completed his first half at Eton, and his daughter Georgina, one of the children of his first marriage to Mary Knatchbull, was to be married in August 1858. As Marianne Sophia Rice wrote to her sister, the tension at the wedding was palpable, not least because Fanny Knatchbull displayed an old prejudice against the entire Portal family, including Edward's entirely blameless children from his marriage to Adela Portal:

> Yes, it makes me very angry Aunt K's inveterate prejudice about Portals and she is the last person I should have told about 'red-faced one' which Derby heard in the train the day before the wedding and Uncle Charles told Aunt K. Don't tell anyone else — I haven't. I like her very much, she is a very nice girl I think, very affectionate and altogether nice. People think her very plain I mean Uncle Charles, Aunt May, etc. She is plain certainly, but I don't think so very ... I saw At. K hating them all — with no reason, for they are very nice children, all of them, and very nicely behaved and brought-up it appeared to me. Charlie is a nice little boy, but hideous.[62]

Yet, despite the unkind remarks, there was nothing more hurtful going on at this wedding than at most, which, given all the anger and resentment over Edward's marriages and disposal of Godmersham, was in itself remarkable. Indeed, as the decade of the 1850s closed, everyone did seem more at ease. Marianne Sophia stayed during Georgina's wedding at the Rectory at Chawton, with Charles and Marianne. 'We were so comfortable at the rectory,' she wrote, 'and liked our short visit so much. Uncle Charles and Aunt May are so comfortable.'[63] Godmersham was gone, in effect if not in fact. Yet, with Marianne's happy resettlement at Chawton, the safe return of almost all the young soldiers and sailors from two terrible wars, and the beginning of the marriages of the next generation, it did appear at last that the extended Austen/Knight family had reached a state approaching equilibrium.

CHAPTER 7

'I CAN'T LIVE BY MYSELF'

Life After Godmersham
1860–1881

She considered it as an act of indispensable duty to clear away the claims
of creditors, with all the expedition which the most comprehensive
retrenchments could secure, and saw no dignity in any thing short of it.

PERSUASION

In the years following the loss of Godmersham, Marianne seemed well settled
in Chawton. Yet, there was no escaping the fact that this home, too, depended
on the goodwill of her eldest brother Edward, and the continued health of her
younger brother, Charles. If either Edward or Charles were to die, Marianne
would be left once more without a home. None of her remaining brothers
would be in a position to offer her refuge and, while she knew she would
always be welcome as a visitor in the houses of her sisters, they were in reality
no more secure than she. If their husbands were to die, they might well find
their continued residence in their comfortable homes in question. Fanny,
Lady Knatchbull, had already experienced this in 1849, when she had been
obliged on the death of her husband to leave Mersham le Hatch, and Lizzy's
husband, Edward Rice, was in poor health. Louisa was even less secure, for
Lord George Hill's estate would pass on his death not to her son, but to her
stepson Arthur who, though also her nephew, would have it within his power
to follow the example of his uncle, Edward Knight, and dispose of the house
without reference to its occupants. Louisa had to hope that he would regard
her not simply as his aunt but as the dowager, traditionally permitted to stay
in the Irish Big House 'for her day'.[1]

Louisa's legal position had always been tenuous in the eyes of the law, and she had already endured the distress of a parliamentary investigation of her marriage. For her, uniquely among her siblings, the good opinion of Irish society was as necessary as the maintenance of position in England. The marriage of her stepdaughter Norah Hill to Somerset Ward in 1859 had been a welcome social success, consolidating two already powerful political families, the Bangors and the Downshires. Apart from the happiness of the young couple, there was no doubt that both families' influence in society and politics could be further strengthened by such a suitable alliance. Lord George's philanthropic efforts and natural gift for publicity had won him the reputation of having saved Gweedore from the worst ravages of the famine: indeed, by 1851, the population, which had been 3,997 ten years before, had increased to 4,300, and it would rise over the next thirty years by another thousand.[2] Yet, this apparent calm was to some extent illusory for, by the time of Norah's wedding, Lord George had a number of opponents who took the view that he had not supported but colonised the land. While his enterprise had been highly successful, subdivision of land continued, no large town had developed, and the district 'had the dubious distinction of having the lowest poor law valuation per capita (6s. 6d.) in the west'.[3]

Some prefiguring of this growing dissatisfaction had been apparent as early as 1849, when Lord George, escorting an admiring Thomas Carlyle round Bunbeg with all its improvements, was approached by a distressed Irish squire, reduced to begging in the streets. Carlyle tells the story almost as an aside:

> Ancient Irish squire actually 'begging' here; follows about in blue camlet cloak, always some cock-and-bull story, which Lord George, unable to escape by artifice, coldly declares in words that he can't listen to. Strange old squire; whisky all along and late failure of potatoes have done it; gets no rent, won't sell, 'a perfect pest,' the fisher calls him.[4]

This oddly jarring tale serves as a reminder that there were, and remain to the present day, varying opinions of Lord George's enterprise. The changes to the system did not benefit everyone, and it is both remarkable and disappointing to observe that neither Carlyle nor Lord George showed any compassion towards the old squire. Moreover, while there seems no doubt that Lord George tried his best to help his tenants, it appears that a substantial number of the population felt that they too had been dispossessed through the establishment of his businesses and his reorganisation of their farming practices. Though, as historian Peter Gray puts it, 'the success of Lord George's paternalist improvements in Donegal was a model for all landowners', the very term 'paternalist' suggests the source of the difficulties inherent in the scheme. As Gray explains, despite the fact that he was considered an exemplary landlord, Lord George's methods 'were not without controversy, and a tenant backlash forced him to discontinue his work in 1856'.[5] This backlash, almost impossible to imagine ten years earlier as the famine took hold, occurred when Lord George introduced English and Scottish sheep farmers as the next part of his plan of improvement. As a consequence, the animosity growing among an increasingly dissatisfied tenantry in the years following the famine began to find expression. Previously, as Lord George had been relatively tolerant of older farming practices and had not been over zealous in asserting his property rights, the changes he introduced to the area had not occasioned widespread resentment. Though he had altered a well-established settlement pattern he had, as Brendan Mac Suibhne points out, 'improved agricultural production; stimulated a more monetised and market-oriented economy; increased the consumption of shop goods; created more agricultural employment; developed the tourist industry and facilitated the expansion of state services in the area'.[6]

Despite the fact that Lord George had encountered some opposition at the outset of his enterprise, no general outcry had ensued, at least partly because the mill, grain store and shop he had introduced were seen to be of benefit to more than the landlords and because, as letters between Louisa and Fanny show, it was known that he had used his own money to ensure a supply of meal to his tenants during the famine. Lord George listened to his tenants, tried to see their point of view and preferred, when it did not conflict with his own interests, to maintain good relations with them. Where his interests were threatened, however, he was quite prepared to protect them.[7] As W.E. Vaughan remarks: 'Lord George Hill was able to enforce a monopoly for his shop in Gweedore by threatening rivals with eviction; but few landlords had such a command of territory.'[8] That command was strengthened by respect, even among those who doubted his motives, for the fact that he lived on the land, spoke the language and, during the time of the great famine, worked to bring relief to his tenants.

Times changed during the 1850s and, while the Knights, Knatchbulls, Rices and the Hills themselves were concerned with the economic and personal consequences of the Crimean war, agrarian crime became a distinct problem in Gweedore. Tenants felt less inclined to allow themselves to be told where they might or might not graze their cattle. One of Lord George's bailiffs had his boat destroyed; a wall on the Hill estate was demolished; cattle belonging to his agriculturalist had their tails docked; papers relating to the estate and rents were stolen from Lord George's office; and his gamekeeper was set upon when he accompanied a process server. Lord George was by nature neither unkind nor ungenerous. Yet, his patience was tried. He took the view that providence had sent this harsh lesson to be heeded by all, landlords and tenants alike. He was not a wealthy man, having sunk most of his 1836 inheritance first into the acquisition of the estate, and subsequently into trying to ensure a supply of food for his tenants during the famine. In addition, he had five children to launch in life – commissions to purchase or university fees to pay for his sons and seasons to finance and marriages to broker for his two daughters – if their place in society was to be maintained.

Lord George clearly felt it necessary to review his own practices, and began raising rents, calling in fees and fines which he had waived in better days. He did not adopt the stringent measures introduced by some of his fellow landlords and, where he raised rents, was less draconian than the rest, allowing some abatement. In 1854, significantly, he stopped his old practice of ignoring tenants' stock trespassing on his land and began impounding strays and levying fees. It was at this time that he began leasing land to English and Scottish sheep farmers. For the first time, tenants on his estates were denied grazing on rough pastures to which they believed they would always have access rights. Donegal, as part of the historic province of Ulster, believed in the 'Ulster custom' of tenant right.[9] Lord George's tenants were affronted to see fields let to those they regarded as outsiders and, as the harvest was again poor, the parish priest, Father Doherty, began to be called in by the tenants to plead their cause. Father Doherty tried to obtain relief from the Lord Lieutenant: he failed, but managed to obtain Indian meal in Dunfanaghy for them. This shift was significant: the priest now took the role assumed during the famine by Lord George. Soon, Lord George himself – who referred to Father Doherty as 'the obnoxious priest' – appeared to his tenants to be part of the problem.[10] As W.E. Vaughan puts it:

> the introduction of imported Scots sheep, accompanied by Scots shepherds, had caused an outbreak of serious disorder on Lord George Hill's estate ... the tenants killed hundreds of sheep because they feared eviction; several tenants were convicted of maliciously killing the sheep and one was transported and several imprisoned.[11]

Unlike the wars in the Crimea and India, where the enemy seemed clearly identifiable, this insidious war at home was one of attrition, where threats and cruelties, large and small, pitted landlord and tenant against one another. Different, too, from post-famine dissatisfaction, which has been compared to the reaction in Scotland to the Highland Clearances, the misery of the sheep war was exacerbated by the active presence of a highly-organised network known as the Molly Maguires: their campaign of terror was met by the introduction of extra police and increased taxes, which the residents of Gweedore struggled to pay.[12] While an uneasy peace was re-established by the end of the decade, matters were never again quite as they had been: smallholders might indeed have regained access to the rough pasture which had been denied to them, but their rents now incorporated grazing fees.[13] As Lord George welcomed his son home from India and gave his daughter in marriage to a veteran of both the Crimea and the Mutiny, he was already landlord to a new generation, lacking even limited trust in landlord–tenant relations.

Even the sheep wars, however, were overshadowed by the shocking eviction in 1861 of forty-seven families by Lord George's neighbour, John George Adair. Two hundred and forty-four people, including one hundred and fifty-nine children, were left homeless as twenty-eight houses on the Derryveagh estate were either levelled or unroofed, and over eleven thousand acres of land, itself almost barren, left desolate. Adair had had the land only since 1859: a quarrel over trespassing sheep and hunting rights had escalated, and Adair's steward, James Murray, was murdered in November 1860. Following the precedent of the sheep wars, where some of the Scots shepherds had claimed, falsely, that they were entitled to compensation for sheep that had in fact not been killed but had died of exposure, Murray appears to have colluded with the shepherds on the Adair estate to perpetrate a similar fraud. He paid dearly for his wrongdoing, as did the families Adair suspected of having had a hand in the killing, all of whom were then evicted in the spring of 1861, and most of whom could not afterwards find work or a place to live.[14] On Lord George's estate, however, matters appeared to settle: yet, the memory of the sheep wars and the knowledge of what had occurred on Adair's neighbouring estate would linger long afterwards.

For Louisa in Ballyare, this gradual disintegration of her husband's philanthropic enterprise, though incomprehensible to her, could not be allowed to interfere with her priority, the care of her family. She might not have been able to understand the tenants' point of view but, subject as she was to increasingly severe and debilitating headaches, she could show sympathy for the afflictions of others in the family: a kindly letter of 1863 shows her giving detailed instructions on travelling in Donegal to her nephew Henry Knight, Montagu's son, a naval cadet plagued with chronic seasickness:

> Whenever you get to Lough Foyle come to see us if you can get leave — if you go to Lough Swilly you will be only 8 miles from us — & a car to Rathmullan will bring you with care — From Derry you must have a car to Fort Stewart ferry — cross in a boat & on here — If you can say when you come we will have a car in readiness for you. The ferry boats cross the odd hours from the Derry side, but you can [ask] for a special boat if you get here when the others are gone — Derry is 9 miles from the Ferry & we are 4 miles this side of it — very stormy weather now — you must have been well tossed — I heard from Uncle Charles today & was sorry to hear Papa was poorly — I wish

he would go abroad for a few weeks & drink mineral waters to wash out the gout.[15]

'Papa' was Louisa's eldest brother Edward who, like Charles and Louisa herself, was increasingly subject to gout. By the 1860s, almost all of the Knight siblings were beginning to feel their age. The exception was Marianne, as bright, energetic and lively as she had always been and content in her life at Chawton Rectory. A description of her at Lizzy's house at Dane Court in 1864, calming an agitated daughter of Lizzy's, Florence Rice, confirms the impression of a woman able to cope without fuss or hysteria: 'Floss looks very poorly,' Lizzy wrote, 'and burst into tears as soon as she came into the room. Aunt May hurried her off "to take off her things" and she soon recovered poor dear and has been cheerful ever since.'[16]

The *Garden Book* which Marianne had begun shortly after she moved to Chawton acts as a kind of objective correlative for her state of mind, indeed for her life, during most of the 1860s. The source of her contentment lay in her care for her brother, for visiting family and, by extension or through substitution, for the plants and trees all around her. She grew roses exotically or improbably named 'La Séduisante', 'Adelaide d'Orleans', 'Imperatrice Eugenie' and even, with a nod to the still fairly recent Crimean war, 'Lord Raglan'. Her hyacinths – 'Jenny Lind' and 'King of the Netherlands' – sat together, history and society reflected even in the tranquillity of a rectory garden. She wrote about the care of geraniums and heathers, noted her own solutions for ridding fruit trees of insects and polishing tiles, wrote out her recipes, or 'receipts', for herb soup, steamed red cabbage, Rockhampton barley water, gingerbread flats, brandy cherries and, perhaps surprisingly for a lady who had travelled no farther than Ireland, 'Indian curry'.[17] It is a record of thrift as well as of happiness: Marianne had only her annuity of £200 per year, and Charles was no more wealthy than she.[18] Yet, the book records their care of the poor and distressed in the parish, work they had begun years before when they were still the comfortable son and daughter of the Great House at Godmersham.

Though now they resembled the old rector Mr Papillon and his unmarried sister, who had been so consistently if gently satirised in Jane's letters, they had no complaints. A list in the *Garden Book* for Christmas 1867 reveals that their provision for the poor included jerseys, blankets, hand-knitted socks, 'linsey gowns' and 'crochet shawls'. Some of these may have been Marianne's own handwork for, like her aunt Jane, who commended her skill when she was seven years old, Marianne was an expert needlewoman; some of their gifts to the poor may have been the work of Lord George's tenants, as the socks and mittens sent to their family and acquaintance in the Crimea had so often been. The gowns and blankets came from Marianne's own wardrobe; the jerseys belonged to Charles. At the top of a page written in late 1867, after noting that four shillings and sixpence had been given 'to help get a greatcoat' for one of the parishioners, she wrote, in brackets, 'Charley'.[19] At the top of the page is the note 'relieved by me' and underneath, ringed, the words '& by Charles'. What Marianne did not record on that page was that her brother Charles had died, two months before.

Unlike his sister, Charles had become very frail in late middle age. By October 1867, aged only sixty-three, his health began to cause such grave alarm that Marianne and John, the brother closest in age and sympathy to him, sat at his bedside, just as Charles and Marianne had done with their brother Henry, and Charles himself had done when John was stricken with smallpox. Now that Charles was failing, it fell to Marianne, John, and John's wife Margaret to tend to their brother. Despite all their care, he sank slowly and painfully, dying on 13 October 1867. A few days later, Margaret wrote to her sister-in-law Lizzy Rice, addressing her rather strangely as 'Aunt Lizzy', giving a moving account of his last days. He had been a somewhat reluctant clergyman, without an overpowering vocation for the life; his diaries show a frustrated naturalist, most fully himself in the company of a few siblings or friends, or with plants, birds, dogs and horses. Margaret Knight's account, however, shows a man at last at peace with himself and his maker, dying in 'sweet calmness and perfect resignation to God's will'.[20] 'I had the privilege,' Margaret wrote to her sister-in-law, with perhaps more emotion than tact, 'of being with him constantly, night and day. I gladly write to give you any little details that I know you will love to have.' She continued:

His death was like his lovely peaceful life, no doubts or fears disturbed his mind but all was perfect rest and trust and faith ... 'He would have liked a few years longer had it been so ordained' but he added 'God's time is best, and pardoned and saved, I am ready to go — I have no wish to live' — One night, as I stood by his side after various expressions, such as these '*Where* am I going to —? *What* is it! I cannot understand' he added in a surprised voice 'Papa!! Papa!! *Yes* — it *is* — (then he smiled & nodded 2 or 3 times and waved his hand) how *wonderful*!!' — And then this — 'I see thousands — thousands (raising his voice) how *beautiful*!! Heavenly! — heavenly — heavenly! Jesus my Saviour' — 'Salvation! Glorious thought' —[21]

Though Charles seems to have experienced in the last days of his life a final, glorious vision of Heaven, and to have felt the certainty of reunion with his beloved father, the family was greatly grieved at his slow dying. Yet, as Margaret recalled, '*He* was the one to cheer and comfort us when we told him we could not let him go, we *could* not do without him.' Margaret was at pains to emphasise her own loss, and her own share of the nursing, hinting perhaps that Lizzy might have done more: 'It is grievous to us *all* to lose him (to me I think really as much as any of you for I have been his constant daily companion by the hour together).' For her sister-in-law Marianne, however, she had nothing but praise, and a compassionate acknowledgement that hers was the greatest grief of all:

For Aunt May I cannot express my sympathy and sorrow! For it is a doubly bitter trial to her — She is herself under it all, & you know what that means — she sends her love & thanks for yr letter, & she did not write yesterday because there was nothing to say. My husband & I are staying entirely with her, only too glad to give her the *least atom* of comfort, but we are a sorrowful trio! My husband is completely upset. I never saw him in such deep distress, he loved his brother *very dearly*, as

all who ever knew him must — Dearest Uncle Charles, no one
will ever supply his place![22]

Margaret's letter is revealing, not just of her genuine affection for her brother-in-law, but also of a rather defensive sense of her own right to have a place within the family, which may emphasise how very tightly knit it was, and how difficult it may have been for an outsider to enter that closed circle. Her letter speaks too of the enormous loss to John and Marianne. John, always deeply attached to Charles, had not had a very successful life. After Cassandra's death, his grief was a matter of grave concern to his sisters; and when Godmersham passed away from the family, Fanny's relief at his having found a wife to care for him was palpable.[23] Yet, only a few years after his marriage, he was living in Bath in poor circumstances, for Margaret was not wealthy. After their one child was stillborn, they seem to have moved about in a rather directionless fashion.[24] John needed the stability of family and, with his earliest mother-figure, Fanny, growing distant through illness and the decline of her faculties, he looked increasingly to Marianne and to Charles for friendship and guidance.

John was, nonetheless, not quite alone now that Charles was gone: Margaret, though delicate in health, emerges in her one surviving letter as a character of sufficient strength and spirit to ensure his care. In John's own postscript to this letter, he gave full rein to his grief over Charles's death, his compassion for May and his sense that Margaret would, indeed, help him recover:

I am sure you will like, my dearest Lizzy, what Margaret has told you, and you will love her when you know what a comfort she was to him — He said to her when she was giving him something — 'dearest Marg: you are a great comfort & help to me — thank you darling!' Poor dear darling May, she has borne up wonderfully, & is utterly miserable. I pray that I may never pass such days & nights as I passed by dearest Charles' bed, waiting for him to die. I could not speak to him, although I wanted so much to do so, 50 things I wished to say but never said one, I knew that the first word would have brought on a burst of grief & I feared to distress him. Today I have looked at him for the last time & wished goodbye to the kindest, best and dearest Brother mortal ever had.[25]

It seems rather odd that Lizzy was to be persuaded to love her sister-in-law as though she had never met her, since John and Margaret had then been married for fourteen years. There remains an underlying sense that the youngest five of the Godmersham children not only formed a separate unit within the family, but were also slightly less regarded by the older, more comfortable Knights, rather as Jane and Cassandra Austen had been, in their unsought poverty. John had considered Fanny his mother, and to Lizzy, always between the two wings of the family, he signed off his letter most affectionately with 'God bless you dearest Lizzy.' None of his other brothers, however, seemed to inspire the affection he felt for Charles, a fact all the more remarkable as Charles was not the only brother to die in 1867. In August of that year, the family had already lost George, Jane's 'itty Dordy', exasperating and greatly loved: yet, it was the loss of Charles which John found hardest to bear. For Marianne, however, 'under it all' and 'utterly miserable', there was no spouse to give comfort and assurance that life would someday resume. Once again, she would be dependent for a place to live on the decision of her eldest brother Edward, who had not shown himself to be remarkably compassionate over the loss of Godmersham. It is difficult to decide whether Margaret's reminding Lizzy that she knew what 'under it all' meant, indicates a depressive tendency in the otherwise resolutely cheerful Marianne, or whether Margaret simply meant that Lizzy, having lost so many members of her own family, might understand what it was to be bowed down by grief to the extent that communication became impossible.

It was the last day of October before Marianne could bring herself to write to her eldest sister, and by implication, to Louisa in Ireland. Fanny was staying with their niece, the former Fanny Rice, now the recently-widowed Lady Winchilsea. By the time Marianne wrote, she had collected herself sufficiently to send commiserations to her nephew Reginald Knatchbull and his wife, who had just lost a baby, and to make kind and detailed enquiries about her niece, Fanny. Whatever her feelings may have been at the time of Charles's death, it is clear that she was not prepared to indulge them. On the contrary, she was readying herself to uproot and, once again, move on:

> I have a joint letter from you & Lou to thank you for — My love to her and thanks for hers. Poor dear Reginald and Maria! I am so very sorry for them, of course they are very miserable, & will be most likely till another Baby arrives — poor little dear thing! What sad things keep happening, but they will end in time, and the … happiness that I pray we may all enjoy in another world, will never end… Fanny will have told you that William's son Edw'd has accepted this Living for 5 Years! We are so very glad not to have a stranger here & he is, & always has been so highly spoken of, & so very popular, wherever he has been, that I think the people will like him better than they w'd anybody else, after our kind, gentle, darling Charles. Drst Ed. very kindly lets me stay on for 3 or 4 months, & will not have the Presentation made out till then — that I may have time to make arrangements. This being the case, and there being constant things for me to do, & see about, I mean to put off paying any visits, except to Lizzy till I leave this for good, so don't mind, drst Fanny, if I leave you out this time! I shd not like to be away long, & I hope to return here in a fortnight, from the 18th Nov., on which day, our little melancholy party will probably break up — Johnny and Marg't will go back to their house & I, to D. Court. Mr Rice kindly asked them to go with me wh[ich] we should all have very much liked, but Marg: continues so weak & unwell, her Dr says she muct have complete rest, & not take such a long journey; so they sorrowfully will have soon, I am afraid, to write, & put off their visit — drst Charley has left me all he had — it is not much, as he lost money like the rest of us, & spent more than £1000 in altering this house — but every little helps, when one has not much — I mean to live with Johnny and Marg: they like it, and I can't live by myself. We don't know yet, where — it will depend on Edw'd — when he has made up

his mind, of course I shall let you all know — but whilst things are so continuing unsettled, there's no use saying more — the days pass sorrowfully away! We can scarcely yet, believe that we shall never again in this world, see dearest Charley's lovely face, or hear his sweet voice! So like Papa, in character, as well as in features! He was universally loved by all who knew him! as the quantities of kind, feeling letters we have received abundantly testify. I must send you such a nice, affec'ate one, from his old friend, Archdeacon Crawley! I am sure you will like it: and will you let drst Lizzy see it please, & beg her to send it back to me. I had a better acc't the other day of Lou's head, I am thankful to say ... We all send our best love to you, dearest Fanny.[26]

It is a brave letter, minimising her own great distress, and overlooking entirely her brother Edward's fairly brisk requirement that she quit this home too within three months. Charles had indeed left her all he had. His will, a simple document barely ten lines long, made her his sole beneficiary. No equivalent of the 'Ulster Custom' existed for sisters of the clergymen who had improved the property; and, as Marianne knew, the money lost fifty years earlier when Henry Austen's bank failed had caused great financial hardship not only to their father but also to his five youngest children.

Yet, like Charles, Marianne had never lacked courage: just as he had nursed John through smallpox, she had performed the same office for Reginald, the nephew she asks about in this letter, when he had the disease at the age of thirty-two. Nonetheless, the death of Charles called for more than her usual fortitude. He was the brother closest in age to her when they were children; and they had lived for fourteen years in harmonious quietude following the loss of Godmersham, she turning for solace to the garden, he to reading and ornithology. Marianne accepted, like Jane Austen before her, her brother Edward's continuing power to decide where she and her youngest brother and his ailing wife would live. It does not seem to have occurred to her or to any of the family that Edward might have offered her a home in Chawton House with his family. Like his father, he does not seem to have thought it necessary to do much more for his sister than give her time to consider her position.

He was, however, more generous than *Sense and Sensibility*'s John Dashwood: he appears to have made a house available, for shortly afterwards Marianne, John and Margaret were living at Highway House, near Bentley in Hampshire. Marianne said little and made the best of it, rather more in the spirit of Elinor Dashwood than her literary namesake.

This dignified equanimity of temper by which, remarkably, she continued to distinguish herself, was about to be tried further. Since 1864, Marianne's cousin and first admirer, James Edward, now James Edward Austen Leigh, had been attempting to collect material for a memoir of their aunt Jane.[27] He had resisted earlier requests to compile such a work and had been accustomed to answer, when urged upon the subject, that as there was so little to tell, he considered it impossible to write anything that could be called 'a life'. At length, however, he agreed to put down whatever he could find. His interest grew as he wrote; he appealed to other members of the family, some of whom he had not seen for years, and he received assistance from several quarters in the form of letters and manuscripts. His half-sister, Anna Lefroy, admitted that, though she had spent much time with her aunt, her memories were fragmented. She remembered, however, that though Mrs Edward Austen, the former Elizabeth Bridges, had never cared as much for Jane as for Cassandra, 'there grew up during the later years of Aunt Jane's life a great and affectionate intimacy between herself and the eldest of her nieces' at Godmersham.[28] This, of course, was Fanny, the niece whom Jane had once considered 'almost another sister'. Yet, James Edward failed to obtain any information from Lady Knatchbull.[29] It had seemed reasonable to him that Fanny would be happy to contribute information and for a memoir to be published. Inexplicably, Fanny resisted, and no application to her, or to her daughters, could change her mind.

She was not simply being difficult: Fanny truly believed, as Cassandra Austen had, that the world had no business knowing about her aunt's private life. James Edward persisted. He wanted to include not only the letters Fanny held but also the manuscripts she had in her possession, including what was later to be known as *Lady Susan*. Fanny would not change her mind. Her daughter, Louisa Knatchbull-Hugessen, gave another reason for her mother's unwillingness to allow the letters to be consulted. Fanny's memory loss had grown so very much worse by the time James Edward made his request that her daughter implored him not to add to her mother's distress:

> We are most willing & anxious to help you about Aunt Jane's letters, but it is more difficult than you can imagine. In fact it is almost impossible to convey to anyone at a distance the real state of the case, which I am told is a very singular one — for tho' my mother's *memory* is gone, her intellect is as clear as ever, & her brain only too active. This makes it impossible to get at her private papers without an amount of argument, & *reiterations* most injurious to her — & at the same time she is quite incapable of looking over the letters herself — I have no doubt that she would gladly enter into the plan, & attempt the task — but it would be *impossible* for her to come to any decision, & as unfortunately she cannot recognise the impossibility she would not allow me to help her.[30]

She added, sadly, 'I only wish the "Memoirs" had been written ten years ago when it would have given my mother the *greatest* pleasure to assist, both with letters and recollections of her own. She has thoroughly enjoyed the book and read it again and again.'[31] Fanny's memory loss, which she herself had noted as early as 1862, gradually became more marked, and with it there developed certain uncharacteristic alterations to her personality.[32] The presence of what may have been dementia may also account for the strange and disturbing letter which she wrote to Marianne in August 1869. Beginning 'Yes my love,' it appears to answer a question asked by her sister, and its timing, weeks before the *Memoir*'s publication, suggests that the question may have been part of an attempt by Marianne either to help the cousin who had once found her so 'bewitching beautiful', or to understand her sister's continued refusal to cooperate:

> Yes my love it is very true that Aunt Jane from various cir-
> cumstances was not so *refined* as she ought to have been from
> her *talent*, and if she had lived 50 years later she would have

Lord George Hill, *c.*1825–1830

The Gweedore Hotel, Donegal, *c.*1890

Marianne Knight's entry in the *Gweedore Hotel Book*, 1890

Lithographic drawing of the New Mill at Bunbeg by Lady
Harriet Clive, from Lord George's *Facts from Gweedore*

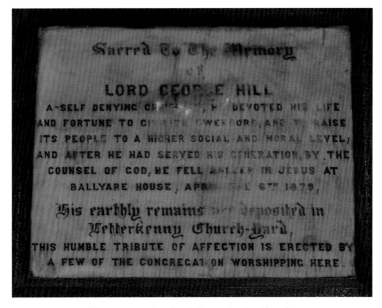

Plaque erected to Lord George in the Church
of Ireland church in Bunbeg after his death in 1879

Louisa Knight, Jane Austen's godchild, later Lady George Hill

Marianne Knight, *c.*1880

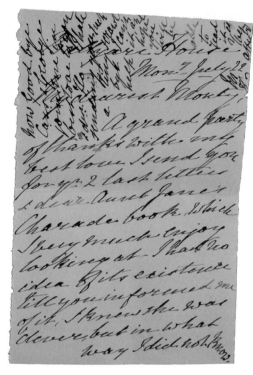

Marianne's last letter, sent to Montagu Knight, 22 July 1895

Montagu George Knight, Marianne's favourite nephew

Capt. the Hon. Somerset Ward, fifth son of
Edward Southwell Ward, 3rd Viscount Bangor

Norah Ward (née Hill), eldest daughter of
Lord George Hill and Cassandra Knight

Isle O'Valla House, outside Strangford, County Down

Ballyare House (now Ballyarr) in Donegal, the last home of the Knight sisters

The graves of Marianne and Louisa Knight at Tully,
near Ballyare/ Ballyarr in Donegal

been in many respects more suitable to our more refined tastes. They were not rich & the people around with whom they chiefly mixed, were not at all high bred, or in short anything more than *mediocre* & *they* of course tho' superior in *mental powers & cultivation* were on the same level as far as *refinement* goes — but I think in later life their intercourse with Mrs Knight (who was very fond of & kind to them) improved them both & Aunt Jane was too clever not to put aside all signs of 'commonness' (if such an expression is allowable) & teach herself to be more refined, at least in intercourse with people in general. Both the Aunts were brought up in the most complete ignorance of the world and its ways (I mean as to fashion &c) & if it had not been for Papa's marriage which brought them into Kent, & the kindness of Mrs Knight, who used often to have one or other of the sisters staying with her, they would have been, tho' not less clever and agreeable in themselves, very much below par as to good Society and its ways. If you hate all this I beg yr pardon, but I felt it at my *pen's end* & it chose to come along & speak the truth …[33]

Such an unwarranted dismissal is excusable if the writer was indeed suffering from a mind-altering illness; yet, even if she were not, Fanny's long years of responsibility and anxiety had long since robbed her of the spirit and joy which so delighted her aunt at the beginning of the century. Where Jane Austen had been a Georgian, a proponent of the middle way and the 'good sense' advocated by the eighteenth-century writers she admired, Fanny was, by 1869, a narrow-minded, intransigent Victorian.

For Marianne, the gradual loss of Fanny, her mentor for almost seventy years, meant that she lived in an increasingly lonely world. There was worse to come. In 1874, Edward Knight decided to sell the entire estate of Godmersham, with its fifteen farms. One suggested explanation is that the decision was reached because of financial considerations, combined with disagreements between Edward's first and second families.[34] Whatever the reason, Godmersham was sold to John Cunliffe Lister Kay, the son of a wealthy manufacturer in the

Midlands.[35] The shock to the rest of the family was enormous: Fanny's relations with Edward and his family had been at best ambivalent since his elopement with her stepdaughter in 1826, yet her illness meant that she was no longer the force she had been.[36] Lizzy, however, felt the loss greatly, writing to her daughter Louisa at Chawton House:

> I am thinking so much of all the dreadful sale which even now seems impossible for Uncle Edward ever to have done, that I cannot help writing about it to someone who feels it and cares about it which alas he cannot do or he never could have done it. I am glad I am not at Chawton. I do not think that I could behave with the affection towards Uncle Edward that I always have had for him especially, he has done such a very wrong and totally unjustifiable thing … Such a thing as this must be felt and never can be forgotten.[37]

Lizzy's daughter Caroline Cassandra, who as a young girl of eighteen had helped her aunts Marianne and Louisa clear Godmersham in 1853, wrote once more about the old house to her sister Louisa:

> I hoped Mama had got over it more — I mean she felt hearing of the sale more than I hoped she would — but still it would have been wonderful if she hadn't … on the whole one may be thankful that it is I trust doing her no *more* harm.[38]

Lizzy, at first so shocked that her head was 'shaky and noisy owing to tears and gout', had eventually collected herself sufficiently to contribute a page to Caroline Cassandra's letter.[39] 'Don't distress yourself,' she wrote, 'about my sorrow for G[odmersham]. It will not do me any harm now and my Head is better & I go on liking my drives & planning work.' For her brother, however, she could not yet find forgiveness, especially when she learned that he did not wish to keep Godmersham's paintings and library: 'Uncle Edward is too dreadful to think of — not care for the pictures & books.' She concluded: 'Don't fancy I think you do not *care* enough about G[odmersham]. I know you do but who can like us who were born there.' [40]

Lizzy was the second of the Knight children to be 'born there'. From the others, no reaction survives. William Knight, the first of Edward Austen's family to be born at Godmersham, who had been Rector for fifty years at Jane Austen's first home at Steventon, had died the previous winter. Marianne, the third of the Godmersham-born children, may well have written to her sisters about it: if she did, the letters were not kept. Equally, it may be that having 'cried out all her tears', as Caroline Cassandra had written twenty-one years before, and accepted the grievous loss of the home she had run since the age of nineteen, Marianne may have kept to herself any new feelings arising from the sale. Unlike Lizzy, Fanny and Louisa, she and John could hardly afford the luxury of indignation.

One by one, the generation of young nieces and nephews whom Jane Austen had known was passing away. Anna Lefroy had died in September 1872 and her half-brother James Edward Austen Leigh, Marianne's first admirer and, like Anna, the fortunate recipient of Jane's critical appreciation of his early writing, had seen his *Memoir* go into a second and third edition before his death in September 1874.[41] Fanny's memory deteriorated further. By 1875, at the age of eighty-two, she was having difficulty recognising her grandchildren and, by 1878, could no longer bear to have her son and grandson with her at meals, thinking them strangers; time had imploded, and her granddaughter Eva was sometimes her sister Louisa, sometimes Lizzy.[42] In the narrowing circle of her generation, Marianne had few to whom she could turn. On 10 January 1878 her youngest brother, John, died at the age of sixty-nine, leaving her once more without a home. There was more to come. 'We are very uneasy about Ld. G. Hill,' Lizzy wrote to her son Walter. 'He is dangerously ill of congested lungs and they say his recovery is … hopeless here. His children are all sent for, & I fear the worst very much — Aunt May is there.' [43] Marianne, no longer needed in England, went at once to Ireland to help her distraught sister.

In the late 1870s, Donegal was a very different place from that which Marianne had seen on her visit in 1853. Following the famine, before the sheep wars of the mid-1850s began, an atmosphere of relative calm had prevailed in Donegal. The young rebels of 1848, such as fiery John Mitchel and the contentious parliamentarian William Smith O'Brien, had failed in their attempt to bring about change in the spirit of revolution then sweeping Europe. Impatient with O'Connell's attempts to have the Union repealed, they had themselves faltered, unable to agree on a coherent policy.[44] Few believed any more, as the dreamer poet Thomas Davis had, that the country would stand up for a cultural ideal; instead, a new and much more militant mood prevailed. The Fenian brotherhood, or Irish Republican Brotherhood, under James Stephens, determined to be more effective than Young Ireland, and looking back to Wolfe Tone and the United Irishmen for their models, had already stirred revolutionary feelings once in 1858.[45] By 1860, the first of a series of land acts had begun to change relations between landlord and tenant yet again. Under this, their relationship was 'deemed to be founded on the express of implied contract of the parties and not upon tenure or service'. This seemed to give the landlord more power to set his own terms. A new act, however, under William Gladstone in 1870, following the principle of the 'Ulster Custom', gave evicted tenants the hope of compensation for improvements they had made, and the hope of purchasing land with a loan from the state.[46] As the 1870s closed, only land was considered worth a struggle.

The culture of resistance spread rapidly. Such cases as that of Charles Cunningham Boycott, agent in County Mayo to John Crichton, 3rd Earl of Erne, received immediate and widespread attention.[47] As a test case, he was perhaps the most famous of those ostracised by the Land League, and his name as a consequence passed into the language. Yet, he was not a landlord, unlike Lord George's near neighbour in Donegal, William Clements, 3rd Earl of Leitrim, whose murder in April 1878 shocked society in both Ireland and England. Though popular memory condemns Leitrim as a tyrant, a body of evidence exists, as A.P.W. Malcomson has recently demonstrated, that he 'sought out the common ground between landlord and tenant, and embarked on new enterprises which promised to conduce equally to the advantage of both'.[48] In this, his efforts were not dissimilar to those of Lord George, known to Leitrim since his time as Comptroller of the Royal Household in Dublin. Indeed, as early as 1840, Lord George had been an object of admiration to Leitrim for his 'superior management' in Gweedore.

As Malcomson makes clear, however, Leitrim did not share Lord George's early tolerance of 'tenant right': he had offended his tenants over his requirement that they pay charges for the seaweed, or 'wrack', which they had been in the habit of collecting, for their own use, from the shores of his estate.[49] Leitrim was well aware that he could become a target for militants. In 1860, he had made a chillingly prescient observation: 'A man's life in Ireland is a simple matter of traffic: how much is it worth? If it be considered a good speculation to take it, slander of the most ingenious kind is resorted to for the purpose of preparing the neighbourhood for his fall.'[50] His prediction was accurate; he was murdered near his home, on the shores of Mulroy Bay, on 2 April 1878. For Lord George, as a fellow-landlord as well as a friend, it was a severe blow. He had been one of the executors of Leitrim's 1859 will, though not of his final will, and the murder was a source of shock and great sadness to him, causing him to regret in the last year of his own life that 'of late years [Leitrim had] always said he could not come to see us because he had so much business'.[51] Though by then Lord George himself was less engaged with the work of the estate as a result of his health, he had already expressed his distrust of the new land agitation.[52] In practical terms, however, unable or unwilling to make the effort to comprehend this new movement, Lord George was no longer in the forefront of change. It was his son Arthur who needed to address what was happening.

It was to this Donegal, wary, and mistrustful of its neighbours, that Marianne Knight, in her seventy-eighth year, travelled to help Louisa care for her dying husband. As Lizzy's letter indicated, very little hope was held out for her brother-in-law's recovery. On 6 April 1879, Lord George Hill died, aged seventy-seven, in Ballyare House. His death was registered in Ramelton twelve days later by his son Augustus, giving his occupation as 'gentleman', and the cause of death as 'senile decay and congestion of the lungs'.[53] He was buried beside Cassandra in Conwal Cemetery, Letterkenny. Though only Augustus was listed as witness to the death, all Lord George's children had been sent for, as Lizzy had told her daughter. The eldest, Norah, Mrs Somerset Ward, was by 1879 the mother of grown children, with a daughter who was herself on the verge of marriage. Arthur, the heir, had been married since 1871 to Helen Emily Trench, daughter of Richard Chenevix Trench, Archbishop of Dublin, who had once joined Lady Campbell in enthusiastic praise of Jane Austen. Arthur, Captain Hill, was settled just outside Dublin, while his two unmarried brothers, Augustus and Louisa's son George, a barrister, spent time between Dublin and Ballyare. The youngest of Cassandra's children, Cassandra Jane Louisa, was in a different position. Born three days before her mother's death, she was thirty-seven, unmarried and without a profession. She had spent her adult life occupying herself like her stepmother and aunts with duties to the poor and, fluent like her father in the Irish language, teaching the children of the tenantry. Thoughtful, lively and intelligent, Cassandra alone was committed to living in Donegal and working with the people there, having inherited something of her father's imaginative understanding of custom and tradition. Yet, primogeniture meant that the estate passed to her eldest brother Arthur, who showed no inclination to follow his father's example and move there, any more than his cousin Edward Knight had wished to move back to Godmersham when his father had died.

For Marianne, returning to England after Lord George's death, it may not have seemed that she would be likely to spend long periods in the turbulent surroundings of Donegal. For the children of her sisters Cassandra and Louisa, however, there was less choice. With sole charge of the estate at Gweedore, Arthur was in no mind to entertain any kind of challenge to his authority. Attitudes had hardened on both sides in a time of widespread economic depression. Following yet another failure of the harvest in 1879, and the consequent absence of provision for his tenants by Arthur, the newly founded Land League quickly gathered strength in Donegal under the leadership of a charismatic and highly intelligent parish priest, Father James McFadden.[54]

James McFadden had been born to a comfortable and ambitious farming family near Carrigart in Donegal in 1842, barely two months after the death of Cassandra Knight. Thirteen years after Catholic Emancipation, Catholic families remained acutely aware that education, whether in the Church or the Law, was still the best and surest route for a clever child to make his way in the world.[55] McFadden was such a child and, moving without difficulty through the National School system to the Diocesan Seminary at Letterkenny, he completed his studies for the priesthood at Maynooth in County Kildare, where he was noted for his scholastic excellence. His natural abilities, combined with the self-confidence which, as a cousin of two important churchmen, he had in abundance, fitted him for the role he discovered for himself in Gweedore.[56] He saw himself, and was accepted, as the guardian of the people and the safe keeper of their money until such times as rents should be set at a level acceptable to the Land League. It was not unusual in Ireland for a priest to be involved in politics yet, with the benefit of hindsight, modern historians can see how such a situation might have increased tensions between landlord and tenant. Terence Dooley considers that this was especially the case in Ulster, where landowners looked to the Orange Order to provide a buffer between them and the tenants' agitation.[57] For W.E. Vaughan, 'the one incontestable fact that emerges is that 1879 was the only year of serious agricultural depression that found a united and powerful political leadership, ready to exploit agrarian discontent.'[58] Though the leader of the Irish Parliamentary Party and President of the Land League, Charles Stewart Parnell – himself a member of the landlord class – may have believed that successful land agitation might pave the way for Home Rule, J.S. Donnelly Jr has made clear that many landlords realised by 1879 that reorganisation might well be necessary for survival.[59] R.F. Foster has further observed that 'some of the more astute among them began to see that land reform, and land purchase, might be their only hope'.[60] Yet, the involvement of the priest was a stumbling block; Foster sees the 'rapid identification of the movement with a revanchist Roman Catholic Church and with the drive for denominational education' combined with 'the language of social revolution and expropriation' as a real barrier to reform.[61]

In his day, Lord George had tried, according to his beliefs, to understand his tenants' point of view and accommodate their wishes, where it accorded with his view of the correct management of the estate. Now, his son proposed to run the estate from the comfortable suburbs outside Dublin. As Maria Edgeworth had her fictional Thady say of an absentee Rackrent:

> Sir Kit Stopgap, my young master, left all to the agent, and though he had the spirit of a prince, and lived away to the honour of his country abroad, which I was proud to hear of, what were we the better for that at home?[62]

For Arthur Hill, there were difficulties in addition to those identified by R.F. Foster. One was his reluctance to deal with the issues in person; another, that the rent reductions required by the League referred to the levels set decades earlier by Griffith's valuation. In the view of many landlords, these valuations bore no relation to the real value of land and, in common with many other landlords, Arthur Hill did not see why he should give in to his tenants' demands.[63]

By 1881, Arthur had clashed with Father McFadden over the payment of rents. His brother-in-law, Somerset Ward, was writing to him in terms of the strongest indignation, urging him to tackle not only the wider problem of tenant refusal to pay rents but also, specifically, the urgent problem of Father McFadden. Somerset Ward had already expressed his frustration in the *Gweedore Hotel Book*: 'Very comfortable,' he wrote, 'in spite of behaviour of natives who have boycotted hotel, stopped supply of bread & coerced male servants into resignation of their appointment — house patrolled at night by constabulary, & loaded revolvers are handed about inside, we suppose in order to protect our eatables.'[64] It was following this that Somerset Ward wrote to his brother-in-law, adamant that Arthur should not give in to the tenants' demands. In 1881, with more legislation imminent and his daughter, Norah Ward, granddaughter of Lord George and Cassandra, about to be married, Ward could not suppress his indignation. He was furious at McFadden's composure, at the boycotting of the Gweedore Hotel and at the ineffectiveness of Arthur's agent.[65] So strongly did he feel about the situation that he offered, once his daughter's wedding was over, to take on the role of agent himself. As old comrades, both veterans of the Indian Mutiny, the attitudes of Arthur Hill and Somerset Ward to rebellion among the 'natives' remained in complete accord:

> I was studiously polite and courteous to [Father McFadden], and he was as oily as he could be — professed his anxious desire for peace — and good feeling between landlord and tenant. The hypocrite! As if he could not restore peace at once if he chose to do so. After some general conversation I asked him what the tenants wanted. He said they wished to have the mountains

restored to them and the rents reduced to what they were 40
years ago, but he was good enough to say he considered their
demands somewhat unreasonable. I told him I knew very well
the influence he had on them — and also that you could not
possibly give more liberal terms than what you have already
offered viz. 10% of rents as I said at once — that you must have
rents paid, otherwise you must enforce payment by legal process
for the charges on the property must be paid …[66]

McFadden, untroubled by any threat of action, indicated that the tenants
were prepared to make sacrifices and 'openly admitted … that the Land League
was the cause of all the agitation for before it was formed the people did not
know their power'.[67] He added that he had exhorted the people not to break
the law, and suggested that an abatement of 25 per cent though inadequate,
might be acceptable. When Ward pointed out that Father McFadden, unlike
Captain Hill, was comparatively well-off, McFadden agreed, but suggested
that the tenants 'wd not take that into consideration'. He left Ward with some
advice: 'We will suppose the rental is £1,000,' he said. 'Well, 25 per cent will be
only £250. This will reduce the rental to £750, and it will be quite worth Capt.
Hill's while to accept of this reduction for the sake of peace.' They parted with
the reluctant agreement of McFadden to Ward's meeting twelve tenants, from
varying districts of the estate, the following day at the Derrybeg schoolhouse.
Privately, Somerset Ward then gave his brother-in-law advice which would
irredeemably alter relations between landlord and tenant in Gweedore.

He is a thorough going rascal — and I am afraid you must push
matters to an extremity. If so I should evict a great many men. 8
or 10 is not enough to cow 800. If they see you are determined
to go on to the bitter end they may yield, but a very firm front
must be shown. They will never yield unless they see plainly that
you are master …[68]

Following the meeting next day, Ward was careful to record his declaration
to the tenants that he was present there 'not … in an official capacity', but

simply as an interested party who wished to see the restoration of peace. He told them he knew of their membership of the Land League; Father McFadden rephrased this as 'passive resistance'.[69] When Ward brought up the subject of 'isolation, commonly called boycotting of the landlord and all supposed to be favourable to them', McFadden countered with 'social ostracism'. Ward then asked the tenants for their terms, and McFadden asked them to speak one by one. They were very specific, 'all unanimous in requiring a reduction of rents to what they were 40 years ago, the restoration of the mountains to the tenants and the expulsion of the Scotch farmers, and further an abatement equal to that given by the Marquess of Conyngham'.[70] Ward told them there would be no reduction, no restoration and no expulsion of Scots farmers, adding that they would be evicted if they did not pay their rents, for 'tho' the Land League was powerful the law was more powerful'.[71] Father McFadden then gave what Somerset Ward described as an 'oration', expressing his hopes for the future:

> The new land bill may do great things for the tenants — he was in great hopes it wd. contain a clause remitting arrears — that the Land League was formed in consequence of landlord tyranny — that tenants were bound to protect themselves, that the Land League exercised a mighty power which compelled M. of Conyngham to grant the abatement he gave, and without the Land League you wd. not have offered them even what you have. He spoke good humouredly but very strongly.[72]

McFadden finished by advising an abatement of 25 per cent, and Somerset Ward made his final offer of 10 per cent: if they thought their rents too high, he told them, they were free to go to court and make their case after the Bill was passed. Ward asked if they would accept an agreement to abide by whatever reduction the courts ordered, in addition to the 10 per cent abatement; there was no opportunity for a response, Father McFadden 'at once jumped up and said he wd. never allow any of them to go into court. They were too poor to incur the necessary costs'.

> The plain English of that was of course that he knew the rents
> were so low that no Court wd. reduce them. He also drew the
> tenants' attention to the fact that you had contributed nothing to
> relieve their distress at which I at once jumped up and said that I
> wd. leave it to any unprejudiced person to say whether you were
> in any way called upon to contribute to those who combined
> together to refuse to pay you a farthing of rent.[73]

Though Somerset Ward emphasised to his brother-in-law that the discussion 'was carried on very quietly and there was no heat on either side', and that he hoped they would think better of their stance, neither he nor Arthur Hill can have been unaware of how dangerous a quiet this was. Every grievance had been remembered over the years: as far as the tenants were concerned, the time of reckoning had arrived. Whatever degree of loyalty some tenants might once have felt for Lord George, there was little for his son. Father McFadden knew of Arthur Hill's failure to alleviate any recent distress, and Somerset Ward as his spokesman had sought to justify this position. There was no escape from the round of accusations, however quietly they were voiced, and there was no avoiding the fact that this was indeed a war.

The last part of the letter above was written from Ballyare, but by the time Ward wrote the next day, he was again in the centre of the dispute at the boycotted Gweedore Hotel, where he looked in vain for Gillespie, the agent for the estate: 'All the men have left. The laundry girl also left last night, but the two maids and cook say they will not go. A nice state of things. There are 50 police in the district and 3 Sub. Inspectors ... Your worthy agent is conspicuous by his absence.'[74] He urged action, specifically the bringing in of 'emergency men to work the farm here'. The blacksmith would no longer shoe the horses, local traders would not supply the police with food, so that provisions had to be brought from Letterkenny, and Gillespie was clearly unequal to the task of collecting rents. In desperation, Somerset Ward offered to come and act as agent himself: 'If I could stay a month here and get to know the people, I might be able to do something'. In the meantime, he went about the estate to survey the extent of the difficulties, finding an old acquaintance, the local baker, about to give up his business, 'such a reign of terror exists here'.[75]

Ward also told Arthur Hill that he had learned from the baker that the tenants felt he 'ought to have come down here [him]self and spoken to them'. There was no avoiding the fact that, while Lord George had made an effort to get to know his tenants in their own language, Arthur Hill's behaviour increasingly recalled that of the traditional absentee landlord. Somerset Ward's high-handed defence of his brother-in-law's actions, followed by the spirited oratory of Father McFadden, could serve only to confirm this impression. Yet, Ward's advice to his brother-in-law was sensible and practical:

> I think it would be wise to inform the tenants again decidedly
> that you require the rents to be paid by a certain date, say 15 June
> and that you will extend your offer of 10 per cent to all tenants
> paying all arrears to Nov last, on or before that date, that no
> abatement will be given to any in arrears after that date, and
> that you will proceed at once against them.[76]

He still hoped that eviction could be avoided, and he felt that many would indeed be relieved to pay their arrears if they were not so afraid. He urged Arthur Hill in the strongest terms to come and settle matters, but added that, if his brother-in-law really could not come in person, he would stay and meet him at Ballyare and work out a strategy.[77] In other words, in a time where compromise was no longer simply desirable but essential, Somerset Ward, well-versed in land management, was convinced that Arthur Hill of Gweedore was in real danger of missing his only opportunity to save the family estate. For Arthur, it was a problem of business. For his siblings, especially his youngest sister Cassandra and his stepmother Louisa, it was becoming more pressing with each day. For Marianne, with so few options left, the troubled country of Ireland would soon represent her only means of avoiding the prospect she most dreaded, that of living alone.

CHAPTER 8

'THE FASHION TO BE POOR'

Lady George, Miss Knight and Miss Hill
1879–1885

'Her letters show her exactly as she is, the most active, friendly, warmhearted being in existence …'

SANDITON

Following the death of Lord George Hill in April 1879, Marianne returned to England. She could not go home for, since the death of her youngest brother, John, she no longer had one. Then, with the death of her last brother Edward on 5 November 1879, her position became even more precarious: there was now no one for whom her care need be a priority. In a sense, as the beloved aunt of so very many nephews and nieces, she had any number of possible options. In practice, this made her situation even more tenuous, for she was everyone's concern, yet no one's responsibility. Fortunately for Marianne, however, she still had three of her four sisters and, though Fanny continued to retreat further and further within herself, and Louisa stayed on in Ireland, Marianne knew she could always go to Dane Court while Lizzy lived. Accordingly, she did so, as her great-niece Marcia Rice recalled:

> In the summer of 1880, when I paid a fortnight's visit to my grandmother at Dane Court — Aunt May was staying there. She was probably on a long visit and seemed to be thoroughly established. I was greeted at the door by her, an active, light, lively little lady in a white cap with lavender ribbons. She greeted me with great kindness and led me into the drawing room, where grandmama lay on a sofa. Throughout my visit Aunt

May was much in evidence, she took full part in the family life and being 'very witty' contributed much to its gaiety. On many mornings she took me for a walk, chatting gaily all the while. She certainly enjoyed herself, darting from one side of the lanes to the other, looking for birds' nests, which were the passion of Dane Court. She encouraged me to pick flowers and was a very happy companion for a little girl.[1]

Marcia's pen portrait of this bright and lively aunt, comfortable with children and prepared to settle wherever she was welcome, may give an idea of the kind of great-aunt Jane Austen, whom Marianne so resembled, might have been. Yet, however well-liked an aunt Marianne was, it was never certain that permanent homes would be available for the unmarried women of the family. Edward Austen Knight's original family was shrinking with every year that passed and Fanny, the eldest of all, died on Christmas morning 1882, some weeks short of her ninetieth birthday. She was followed in 1884 by Lizzy, whose eldest son Edward Bridges Rice inherited Dane Court. Yet again, in an unsettling repetition of 1853, the unmarried daughters of the house, Caroline Cassandra and her sister Louisa, the young girls who had helped Marianne clear Godmersham, found themselves at forty-nine and sixty years old having to uproot from their lifelong home. Though their brother Edward was 'very kind indeed … to the girls', finding them a pleasant house nearby, Lizzy's son Walter Rice thought 'the experience for Louisa and Caroline Cassandra was a traumatic one'.[2]

Marianne, by implication, was left once more without anywhere to go, and no record survives of her having been offered a permanent home anywhere in England. What is certain is that she travelled by land and sea to Donegal in October 1884, breaking her journey first with her niece Fanny, Lady Winchilsea, at Haverholme in Lincolnshire, then again in Ireland with her elder Hill niece Norah Ward, in County Down. She wrote from Norah's home at Isle O'Valla House outside Strangford to her favourite nephew Montagu Knight, the new owner of Chawton, describing her arduous journey. Her letter, in which she asked Montagu to arrange to send on some luggage, seems to suggest that she moved permanently to Ireland at that point.[3] It was hardly a propitious time.

Though Ireland may have seemed the most logical destination for Marianne, it was still far from safe, despite or perhaps because of the series of land acts, begun over twenty years earlier, which were gradually altering all the old certainties.[4]

Marianne, however, with little alternative, travelled to Ireland. Her letter of 11 October 1884 was the first of a series which would continue almost until her death. They were directed to her favourite nephew, Montagu Knight, and his wife, the former Florence Hardy of Chilham Castle, where Fanny's one-time suitor Mr Wildman had lived. Marianne wrote while resting, before she travelled on to the untamed landscape of Donegal, in the far north-west of the island. Rest was necessary: the sea journey from Stranraer to Ireland, often uncomfortable and hazardous in stormy weather, was not pleasant for Marianne, who had recently celebrated her eighty-third birthday and had, moreover, always been prone to travel sickness:

Most thankful am I to tell you that my journey was safely over, *just* before the violent gale which is still raging commenced. I left Haverholme last Wednesday & sailed in fog & rain to Dumfries, quite calm it was, & the sun shone brilliantly the next morning. I watched it rising as we sailed along. I had to rise at 5.30 & the train started at 6.30 from Stranraer — 2½ hours brought us there: the sea was *almost* quite calm, but there was a slight swell, which I hated, but managed to preserve my equanimity all the time, tho' with difficulty! We sailed on to Belfast & thereafter ½ an hour to Downpatrick, where a Fly waited for me & deposited me … quite safely here at 4 o' clock! I know you & Florence will be glad to hear of my being alive and well after all my fatigue — I was pretty tired, but a good dinner & 7 hours' sleep through the night quite refreshed me. The wind began to rise before I got here, & tore on, to a perfect gale, with hail & rain through the night; & all yesterday, tho' there were a few intervals of sunshine. Today is bright & fine, but the wind is still boisterous & it is *very cold*. I was *very* sorry to leave H — & very glad I did, & was not persuaded to stay longer, as they most kindly urged me to do — I

shd have been still waiting at Stranraer probably if I had staid
till the next day only — I believe I go to Ballyare on, or about
the 20th — I will let you know when to send my portmanteau
to Liverpool. I hope you both are well & the Rectory too ...
Norah sends hers to you. Norah jnr is here for her confinement
w[hic]h is to be soon.[5]

The liveliness of Marianne's description of her journey accords with her
great-grandniece Marcia Rice's account of her at Dane Court in 1880. Yet,
Marianne, for all her gentility and mildness of disposition, had learned to be
intrepid. She had run the great house at Godmersham for thirty years and,
indeed, one reason for her going to Ireland at this time may have been to assist
Cassandra who, in 1884, perhaps anxious about her own security of tenure
in Ballyare, had shown interest in setting up a convalescent home in nearby
Ramelton.[6] It may be that Marianne had in mind either to help her niece run
it – she certainly did not lack experience – or to be, with her ailing sister Louisa,
one of its first residents, for both were now in their eighties. Cassandra, now in
her early fifties, was very active and able, as Marianne herself had been, and they
formed a quiet, comfortable relationship in the house in Ballyare. The proposal
to open a nursing home shows the resourceful spirit of Cassandra who, like her
father, was a fluent Irish speaker and greatly involved with the education and
physical welfare of her family's tenants. She was, in many ways, as conservative
as the rest of her family, yet maintained a wide circle of friends with varying
political views. One of her closest friends, Charlotte Grace O'Brien, was the
daughter of the former Young Irelander, William Smith O'Brien. Charlotte's
nephew, the writer and Home Rule MP Stephen Gwynn, later described the
difference in the Gweedore he recalled from his childhood, and that of the
late nineteenth century:

In the old days, now unhappily almost forgotten — when
one used to hear that if Lord George's horse broke down the
tenants would gladly draw his car back the twenty miles to
Ballyarr, on the Lennan, where he lived — things may have
run smoother.[7]

Things were not running smoothly in the early 1880s. While continuing land acts slowly shifted the balance of power between landlord and tenant, they could not stabilise the already volatile state of public feeling. Though Parnell thought he had succeeded in settling matters concerning arrears and rent strikes in April 1882, the murder of the newly-arrived Chief Secretary, Lord Frederick Cavendish, and his under-secretary, Thomas Burke, in Dublin's Phoenix Park on 6 May 1882, outraged moderate opinion in both Ireland and England. Parnell, who had no knowledge of or involvement in the murder, condemned it, as did the IRB. While arrests were made and those convicted hanged, it could not have been considered an ideal time for an English lady of eighty-three to emigrate to Ireland.

If, as Amanda Vickery has recently observed, 'letters build community out of absence', Marianne's letters from Ireland served an important function in her life. In addition, they leave a clear picture of a clever, stoic and perceptive woman.[8] She had her own means of coping with her exile for, like Jane Austen herself, beyond the hazards of weather and travel, she almost always avoided reference to the real dangers of life in Ireland during the last two decades of the century. Instead, she made for herself a version of the life she had known in England, as Marcia Rice, quoting her sister's recollection of visiting Marianne in Donegal, confirms:

> Her favourite expression was 'Gadge my love.' My sister re-
> membered the same. 'Gadge my love, what filth,' she exclaimed
> when out for a walk on a typical Irish day ... My grandmother
> was dead and Aunt May had left England to make her last
> home with her niece Cassandra Hill at Balyare [sic] in County
> Antrim [sic]. She was then naturally much older and frailer, but
> she still took little walks, visiting the poor in the village. 'Who
> is my neighbour?' she said one day, looking across the table at
> my sister. 'That is Cecil's child, Aunt May.' 'Law, my dear, then
> I must get up and give her a kiss.' My sister said she was 'very
> charming, always bright and gay and never out of humour'.
> Though celebrated in the family as 'very witty', her remarks
> were never unkind. One little incident has been handed down, it

always caused her great-nephew, Arthur Hill, much amusement. It took place at a railway station – Aunt May was at the booking office when an ungallant man tried to push her from her place. 'You may have heard,' said he, 'that the first shall be last, and the last first.' 'Very likely,' was her rejoinder, 'but I am first now,' and she stood her ground![9]

It may have amused Arthur that Marianne had learned when to stand her ground: yet, unlike him, she had also learned how and when to move with the times. Her Rice great-nieces' accounts of her, supported by her letters and the *Garden Book*, indicate that this frail, elderly little lady with lavender ribbons, who had lived her life between great houses and rectories in Hampshire and Kent, her very expressions speaking more of the *bon ton* of the eighteenth century than the demotic of the late nineteenth, should have been an unlikely candidate for life in the cold, stormy and often dangerous county of Donegal in the 1880s and 1890s. Yet, the opposite was true. Just as Elinor Dashwood could adapt to comparative poverty more easily than her supposedly unworldly sister and, just as Anne Elliot managed to leave her home in a dignified fashion when her elder sister could not, Marianne had the quality of endurance, of grace under pressure, which Jane Austen so admired, and attributed to her favourite characters. There were birds and flowers to enjoy in Donegal, a parish to look after, and nieces and nephews to write to or even, weather permitting, to visit. Until her very last years, Marianne regularly travelled to London and Chawton, despite her dislike of the journey, and she made every effort to go to County Down to visit the two Norahs, her niece and great-niece.

Visits to Ireland in the mid-1880s presented problems for other members of the family, as one of Marianne's great-nephews found out. Cecil Knatchbull-Hugessen came to Ireland by ship, disembarking at Derry at the end of August 1887, and travelled to the Donegal estate owned by Wybrants Olphert of Ballyconnell for some shooting. Writing to his sister Eva from Falcarragh he described, with a casual disregard bordering on contempt, his views of the place, 'a little collection of dingy white houses about fifty in number, & situated about half a mile from the town & 6 miles from the mountains'. He went on to give his opinions of Donegal people, and of the dangerous state of the country:

We have comfortable rooms in the house of one Bankhead, a pensioner of the Royal Artillery who says he is the only loyal man in the country. We have been recommended by Greene's friend who told him of his plans to change our abode as Bankhead besides being a loyalist is bailiff of the Stewart estate and in rather bad odour with some of the people who might possibly interfere with us while fishing in annoyance; but we have two tolerably able-bodied blackguards in our pay. Condy Wilson, an ex Fenian, & now water bailiff to Olphert, & John Ferry a whisky sodden brigand who is the caretaker of the property of Dick (Greene's friend) who is Station Director of the medical appointment of the Navy. I certainly have no intention of leaving this house, & I don't believe there is any reason for doing so ... This place seems fairly quiet & probably will be so till October when Olphert has 80 more tenants to evict. I have just seen a letter of his to Dick in which he says he has had no rent at all for 5 years. We had a long talk yesterday with one of the coastguard who said among other things that lots of the evicted people had told him that they would be only too glad to pay their rent & go back to their holdings but that they daren't do it. As old Bankhead says the people are not to be blamed for all this trouble but their advisers, the blackguardly agitators & the priests through whose hands the money for the Land League passes.[10]

What was being described was known as the Plan of Campaign, the next phase of the Land War, adopted in 1886. Though Parnell had no connection with the infamous Phoenix Park murders, the atrocity deflected attention from and perhaps delayed his attempts to bring about some approach towards Home Rule. By 1886, however, a change of government from Liberal to Conservative seemed to present another opportunity. Parnell urged his new organisation, the National League, successor to the Land League, to avoid violence in order to allay fears in England: another recession in the mid-1880s, the failure of tenants to pay their rent and the consequent evictions and outbreaks of violence led to the formation by the left wing of Parnell's followers of the Plan of Campaign. Under this plan, landlords would be offered affordable rents and, if this were not acceptable, the money would be withheld as a fund to help the evicted.[11] As Robert Kee points out, 'Parnell took care to remain aloof.'[12] Meanwhile, another organisation, the Irish Landowners' Convention, had been set up in 1886. The aim of this was to protect landlords' interests from the Plan, from the National League, and from the negative effects of continuing legislation.[13]

In Gweedore, Somerset Ward's old opponent, Father McFadden, was perfectly ready to play his part in implementing the Plan of Campaign, simplifying the issue as 'a struggle between planted Protestants and native Catholics.'[14] To him, Lord George Hill was a 'speculator', his son an ineffective inheritor of an inglorious legacy, and the Gweedore Hotel little more than a barracks for the housing of eviction agents.[15] He knew his capabilities as an organiser and used them to good effect, coordinating not only rent strikes but also civil disobedience.[16] He carried his point: Arthur Hill, who had carried out the evictions urged by Somerset Ward, was obliged by November 1887 to reinstate more than one hundred and thirty tenants who had lost their homes, to give a reduction in rent of 30 per cent, pay legal costs of £900 and reduce the tenants' arrears by 60 per cent.[17] As president of the parochial branch of the National League, Father McFadden kept a 'war chest' of money paid in by the tenants who withheld rent: with this, he set up negotiations with the landlords. On 4 January 1888, at a meeting in the nearby parish of Doe, attended by Michael Davitt, founder of the Land League, he made the statement which defined his role in the eyes of the tenants:

> [Spoken in Irish] If ye pay behind backs, ye will be watched. If you stick together, I will give you my blessing.
> [Spoken in English] Mrs Boner was put out. Mrs Boner is since gone to her account and somebody must account for her death. One man had a fork, another a stone and they could only get out one that day. Now that is a sample of how you ought to conduct the campaign. Let them [constabulary note takers] take a note of it. I don't care about all the note takers. I am the law in Gweedore. They could not arrest any person without my consent. I despise

the Coercion Act. If I got a summons, I would not reply to it. I say your methods are strictly honest.[18]

This statement made many enemies, and may have been a factor contributing to a tragic event just over a year later. At the time, Father McFadden was arrested and imprisoned for three months, and Cecil Knatchbull-Hugessen's host Olphert was boycotted, suspected by his tenants of having used his son's position within the household of the Lord Lieutenant to bring about the arrest. When released, however, McFadden returned in triumph to Gweedore, an attraction in himself, and such public figures as the flamboyantly nationalist Wilfrid Scawen Blunt and Yeats's first love, Maud Gonne – who arrived on horseback – made the journey to Donegal to see him.[19] McFadden was suspicious of the motives of such visitors. 'What did she want in Gweedore?' he later asked of another friend of Yeats, the poet Katharine Tynan, who he hoped would present his side of the struggle to the world. 'He always wanted to know what any person from the outside world wanted in Gweedore,' Tynan recalled. 'Donegal "of the Strangers" was well-guarded at this outpost from foreign invasion.'[20]

Yet, some visitors who, in the spirit of Thomas Carlyle, admired Lord George's work in Gweedore, unexpectedly found Father McFadden a powerful and persuasive force. One of these, an American named William Henry Hurlburt, published an account of a meeting with him. Despite his regard for Lord George's work, Hurlburt did not admire Arthur Hill, or his 'vacillation'. Captain Hill, he was given to understand, was 'always of the mind of the last man that speaks to him', giving Father McFadden a constant advantage.[21] When Hurlburt went to see McFadden in his impressive house, he found him able, intelligent and persuasive, convinced that agents were 'the curse both of Ireland and the landlord', ready to explain that he kept the people's money to be ready to pay as and when a settlement was reached, and convinced that he was not simply the only possible buffer 'between my people and obligations which they are unable to meet', but also the only conduit by which the landlord might receive any remuneration.[22] Just before Hurlburt left, the almost teetotal Father McFadden offered him a glass of wine. Hurlburt, who accepted, was later informed that Arthur Hill's 'declining that same courtesy under Father McFadden's roof' had brought about the priest's implacable enmity.[23] Whatever the cause, McFadden and Captain Hill were sworn opponents, and Father McFadden retained the advantage of tactical superiority.

Matters finally came to a terrible conclusion in early 1889. In late January of that year, Father McFadden ignored a summons to appear in court, where he was to be charged with incitement to discourage rent payment. A warrant issued for his arrest precluded forcible entry and McFadden refused to give himself up to the constabulary. Then, on the morning of 3 February 1889, after Father McFadden had said Mass and left the chapel at Derrybeg to climb a flight of steps and walk the short distance to his house, District Inspector William Martin of the Royal Irish Constabulary, with a considerable force of policemen, stepped forward to arrest him.[24] Martin, whose short temper had involved him in confrontation on earlier occasions, had been given to understand that Father McFadden was saying Mass at another parish that morning, and may have been irked by the necessity of having to begin again at Derrybeg. Sword unsheathed, he confronted the priest as he left the church, taking hold of the collar of his soutane, and causing McFadden to stumble. The cleric righted himself, but his stumble had been seen by some of his parishioners, and a cry went up that Martin was killing the priest. Alarmed and incensed, the congregation surged forward. Suddenly, in a terrible reprise of the situation Father McFadden had seemed to commend in his much-quoted speech of January 1888, someone threw a stone and others picked up paling posts. As hysteria and confusion increased, Inspector Martin was corralled within the confines of Father McFadden's garden, cut off from his officers and, in a matter of minutes, horribly bludgeoned. He collapsed at the front door of the parochial house; upstairs McFadden who, separated by the crowd from the officer, had finally gained the safety of his house, called in vain for calm. It was too late. Though Father McFadden surrendered to the County Inspector when he arrived, gave his word that he would not try to escape, and made his house available to the wounded, the inescapable fact was that Inspector Martin lay dead at his feet.[25] McFadden later described his distress at what had occurred to Katharine Tynan, as he walked with her over the scene of the crime:

> He was a brave fellow and he faced them like a lion. I wish he
> hadn't been so brave for his own sake. I struggled to get to him

to protect him, but the people were determined to save me whether I liked it or not. Here he stood up among them, just in this spot … It was terrible that I could not help him … They were completely out of hand. It all happened in a few minutes. It has been a great trouble to me ever since that I could not save him … He died there on the hearthrug at your feet. The anger died out of them when they saw what they had done. They carried him in here. The poor fellow: he was beyond all help.[26]

As Katharine Tynan later wrote, 'After this affair, to a great many good folk Father McFadden was a very terrible person. Others knew him as a zealous, devoted priest.'[27] In the aftermath of the murder, however greatly Father McFadden regretted it, consequences for his parishioners were severe. Within a week, in what came to be known as 'the Gweedore Terror', police and soldiers were dispatched to Donegal in large numbers; gunboats were stationed off the coast in search of fugitives trying to escape to the offshore islands such as Gola; houses were unceremoniously searched; and forty-eight people were arrested. Father McFadden was one of ten charged with murder, while thirteen others were charged with conspiracy. At the trial at Maryborough (now Port Laoise) in October 1889, where Edward Carson was one of those assisting the Attorney General in conducting the case for the crown, Father McFadden pleaded guilty to obstruction. He was released, while seven others, of whom six pleaded guilty, were convicted of manslaughter and given sentences from six months' hard labour to ten years' penal servitude. The case became notorious, entirely enmeshed in the debate over Land Reform and Home Rule and, for some years afterwards, the degree to which tenants or clergy were responsible was constantly referred to as argument for or against self-government for Ireland.[28] As a talking point it was displaced only by the growing storm over the Katherine O'Shea scandal, which shortly engulfed Charles Stewart Parnell. Once he had been named as co-respondent in the divorce action taken against Mrs O'Shea by her husband, his status as 'the uncrowned king of Ireland' was in question. As J.C. Beckett explains, 'Popular opinion in Ireland was deeply divided; but the whole weight of clerical influence was against Parnell, and it was his morality, rather than his policy, that seemed to be on trial.'[29]

It was to this complex, turbulent 'Donegal of the strangers' that Marianne Knight had come in late 1884, a quiet English gentlewoman with no experience of violence or agrarian agitation and, as her aunt Jane might have reminded her, no knowledge of 'the manners there'. Beyond the first, which had described her journey to Ireland, no letters have survived for the first three years she spent in Ballyare. By the time the series can be seen to resume, February 1887, Parnell had not yet fallen, yet the Plan of Campaign had already been denounced by the British government in December 1886 as an 'unlawful and criminal conspiracy'.[30] In parliament, debate continued over the introduction of a Coercion bill, the Criminal Law & Procedure (Ireland) Act which became law on 19 July 1887, closely followed in August by the suppression of Parnell's National League.[31] While the debate was going on Marianne, normally so reserved, and perhaps unusually exercised by the struggle in which her nephew was then engaged with his recalcitrant tenants, for once spoke her mind:

> How they go wrangling on about the address to the Queen's speech, wasting all this time, instead of making stringent laws to enforce the Queen's laws in Ireland, & to punish *severely* & *immediately*, every rebel who makes disloyal, treasonable speeches urging the Tenants to rob their Landlords more than many of them have already done.[32]

However kind and sympathetic they may have been to individual tenants or their families in distress, none of the Knight family would have supported a tenant against a landlord. In Chawton, at about the same time, her nephew Montagu Knight's agent questioned a prospective tenant on his politics and religion to make sure they accorded with those of the landlord, and Montagu kept a cutting describing the incident in his family scrapbook.[33] Maria Edgeworth, the pioneering novelist who had so completely understood the world of the tenantry that she could write *Castle Rackrent* as though she were one of them, had described many years earlier how she collected punitive fines from two Edgeworthstown tenants she had known all her life. They had voted against the interests of the family because it had been required by their parish priest and, though tears ran down her cheeks and she felt 'it was all shameful', Maria Edgeworth had no doubt where her loyalty lay.[34]

Marianne Knight was no different. While she condemned and required punishment for her nephew's rebellious tenants, she was at the same time sending a regular sum from her small annuity to an elderly and ailing former gardener to the family in Chawton. Yet, if the old Chawton gardener had in any way defied the family, she would undoubtedly have called for his punishment even if, like Maria Edgeworth, she felt the tears come to her eyes as she did so. It is a curious if revealing contradiction: Marianne knew what it was to face losing her house, and did not forget her father's old servant, or his family, in their time of need. Yet, she could not extend this compassion to the poverty-stricken tenants facing eviction on her nephew's land because they, like the mutinous Indians who had threatened the lives of her nephews thirty years earlier, were 'rebels'.

Her real concern, however, much deeper than her views on the Irish question, was Louisa's health. In the spring of 1887, even as she awaited a visit from the Wards of Isle O'Valla, she feared Louisa might not be able for the visit. 'My dearest sister is only pretty well', she wrote. 'She is very unequal to much talking & I am afraid will often have to retire upstairs & take refuge in her bedroom for a time to rest her head.'[35] A year later, she continued to be concerned. On 10 April 1888 she wrote again to Montagu and Florence, the dry irony of her tone recalling the wry amusement of her famous aunt. Once she settled into life in Ballyare, she tried to give the impression to her family that she was once more Miss Knight of Godmersham and Chawton, largely unaffected by much beyond the vicissitudes of the weather, finding her happiness in the house and garden about her, and in news from her family:

> Many thanks for your letter & enclosure, giving me the interesting news of Mrs Fletcher's arrival in London from Paris, loaded with novelties for dresses, bonnets &c &c for the coming spring, if it ever arrives! Your weather does not sound like it, I must confess. Ours is, I hope, improving. We have had no snow, showers or frost for some days, tho' the wind still persists in the North and

East; but there is very little of it, & when the sun condescends to shine out, it is pleasant enough. Everything is very backward, which probably saves their lives. We have had delicious violets in the garden for some days, & now the beds are filling fast with daffodil bulbs — Hyacinths in full bloom, Narcissus, Jonquil, a few tulips & polyanthus besides wallflowers: so the borders just outside the drawing room window look quite gay and springlike.[36]

The letter, bright and optimistic in tone is, nonetheless, deceptive. While relishing the doings of her nieces and nephews and all their children as far away as India, remembering who was getting married, who was rowing for Oxford, who was playing in the cricket team against the villagers, Marianne was uneasy. At the end of her letter, she added a postscript which shows something of her efforts to spare her family the knowledge that Louisa was far from well: 'We go on very peacefully here. My drst Sister still suffers sadly from acute inflammation, otherwise she is really well.'[37] When next she wrote, in May 1888, it was with the same fluent ease and sharp-edged humour that Jane employed in her letters to her sister Cassandra, as though they were together in the same room. Yet, there is a difference: she no longer tried to minimise the degree of Louisa's illness. Marianne's expressions here, such as the archaic 'thanky' for 'thank you', are reminders that she was just a few years short of ninety, not as strong as the voice in her letters would suggest and, for the first time, dreading the prospect of travelling. This was a woman, increasingly fearful of the future, trying not to sound lonely for her old home and the life she knew:

What good pens you always get. I wish I did. How do you manage, I wonder? Thanky kindly for your letter received yest'y. I like so much hearing about you all, & I seldom do it seems to me. No, I have not made any plans for the summer, and have no idea what I am likely to do yet. Many thanks for your kind say about Chawton, if I do visit England I will gladly avail myself of your noble invitation — but the long, weary journey begins

to frighten me & I feel as I approach the 87th year of my reign
that I am neither as young, or as strong, as I used to be.[38]

Though by the end of June 1888, Louisa had been well enough to be
'carried downstairs and into the garden the 3 last days, and staid longer each
time — yest'y more than 2 hours, & not too tired after a good rest on her bed',
Marianne does not appear to have travelled to England that summer. The
'lovely, bright sunny days' in Donegal reminded her of England's 'beautiful
Jubilee weather' the previous year, which, she said, 'I have not forgotten.'[39] A
year later, she chose to believe her sister was stronger, 'excepting her side & leg
which were first attacked', but added, a little despondently: 'I fear there is no
improvement in them, or very, very little', and then, in a brief return to her old,
teasing manner, she wrote: 'I don't know what I shall do; pick up, join you in
Scotland, & get a little shooting!'[40] By her next letter, dated 9 July 1888, the old
Chawton gardener Richard Knight had died, and she wrote offering to continue
her regular remittance in order to help his widow. It was a generous offer, from
one who had little. Indeed, almost as though she did not wish to dwell on this
act of generosity she moved quickly to safer topics. She was a countrywoman
at heart, and had always been used, not least in her capacity as mistress of her
father's estate at Godmersham, to the rhythm of the seasons: she understood
the importance of the opening of the fields, and the later saving of the harvest:
'The weather continues dull & showery', she wrote, 'the meadows were to have
been begun today but it was decided to wait a little longer — I hope the new
moon may do us some good: the last was a very bad one.'[41]

The next letter is dated May 1889, three months after the murder of Inspector
Martin. Marianne, though she must have been aware of all that had happened,
did not refer to it even obliquely for, by then, Louisa was extremely ill:

> She has slept well for several nights which is a great blessing;
> her appetite has been better, and she has not complained of
> breathlessness lately. We are indeed most truly thankful for this
> gracious answer to our prayers. She is still very weak; but she gets
> up, & is wheeled into her dressing room every day, where she
> remains lying on the bed for 2 or 3 hours which refreshes and

amuses her. She can't talk much at a time, on acct of her head, or be talked to for long, but we must not expect too much, & we are very thankful for God's great goodness to us in hearing & granting our prayers.[42]

The condition of her last sister, indeed her last sibling, continued to be Marianne's main preoccupation in that volatile time of 1889. Though she made light of it, she was beginning to feel her age: 'I am very well, thanky, except not being as strong as I was, having pains occasionally in my back; which as I am nearly 100 is not odd.'[43] By 10 June 1889, she was prepared to travel as far as County Down to visit Norah Ward. Louisa's state, she wrote, was 'so critical that I cannot make up my mind to leave her for more than a few days, unless she makes greater progress this week than she has done'. Only if she received very encouraging reports of her sister from Cassandra, she said, would she travel on to England.[44]

After 'a comfortable report ... of dear At. Lou', she made the journey, and her next letter, of 29 June 1889, sent to her nephew Montagu from 58 Eccleston Square in London, showed her to be in excellent spirits. 'I hope to present myself at good old Chawton on Tuesday next,' she told him, '& to regale you & Florence with my company for a fortnight, if you can bear with me for so long.' Yet, she was feeling the effects of the journey: 'I am grown (really) old enough to be everybody's Grand-Mother, & am as deaf as an adder, as blind as a beetle, and as weak as a wagtail.' She was much less active, postponing some family visits she had engaged to make, and making a point of asking for Montagu's help in getting herself and her luggage to his 'venerable Mansion'.[45] By 10 July she was at Dover, once more in good spirits as she wrote to Florence thanking her for the 'delicious visit' she had passed at Chawton, and describing a meeting which might have come straight from the pages of a Jane Austen novel:

I was too early at the Station & had to walk up & down the platform many times, to avoid Mrs Howlett who pounced upon me as soon as I appeared; I did not know her at all, & she had to tell me her name — her 'Caro Sposo' was there, busy taking train tickets & I did not speak to him; I suppose they went 2nd

or 3rd Class, as I saw no more of them save a passing glance &
bow at Waterloo.[46]

It serves as another reminder that, like her sisters, Marianne, for all her
compassion and understanding of human nature, never forgot her station in
society. However precarious her own circumstances, she was still Miss Knight,
and she did not choose to mix, any more than Emma Woodhouse did, with
this latter-day Mrs Elton, or her 'Caro Sposo'. When she reached London, she
enjoyed the company of her nephews Augustus and George Hill, 'cabbed about',
forgot her umbrella in a shop, had the pleasure of having it returned beautifully
wrapped up, and altogether had a delightful holiday. A note of anxiety creeps in
at the end of the letter, however: 'I haven't heard from Ballyare again, wh[ich]
I hope means good news.'[47]

It did not. Her next letter to Florence, two days after her eighty-eighth
birthday, was warm and open, telling her she 'lov'd both [their] dear affec'ate
letters very much'.[48] In common with the rest of her family, Marianne had always
relished the celebration of her birthday: she had, after all, once been brought
to the theatre by Jane Austen to mark the occasion. For the first time, however,
she did not feel like celebrating. While Marianne was in England, Louisa, in
her eighty-fifth year, had died of a sudden cerebral haemorrhage: [49]

My birthday this year was indeed a sadly different one from
any of its predecessors: I missed my darling *last* Sister, as I have
done, & still do miss her every hour of every day; though at the
same time I try to be truly thankful to our merciful God for His
Goodness to her in releasing her from her suffering, weary life
here: if I *had* returned in time to have seen & kissed her once
more, I shd be more thankful, & I cannot help grieving for my
absence, but God's will be done. He orders everything for the
best. Augustus & George are still here, & are of the greatest use
to Cass'ra as well as a great comfort to both of us — I hope they
will stay some time longer — George looks pale & ill poor dear,
but is pretty well I think. Arthur & his wife & 1 girl staid here
about a week, & then went to Gweedore, taking Cass with them

> & George joined them there a little later, & Aug's & I kept house
> here together for nearly ten days, when they all returned, & the
> Arthurs went home soon after; he seemed well satisfied with his
> visit & reception, though I am afraid it has not brought him in
> any more money yet.[50]

As usual, Marianne concerned herself what had happened in the family,
not with the implications of her own last observation. Yet, it seems to be a fact
that Arthur viewed his estate in Donegal purely as a business. If money did not
come in, the business would require restructuring, and the position of his aunt
and sister might become even more tenuous. The family, from Edward Austen
Knight onward, had not laid great store by any attachment of aunts and sisters to
properties which were not paying their way. So, while Marianne moved straight
on to the September weather and its effect on the harvest – 'little sunshine, but
happily not much rain lately, and the harvest progresses I hope satisfactorily
tho' slowly' – and though she tried to show interest in the engagement of one
of the younger members of the family about to be married, she struggled to
find her old enthusiasm. 'I suppose somebody has left him a good property,'
she wrote, '& I am glad of it, my coffee pot will do very well'. [51]

Unsurprisingly, she seems to have been very depressed or, as Margaret
Knight had once described it, 'under it all'. Louisa's dying while she was absent
from home might have accounted by itself for Marianne's low spirits, yet there
was another cause. On the inside of the envelope of her birthday letter, she
had written a note to her favourite nephew: '1000 thanks d'st. Monty for yr
most kind invite to me — I hope to be able to accept it'. Montagu had offered
Marianne a home at Chawton if she should have to leave Ballyare. He had not,
however, extended the invitation to Cassandra:

> Cass sends her love & bids me say to Monty that as he does
> not invite her to go to Chawton with me, she shall do her best
> to make other plans for herself, *or* stay on here!! I cd not live
> anywhere else happily: this place is so full of dear At. Lou, I shd.
> hate to leave it & Cass could not live here alone.[52]

It was all happening again, a grim repetition of Marianne's experience after the deaths first of her father, then her brother Charles, when she had written to Fanny: 'I can't live by myself.' Now, Cassandra Hill, who had been, on her first birthday, the whole family's 'poor little darling', became the latest woman in Jane Austen's family to face the likelihood of losing the only home she had ever known.[53]

It was a time of evictions; Arthur, unable to outwit McFadden, and watching his chances of recovery diminish with each successive land act, had to consider his position in Donegal. By implication, this meant that he had also to consider the position of his aunt and his sister and, while they did not face, like Arthur's tenants, the misery of watching while the roof was removed or the door broken down by a battering ram, they too were facing eviction. Marianne, with more experience of the process than most of her family, had cause to be depressed. On 28 September, she wrote directly to Montagu to thank him for his offer of a home at Chawton, and to tell him how matters stood with his cousin Arthur. Her tone was kind and friendly as, necessarily practical, she accepted his invitation for herself without mentioning his omission of Cassandra. Her niece's spirited declaration of independence had already been conveyed through Florence and, while she continued to worry about Cassandra, Marianne could not afford to refuse her only offer of a home:

> Your most kind letter must be answered at once with 1000 thanks from me to Florence as well as to your dear self for offering me your own beloved home as a safe & comfortable refuge for my old age if I leave this — nothing decided can be known till November when Arthur will examine his accts & discover whether we have lived within our income or not, and act accordingly. If we may stay on here, I had rather do so: the place is so full of reminiscences of my last darling Sister. I shd very much grieve to leave it and so wd. Cass'ra for many reasons — at the same time if we have to go, I shall be delighted to accept your most kind and affectionate offer … if I am spared, I trust to pay you all a visit in the spring.[54]

A week earlier, Marianne had written another letter of thanks for birthday greetings, this time to Edward Bridges Rice, the eldest of Lizzy's fifteen children. As a young girl still in her teens, she had assisted Lizzy at Edward's birth in 1819 and, a year later, when Fanny and Lizzy went to London to choose Fanny's wedding clothes, the child had been left in her charge. He must have referred to this in his letter, for Marianne, so stoic since her last sister's death, briefly became the light-hearted, joyous young girl who had climbed with her sister to the top of the cow-house, and danced in white slippers at the first ball of her life:

> Yes! I had the honor [sic] to teach you to walk in the dear old Library at my darling home; we were near the little low white door when you took your first step alone to my great delight — dearest Mama had gone to London to help Aunt Knatchbull choose her wedding finery, & you were left with me & drst Grandpapa & Cakey — Oh dear! It wrings my old wizened heart to think of those blissful times passed in our beloved Paradise — I cannot write much so please to excuse a short stupid letter.[55]

Seventy years had narrowed the gap in their ages: now they were ailing, and in the winter of their lives, the past brighter and more real for both of them than the exhausting present. Cassandra too, though forty years Marianne's junior, had been suffering from low spirits since the death of Louisa and the consequent uncertainty of her future, and went to stay with her sister Norah at Isle O'Valla. It was well that she was there, for something happened which meant that she had to support Norah, rather than have Norah cheer her. Somerset Ward had sustained a serious injury, 'having been dragged on the ground about 40 yards or so by his runaway horse, & concussion of the brain following'.[56] Cassandra, who had once considered opening a nursing home, was well able to care for her brother-in-law and her sister, for Norah became ill with the shock. Yet Marianne, who now depended on her niece as her father had once depended on her, did not feel happy until Cassandra came home. When she did, however sorry she was for the Wards, Marianne was 'delighted to have her back again'.[57]

In Gweedore, meanwhile, the hotel had begun to recover from its boycotting, and even to benefit from the aftermath of the murder of Inspector Martin. A party of ladies from London wrote in the *Hotel Book* for 13 September 1889: 'We regret that this comfortable hotel is not near Derrybeg as the walk is a long one to Father McFadden where the interest of the district is centred.'[58] Marianne understood that Arthur, when he visited Donegal, wanted to see a return from his investments in the property and the business. She understood too that, like the tenants, she and Cassandra were expendable. With all that was happening in her immediate family it is perhaps unsurprising that Marianne's letters do not, after that unambiguous statement of 1887, comment on the social upheaval all around her, though in a sense, her carefully apolitical letters may make in themselves an oblique comment on the uncertainty of the times. In every way, it would have been inappropriate for her to comment on Inspector Martin's death.

The only passage which could be taken to refer to the volatile state of the countryside in 1889 came in November, when she apologised to Montagu and Florence because she could not invite their son, Henry Knight, then stationed in Ireland, to come and visit. Fourteen years before, when he was a chronically seasick naval cadet, Louisa had sent Henry detailed instructions on finding Ballyare. Now, Cassandra had met him, and been concerned for his appearance of ill-health: yet, he could not be invited. November, the month when he might have come, was when tenants were required to pay their rents.[59] Arthur, in examining his accounts, would decide the future of his aunt and sister. November 1889 would be too tense a time to have a visitor in Ballyare. 'I greatly dislike,' Marianne wrote, 'knowing he is in Ireland, & not being able to ask him to come here & pay us a visit: but I am afraid it can't be — but if affairs mend, & we can invite him sometime or other I trust he will be able to come & see us.' Marianne missed her family and this letter, like so many following Louisa's death, reflects an ever-deepening loneliness, which she no longer tried to conceal. 'I have grown in my old age so idle, & get so soon tired of writing that I put it off ... but that does not mean that I forget my dear relations, be they at Chawton or elsewhere, & I highly enjoy hearing tidings of them.'[60]

To add to Marianne's loneliness, Cassandra was again with her sister Norah in November 1889. During that long, difficult autumn, Marianne stayed at

Ballyare, accompanied only by her nephew Augustus Hill and, though she continued to interest herself in the garden, the weather and the rituals of everyday life, her sadness and anxiety were palpable:

> Our weather too has been beautiful & mild till the few last days, when rain & wind, & now snow have succeeded, & I have not been out of the house since Tuesday, & then only to Church in the carriage. Today seems better, between the snow showers, sunny & nice — Augustus & I have been here for nearly 7 weeks, whilst Cass. is holidaying — she gives us hopes of returning home next week, & I hope very much she will, & will be much the better for her visits.[61]

In the end, having examined his accounts in November, Arthur allowed his aunt and sister to stay on at Ballyare. Marianne, with her niece and one of her nephews, visited the hotel in person in September 1890. It is unsurprising that no comment beyond the careful, 'Hotel very comfortable', was made in the *Hotel Book*. Interestingly, it was eighty-nine-year-old Marianne and not her middle-aged nephew who signed the book for all three.[62] Though they had been permitted to stay on at Ballyare, however, Marianne had enough experience to know this could not be more than a stay of execution. The death of Inspector Martin and its aftermath had altered irretrievably the relation of landlord and tenant in Gweedore. Arthur's making it clear that Marianne and Cassandra's tenure depended on their ability to manage their finances, and Montagu's offer of a home for one but not the other, brought home the reality of their situation.

Isolated in Donegal, they were at the last outpost, almost at the edge of the world as far as their family was concerned. Marianne's last letters, sent between the death of Louisa in 1889 and her own six years later, reflect a growing sense of detachment, despite the realisation that Arthur could and might at any moment ask her to find herself another home. She did not want to be parted from her dear niece, the youngest Cassandra: they had come to share, in a late-found symbiosis, a certain ironically mordant humour, ostensibly mild, yet just short of acerbic, reminiscent of their aunt Jane. The letters of this period reflect that bittersweet acceptance of life as it was, not as they might have wished it to be.

Their experience did not harden Marianne and Cassandra towards anyone, even Arthur, for when he came down with a cold while visiting Ballyare in February 1890 – coincidentally, on the first anniversary of the murder of Inspector Martin – they nursed him through it with their usual care and affection.[63] Nonetheless, Marianne clearly felt her own increasing infirmity. 'I can do very little,' she wrote in July 1890, 'indoors or out.' Unable to engage in her greatest pleasure, she had to be content to watch. 'This fine weather is very pleasant for being out in the garden & sitting on benches admiring the flowers,' she told Florence, 'particularly my favourite roses which had been abundant & delicious, & so has our fruit been.'[64] In that winter, with frosts and what she described as 'an immense flood', she felt the cold, keenly, and had to make an effort to finish her letters, rather than rest by the fire.[65]

Despite her increasing infirmity, Marianne did not become selfish or inward-looking, though she tended to wish for more letters than she received. She continued to try to cheer the others, keeping a faithful record in her head of all their joys and problems, rarely failing to enquire or offer to help. When Florence Knight fell ill in January 1891, Marianne comforted her with the words of the eighteenth-century poet James Thomson, whose work Jane Austen had known : ' "Gentle Spring Ethereal, mildness come", — as Thompson [sic] prettily says in his Seasons —.'[66] She would write that Cassandra was recovering from her own ill-health, or had just come in from the garden, and regret again that she could not join her and work with her. 'I have not been out of the house for many weeks,' she wrote in early April 1891, 'though I am very thankful to say I am almost, if not quite well again; but the Doctor begged me not on any account to go out whilst this bitterly cold wintry East Wind continued, & as it still keeps on, I obediently stay in the house longing daily to pace round the garden.'[67]

Home was still 'beloved England', yet, even when summer came, though she travelled as far as Norah's house in County Down, she was in two minds about travelling further: the journey was too long and wearying and, though she hated to admit it, she felt too 'shaky and tottery'.[68] In the end, she appears not to have gone: her spirits were low and, writing to Florence, feeling deprived of news for a long time, she was uncharacteristically distant. 'I have but little to say,' she wrote, with a touch of asperity, 'so my epistle will not detain you long from more important business.'[69] By September 1891, however, she had clearly received a series of kind letters from Montagu and Florence, who may have realised how lonely and unwell she was beginning to feel. 'They all rejoiced my heart, & my warmest thanks are due to each beloved writer,' Marianne wrote in gratitude. That winter was severe, with a 'terrible gale' which cost the grounds of Ballyare many trees. 'It was wondrous fierce,' she marvelled, in one of those expressions which, so reminiscent of eighteenth-century diction, serve as a reminder that she was more familiar with that world than the more modern one around her.[70] In the summer of 1892, Ballyare House was to be painted, and Marianne, Cassandra and Augustus all decamped, not to the Gweedore Hotel, but to Moville – just as almost eighty years before, the young Marianne and her family had moved to Chawton while Godmersham was redecorated. Then, in addition to her father, brothers and sisters, Marianne had had family nearby in her grandmother and her aunts Cassandra and Jane. Now it was one very old lady, with a middle-aged niece and nephew, who moved out for the summer. To their surprise, the change suited them all: yet, as none of them was rich, 'expense [was] the counter-irritant for', as Marianne wrote, 'we like being here very much.'[71]

The following winter weakened her further and, in February 1893, once more unable to go out, she was greatly cast down by the deaths of Lizzy's son Cecil Rice, and Fanny's eldest son, Lord Brabourne. Increasingly conscious of her age and frailty, she began to withdraw into herself. 'I can't write fit to be seen,' she wrote to Florence in April 1893, 'as you will see, for which reason I very seldom now write any letters and very rarely receive any.' Her nephew George had gone to visit the Wards, and she felt the loneliness of the house, unrelieved even by the presence of Cassandra.[72] Cassandra had been ill again, and by May was 'gone for a fortnight to her brother Arthur's to be braced up'. Left alone with George, Marianne sorely missed her niece.[73] On her ninety-second birthday in 1893, she thanked Florence for 'remembering my old birthday', adding ruefully, 'my writing power is well nigh over, & I shall be obliged to ask you to put up with a few lines only'.[74] By her next birthday, 15 September 1894, she had not only Cassandra, but also Augustus and George with her in the house. She was

now very frail, and her mode of conveyance was similar to that used by Jane
Austen when, in her last illness, she could no longer walk:

> I am steadily losing strength and the use of my limbs — I can
> scarcely walk at all but I do not complain as I am well-provided
> with vehicles from some of our kind neighbours and also have
> a very comf. basket chair, drawn by a capital donkey led by a
> famous boy … We keep one horse, a very good one who draws
> the very nice little Phaeton our friend lends me — So you will
> see that I am very well off. I dislike cars and never get into one
> if I can help it.[75]

Marianne had now entered the last year of her life. She was obliged to
have letters read to her; yet she managed in February 1895 to write in her old
conversational teasing style to her eldest nephew, Edward Bridges Rice, on
the occasion of his son Henry's forthcoming marriage. Though now in his
mid-seventies Edward was still, to Marianne, the first child she had welcomed
into the world; and their shared history seemed to awaken her old brightness
of spirit:

> … if I were as young as you are I would write my thanks & congrats
> on a larger sheet of paper, but as the case stands, I am obliged
> to content myself with this tiny miserly scrap which I hope you
> will manage to read, before you throw it into the blazing fire.
> I hope writing your very nice letter to me did not tire you too
> much. I liked your letter so much, & so did Cassandra, who
> helped me read it. I think the sound of Henry's Missis a very
> nice one, and I send him and you my hearty congratulations, &
> best love. It seems to be the fashion to be poor, so of course I
> am, but if I can hunt up a new 6d before very long, I shall send
> it to Henry to spend on a wedding present for himself — if it
> never arrives, tell him I am probably frozen, or in prison. I am
> so very sorry you have been ill, dearest Edward, and sincerely

trust you are getting better, and will soon be well again. What severe weather we are having! Not at all pleasant, and very cold indeed. I have not been out of the house for ever so long, & I hope you have not either. I am pretty well, thank you, but weak enough to satisfy anybody — this is very pretty and nice to write upon — the paper I mean — I can't write any more now; so Goodbye my dearest Edward ...[76]

It is a return to the lively, funny, generous Marianne whom Edward Rice had undoubtedly known, the sadness and depression following her last sister's death and the possibility of yet another house move seeming, however fleetingly, to recede. She was aided in her enjoyment of this forthcoming wedding by Cassandra's adding her own postscript to the cousin who had once, long ago, been in love with her sister, Norah. The same tone, the same ironic, playful turns of phrase, indicate how well attuned she and her aunt were:

So 'the girl that had hold of the tow rope' has landed her 'boy' safely! & I enclose a line in Aunt May's letter to wish you & Cecy joy very heartily, as Miss Godley sounds so nice & moreover has *Irish* blood in her; I do not think that is a drawback in your opinion (remembering pathetic reminiscences of Julia O'Sullivan!) (poor thing, I always think you behaved rather badly to her, so you had better be doubly kind to Miss Helen Godley on the other's account. Of course you won't show this to Cecy). An't I a bad girl? I mean *old woman*, how one does forget that one gets old ...[77]

In this, which may be Cassandra Hill's only surviving letter, it is possible to see that something of Jane Austen's liveliness of spirit had transferred itself to her. Yet, unlike most of her English relatives, as Jane herself might have been the first to acknowledge, Cassandra clearly valued her Irish heritage. It is unlikely that Jane Austen would have told this great-niece that she did not know the manners of Ireland.

Happy though they were, Marianne and Cassandra did not have much longer together. Marianne's last letter of all was written to Montagu on 22 July 1895 and, rather poignantly, concerns a gift he had made to her of Jane's charade book.[78] Marianne, struggling to write her thanks, was indeed touched by the gift. Yet, she had clearly quite forgotten that her aunt was also the acclaimed novelist, Jane Austen:

> A grand party of thanks with my best love I send you for yr 2 last letters & dear Aunt Jane's Charade book, which I very much enjoy looking at. I had no idea of its existence till you informed me of it: I knew she was clever, but in what way I did not know. I am very nearly an idiot & can scarcely do anything — that's why I directed my letter wrong just now — but I have made it right now I hope — I have burnt it — I thank you very much, drst Monty for yr famous act of the Rice wedding —it did famously... Now Good bye, Cass & George join me in best love to you and drst Flo — I hate sending you such a tiny scrawl, but I can't help it, and hope you will be able to read it.[79]

This was, indeed, goodbye. It is strange to see Marianne, who remembered for so long the disappointment and frustration she felt on being excluded from Jane Austen's readings, unable to remember at the end of her life what it was that made her aunt Jane clever. Nonetheless, in this gallant last letter, she held on to her own mind and her wit long enough to remember the family members she was used to, if not the one she had last seen almost sixty years before.

Born in the first year of a new century, Marianne Knight almost saw it out. In a life of genteel servitude, she was able to accept and support the tradition which shunted her about from house to house in the wider interests of the family and of the society she knew. The series of land acts which effectively signalled the end of the privileged life prized and sustained by landowners, not only in Ireland but also in England, almost over-stretched her comprehension and her compassion. In the end, however, through her own ability to be at home wherever she found herself, and through her deep bond with Cassandra Hill, who was as conscious of her Irish blood as of her English, Marianne appears to have become resigned to Ireland and its contradictions.

'She was a humble, believing Christian,' James Edward Austen Leigh wrote, in his *Memoir* of his aunt Jane. 'Her life had been passed in the performance of home duties, and the cultivation of domestic affections, without any self-seeking or craving after applause. Her sweetness of temper never failed.'[80] He might have said the same of his cousins May, Lou and Cass. Quite unacquainted with the ways and the history of Ireland, struggling with varying degrees of success to come to terms with the place, they all ended their days and lie buried there. On the grave of the youngest, Cassandra, the inscription chosen by her husband speaks to his grief at her untimely death: 'The Lord giveth and the Lord hath taken away: blessed be the name of the Lord.' Death indeed came early for Cassandra Knight, as it had for her mother, and for the aunt who admired the young girl's bright eyes and stoic spirit. Yet, of the three youngest daughters of Edward Knight, indeed of the five youngest children left outside on the stairs while their sisters listened to Jane's story, only Cassandra seems to have experienced the heights and depths of romantic passion. She paid dearly for it, dying far from her family and the home she had loved, leaving behind a devoted husband and four little motherless children.

Louisa knew a different kind of love: equally faithful and openly affectionate, she left all she knew first from loyalty and kindness, and later through a genuine attachment. For her, there was the comfort of a companionate marriage. Doubtless, she was loved and valued by her husband and stepchildren, and by her only son; yet, her husband chose to be buried beside his first love, Cassandra. When Louisa died, she lay alone for six years until Marianne joined her. It may indeed be for Marianne, the eldest and last of the three Knight sisters in Ireland, who so reminded James Edward of his aunt that he fell in love with her, that his tribute to Jane Austen has a particular relevance. Despite her likeness to the aunt they both so admired, when Marianne Knight died at Ballyare House on 4 December 1895, the world she had inherited and understood was rapidly disappearing.[81] If death came too early for Cassandra, it left Marianne until she had outlived not only her own generation, but a number of the next. She had never known the joys or troubles of marriage and children; yet, she had lived, and she, too, was loved. Something of the eager young girl she had been stayed with her to the end: her never-failing delight in her garden; the remembered joy of charades played with Jane and her family during long-ago winters; a sudden recollection of the excitement of teaching her first nephew to walk. Even when she had put away her dancing slippers, long after anyone thought her 'bewitching beautiful', Marianne's quick humour and lively sympathy, her dignified bearing in loss and adversity and, above all, her own natural grace endeared her to those who knew her, and enabled her to find her way in an increasingly incomprehensible world. At the end of her life, as ever, she went where she was welcome, slipping quietly into a space beside her sister.

They are buried side by side in the little graveyard of Tully, close to Ballyare House, not far from the small town of Ramelton. Set high on a hill, Tully is a beautiful place, shaded by yew trees from the worst effects of the winter winds.[82] The sisters lie together by a sheltering wall, one headstone leaning toward the other. Their inscriptions are simple: Marianne is remembered as the third daughter of Edward Knight Esquire of Godmersham Park, Louisa as the widow of Lord George Augusta Hill, of Ballyare and Gweedore. Two scriptural quotations, almost obscured, serve as reminders of the essential beliefs which sustained them in their exile: 'I shall be satisfied when I wake with thy likeness,' is inscribed below Louisa's name; below Marianne's, even more simply, 'I am the Resurrection and the Life'.

POSTSCRIPT

A New Century

Ah! — ' said Mr Parker. — 'This is my old house — the house of my
forefathers — the house where I and all my brothers and sisters were born
and bred — and where my own three eldest children were born — where
Mrs Parker and I lived till within the last two years — till our new house
was finished … It is an honest old place — and Hillier keeps it in very good
order. I have given it up you know to the man who occupies the chief of my
land. He gets a better house by it — and I, a better situation!'

SANDITON

The life of Marianne Knight, beginning so near to the start of a new century,
drew to a close almost at its end. Her youngest sister, the enigmatic, strong-
willed Cassandra, died only five years into the Victorian era: she did not live
to see the the gradual erosion of her husband's power and standing. Louisa, on
the other hand, lived through the great changes wrought in the second half of
the century, feeling their full effect and unable to comprehend why her own
efforts seemed to yield so little result. Yet, though she had the longest life of all
her family, Marianne did not ask herself the questions that so troubled Louisa.
Instead, an exile from the home and land she loved, she became increasingly
distant from the changes all around her so that at the end she found it easier,
as the very old sometimes choose to do, to return to the memory of what she
termed 'our lost paradise' – Godmersham in Kent. It was not a strategy which
could work for everyone. The youngest child of Lord George and Cassandra,
Cassandra Jane Louisa Hill, the last companion of Marianne's life, had no such
memory to return to as she witnessed the collapse of the life and the system to
which she had been accustomed, and which she had expected to continue.

Cassandra Hill, brought up by Louisa, was imbued, like the Knight
sisters, with the Georgian sense that, while politeness was all, borders must be

maintained between the classes. The only one of the Hill children to be born in Ireland, she cared for the tenants of the estate, instructing them in, among other skills, the Irish language, which as her father's daughter she knew and loved. In some ways Cassandra's situation anticipated that of the novelist and daughter of the Big House, Elizabeth Bowen, born in 1899: living through the troubled times of a century Cassandra would merely glimpse, Elizabeth Bowen understood the fine line between absolute politeness and the maintenance of protective barriers. She believed that 'politeness is not constriction; it is a grace; it is really no worse than an exercise of the imagination on other people's behalf'.[1] Cassandra Hill's closest friend, Charlotte Grace O'Brien, was the daughter of a convicted felon, the Young Irelander and fellow-member of the Protestant Ascendancy, William Smith O'Brien: it was a matter of politeness to Cassandra Hill to ignore the fact that her friend's father had once been sentenced to be hanged, drawn and quartered for treason, and that he had in fact been transported for his part in the rising of 1848. Cassandra was capable of admiring Charlotte's good mind and independent stance, commending in principle her desire to improve the social conditions of the oppressed, while disagreeing completely with her support for Home Rule. The movement baffled and saddened Cassandra: unlike Marianne, she could not simply state that the tenants ought to be severely punished, and leave it at that. Cassandra Hill, like Elizabeth Bowen and unlike Marianne and her sisters, was one of the Anglo-Irish gentry who, all over the country, were seeing the disintegration of all that their families had built up. As Charlotte O'Brien's nephew, Stephen Gwynn, later recalled:

> One of Charlotte O'Brien's closest friends in Donegal, Miss Cassandra Hill, daughter of old Lord George Hill, laboured strenuously to promote among the peasantry pleasant social life – reading, writing, dancing, and the study of the Irish tongue – but to promote only what she herself would entirely approve. She could never have been what Charlotte O'Brien was – a link between Will Upton, the Fenian, prouder of hs Fenianism than of anything else, and Aubrey de Vere, the cultivated Irish

Unionist, lover of his country and of his people, but opponent
of their ideals.

The result appeared when a new revolution began. It drove
Miss Hill and all of her kind, good kindred into despairing
opposition to those whom they had loved and for whom they
had laboured – those peasants of Gweedore, who in my boyhood
would have drawn Lord George's old pony phaeton from the back
of Errigal to his hall door at Ballyarr [sic]. It found Charlotte
O'Brien confident in her faith that justice must be done, even
though the sky should fall upon herself and her own class.[2]

The sky would fall upon the class of Charlotte O'Brien, Elizabeth Bowen
and Cassandra Hill even though, as Gwynn himself had observed, the pursuit
of justice had been the stated goal of Cassandra's father, Lord George. 'Over
the harbourmaster's office [in Bunbeg] you will trace Lord George Hill's hand
in the inscription from Proverbs, set up there in Irish, "A just weight is a
pleasure to the Lord, but an unequal balance is an abomination in his sight." '[3]
Cassandra clearly believed that in educating the tenantry, with regard for the
language and customs of Ireland, she was acting in the best and just interests of
everyone. In this she had, for eleven years, the support of Marianne, and their
close, almost symbiotic relationship was only slightly marred by anxiety over
where they might live if Arthur Hill should, as he indicated he might, dispose
of Ballyare. Yet, despite Cassandra's declarations of independence, Marianne
worried, until the detachment of approaching death removed from her the
need or capacity to do so, that Cassandra would be left to manage alone at
Ballyare. It did not happen. Cassandra did not endure the distress of seeing her
house demolished, as Elizabeth Bowen eventually did: yet, like Marianne and
Jane Austen, she lost her home. Shortly after Marianne's death, Arthur Hill,
following the precedent set by his uncle Edward Knight in 1874, sold the family
home.[4] Cassandra was obliged, after all, to find herself somewhere else to live.
No record exists of the offer of a refuge from any of her cousins in England: yet,
Cassandra was not without support. Just as the rebel Lord Edward's daughter
Pamela had aided Louisa's passage through the complications of Irish society
in the middle of the nineteenth century, so the convicted felon's daughter,

Charlotte O'Brien, proved herself Cassandra's true friend at its end. As Stephen Gwynn later explained, Charlotte decided to build a house outside Dublin in Foxrock, 'then a place of whins and stone'.[5] She called it '*Fáilte*', the Irish word for welcome. In a time of loss and sadness, *Fáilte* became Cassandra's refuge and, before long, her last home.[6] Charlotte O'Brien, finding that her relatives, the Gwynns, had decided to leave Foxrock, lived there only a short time. 'After a few years,' Gwynn wrote, 'she sold it to the friend who had been its most frequent tenant'.[7] It was at *Fáilte*, on 16 August 1901, that Cassandra Hill died after an illness lasting over a week; her death certificate giving the cause as 'haematoma, 8 days' and 'exhaustion'.[8] She was fifty-nine years old.

As Estyn Evans, editor of the only twentieth-century edition of *Facts from Gweedore*, pointed out in 1971: 'You cannot send those of planter stock back across the water, any more than you can recall millions of Irishmen from America.'[9] To him, the 'clash of native and newcomer … struck the sparks in Irish culture'.[10] Cassandra, Louisa, and their sister Marianne had been newcomers: the children of the next generation were not. They were, however, by the beginning of the twentieth century, suffering from the weary exhaustion experienced by many of the Anglo-Irish gentry. Cassandra's brothers, Augustus and George, neither of whom married, did not live to see old age. Augustus, who was present at the death of his younger sister, was sixty-nine when he died in 1908 and the youngest brother George, Louisa's delicate only son, who had retired from the practice of the law and come to live with Cassandra at *Fáilte*, died on 22 March 1911 of 'malignant disease of liver' and, like his sister, 'exhaustion'.[11] He was aged sixty-two. Arthur, who outlived all his siblings, died in 1923. He had been married since 1871 to Helen Emily Chenevix Trench, daughter of the Archbishop of Dublin, and the couple had seven children. Arthur based himself at Wilford House, Bray, in Wicklow, not far from Foxrock, so that the family, though no longer involved in the life of Donegal, were together in the capital. Ireland was still part of the Empire, and the careers of two of Arthur's sons reflect their sense of belonging not only to Ireland but also to that Empire. His eldest son, Arthur Fitzgerald Sandys Hill (1876–1961) succeeded to the title, and became 6th Lord Sandys, Baron of Ombersley; his second son, Vice Admiral Hon. Sir Richard Augustus Sandys Hill (1880–1954) fought in the Somaliland Campaign from 1902 to 1904, and in the Great War of

1914–18, later serving as aide-de-camp to George V in 1930, then seeing active service in the Second World War.

Though Cassandra's elder daughter, Norah, died in 1920, before Partition, her children became deeply involved in the unfolding history of Ireland, and especially in the emergence of what became Northern Ireland. When Somerset Ward wrote in 1881 to his brother-in-law Arthur Hill that he would help him deal with his unruly tenants once 'the wedding [was] over', he was referring to the marriage of his daughter, Norah Louisa Fanny Ward, to a young man named Henry Lyle Mulholland.[12] He was the son of John Mulholland, a businessman in the linen trade, who had been MP for Downpatrick from 1874 to 1885: 'a strong supporter of Tory politics', he was raised to the peerage in 1892 to become 1st Baron Dunleath of Ballywalter, County Down.[13] Norah Ward's husband became the 2nd Baron Dunleath on the death of his father in 1895, and the family lived at Ballywalter Park. The Mulhollands' eldest son, Andrew Edward Somerset, of whose imminent birth Marianne had written from Isle O'Valla in September 1882, died in September 1914 at Ypres.

Henry Lyle Mulholland, who lived until 1931, was a Justice of the Peace for County Down, and MP for North Londonderry from 1885 until 1895. Ballywalter Park was a meeting place for prominent political figures, such as Col E.J. Saunderson. Staunchly Unionist, and utterly opposed to Home Rule, he had been compelled to retract a condemnation of Gweedore's Father McFadden as a 'ruffian' after the murder of Inspector Martin in 1889.[14] His family made an alliance with that of the Knights when his son John married the Mulhollands' second child, Eva Norah Helen, while two of Eva's brothers, Charles and Henry, married into another significant political family. Charles (1886–1956), who also fought in the First World War and was awarded the DSO, acting as Military Secretary to the second-last Lord Lieutenant of Ireland from 1919 to 1921, succeeded to the Dunleath title in 1920 and married Sylvia Brooke, daughter of Sir Arthur Brooke of Colebrooke. Sylvia, who died in 1921, a year after her marriage to Charles Mulholland, was the sister of Basil, later 1st Viscount Brookeborough, Prime Minister of Northern Ireland until 1963. Charles's younger brother Henry, or Harry (1888–1971), another veteran of the First World War, had married Sylvia's sister Sheelah Brooke. As the Rt Hon. Sir Henry Mulholland, he was elected MP for County Down to Northern Ireland's first Parliament at Stormont, in 1921, becoming Speaker of the House in 1929. These great-great-grandnephews and nieces of Jane Austen could not have been more involved in the setting up of Northen Ireland, a fact which might well have awakened the ironic amusement of their distant aunt, in the light of her warning to her niece Anna to avoid writing about Ireland, since she knew nothing of 'the manners there'.

Other, more personal legacies came down to the Irish descendants of Jane Austen's brother Edward. Norah Dunleath expressed a marked disdain for too much heating in the house, a characteristic inherited from the Knights of Godmersham and Chawton, used to dealing with grand, cold houses. Even on a bleak winter's day in Donegal during late November 1890 Marianne, aged eighty-nine, struggled to finish her family letters before allowing herself to go and sit by the heat of the fire.[15] 'The house was cold in winter,' 4th Baron Dunleath remembered of his childhood in Ballywalter Park, 'as my grandmother had dispensed with the 1849 hot air central heating system since she considered it to be unhealthy'.[16] A frugal refusal to give in to cold, like the inherited love of the natural world, continued as the generations changed. At Ballywalter, the gardens were developed and tended by successive generations of Norah's family, as her grandson ruefully recalled: 'My grandparents were responsible for designing the rock and water garden and there have been many times when both my father and I wished that they had not bothered.'[17] Norah Dunleath, known to her grandchildren as Gogo, loved to entertain and give house parties, quite in the style of the Godmersham of Jane Austen's time. She had, moreover, another passion inherited from the Knights, as her grandson wrote:

> My grandmother was also a compulsive ornithologist and had an aviary with adjacent enclosed pens which contained exotic and screeching birds. This cannot have added much to the appearance of the garden anymore than could have the deerpark in front of the house which must have looked something like the Maze Prison with a ten foot high fence round it to prevent

the deer from escaping ... Whatever happens we shall always do our best to maintain this garden's personality ... I am thankful indeed to my forbears for having left me with a framework of such potential ...[18]

This love of the garden and birds provides one enduring link between Jane Austen and these, her Irish family. Where politics was concerned, however, though generally conservative and unwilling to condone the need for violent action in the great or the small, Jane Austen could not be cited as their most powerful influence, for she preferred to keep her political opinions to herself.

None of Edward Knight's children were required to face the terrible recurring bitterness of Ireland in the twentieth century, yet one of his descendants, many times great-nephew of Jane Austen and of May, Lou and Cass, had to face the consequences of that long struggle. 'If I were to be reborn and God asked me how I would like to come back,' wrote Timothy Knatchbull in 2009, 'I would say English. But if there were no positions available, I would be sorely tempted to choose Irish.'[19] Few of Jane Austen's family in England could have made such a statement, especially if they had been through all that Timothy Knatchbull had endured. His grandfather, Lord Mountbatten, and his twin brother Nicholas were among those killed in August 1979 by an IRA bomb at Mullaghmore in Sligo, close to Donegal. Yet, Timothy Knatchbull, like Cassandra Hill and her brothers, knew Ireland well from childhood, and found himself able not only to forgive what had happened, but also to understand the motivation of the perpetrators. 'By revisiting Ireland,' he wrote, 'I slowly became better informed, and as I re-evaluated my experiences I eventually found the path to being able to forgive.'[20]

He went further still. Cassandra Hill had, while disagreeing with Charlotte O'Brien's politics, been able to accept that her friend held radically different beliefs: Timothy Knatchbull found himself able to understand and forgive the extreme political beliefs and terrible actions of a man he had never known. This was Thomas McMahon, one of those convicted of the bomb which killed Timothy Knatchbull's grandfather, brother and friend, and severly injured his parents. 'Perhaps the most difficult question was how I felt about Thomas

McMahon,' he wrote of his time spent trying to comprehend what had happened. 'At the end of the year I accepted at least this: that if I had been born into a republican stronghold, lived my life as dictated by conditions in Northern Ireland, and been educated through the events of the 1960s and 1970s, my life might well have turned out the way the way Thomas McMahon's did. In this respect I felt ultimately inalienable from him.' [21]

This extraordinary act of compassion, the ultimate encapsulation of Elizabeth Bowen's definition of politeness as the imaginative consideration of others, recalls a fundamental faith held by Jane Austen. Never called upon to deal with Ireland, and opposed to her niece's even contemplating it, she knew that each human being is 'ultimately inalienable' from the others. When she warned Anna Austen that, without knowing the manners of Ireland, she might be liable to give a false picture, she spoke a simple if inconvenient truth. Marianne, Louisa and Cassandra all found out for themselves that they were in a country so different from England as to be initially incomprehensible to them. Yet, they learned from Jane Austen. In the six novels and those letters which have survived, she left a record not only of elegance and wit but also of compassion for the frailty of the human condition, no less profound because couched in irony, and bounded by the politeness which governed all. It may be this quality of detached compassion which Marianne, Louisa and Cassandra, in their own different ways and according to their own human limitations, brought with them when they made the long and difficult journey to Ireland and which, having learned to love the place, they tried to pass on to the next generation. Timothy Knatchbull is, through Fanny, Edward Knight's descendant; his profound and moving declaration of imaginative compassion indicates that Jane Austen's family did indeed possess the capacity to learn 'the manners there'. Perhaps, in the end, the fact that the graves of Marianne, Louisa and Cassandra Knight lie, not in Godmersham or Chawton but in Donegal, not far from the spot where Timothy Knatchbull's terrible epiphany occurred, stands testimony to the efforts of Jane Austen's nieces to understand and declare their solidarity with their nearest and most distant neighbour.

LIST OF ABBREVIATIONS

CBK	Charles Bridges Knight
CEA	Cassandra Elizabeth Austen
CKS	Centre for Kentish Studies, Maidstone, Kent
EKR	Elizabeth Knight Rice, formerly Austen
FCK	Fanny Catherine Knatchbull, formerly Austen
GHB	*Gweedore Hotel Book*
HRO	Hampshire Record Office
JA	Jane Austen
JAHM	Jane Austen's House Museum
JEAL	James Edward Austen Leigh
LGH	Lord George Hill
MAAL	Mary Augusta Austen Leigh
MK	Marianne Knight, formerly Austen
PRONI	Public Record Office of Northern Ireland

TIMELINE

1775 Birth of Jane Austen (JA) at Steventon, Hampshire, 16 December
   The American Revolution begins

1779 Birth of JA's brother, Charles Austen

1783 Adoption of JA's brother Edward Austen (b.1767), later Knight, by
    Thomas and Catherine Knight of Godmersham, Kent

1785 JA and Cassandra (CEA, b.1773) sent to Abbey School, Reading

1786 Marriage of Arthur Hill, later 2nd Marquess of Downshire, to
    Mary Sandys

1787 JA begins writing

1788 Birth of Arthur Blundell Sandys Trumbull Hill, later 3rd Marquess
    of Downshire, 8 October

1789 The French Revolution begins
   Arthur Hill becomes 2nd Marquess of Downshire

1791 Edward Austen marries Elizabeth Bridges of Goodnestone Park,
    27 December

1792 JA's eldest brother, James Austen (b.1765) marries Anne Mathew
   CEA becomes engaged to Rev. Thomas Fowle

1793 Birth of Anna Austen, later Lefroy, daughter of James
   Birth of Fanny Catherine, later Knight (FCK), daughter of
    Edward and Elizabeth Austen, 23 January

1794 Death of Thomas Knight
   Edward Austen inherits estates at Godmersham and Chawton
   Birth of Edward (later Knight), son of Edward and Elizabeth
    Austen
   Death of Anne, wife of James Austen; Anna Austen makes
    prolonged stay in Steventon
   Thomas Lefroy meets JA

1795	Birth of George, later Knight, known to JA as 'itty Dordy', son of Edward and Elizabeth Austen
1796	Attempted invasion of Ireland by Wolfe Tone, with the assistance of the French
	Thomas Lefroy leaves for London
	Rev. Thomas Fowle leaves for West Indies
1797	JA's novel, *First Impressions* (later revised as *Pride and Prejudice*), completed; *Lady Susan* begun
	Birth of Henry, later Knight, son of Edward and Elizabeth Austen
	James Austen marries Mary Lloyd
1798	Rebellion in Ireland; Cornwallis succeeds Camden as Lord Lieutenant
	Birth of William, later Knight, son of Edward and Elizabeth Austen, first to be born at Godmersham
	Birth of James Edward, later Austen Leigh (JEAL), son of James and Mary Austen
1799	JA's brother, Henry Austen (b.1771) in Ireland, serving under Cornwallis
1800	Birth of Elizabeth Austen, later Knight (EKR), daughter of Edward and Elizabeth, January
	Rev. George Austen decides to retire as Rector of Steventon, December
1801	Act of Union of Great Britain and Ireland, 1 January
	Rev. George Austen moves his family to Bath; James Austen becomes Rector of Steventon
	Death of Arthur Hill, 2nd Marquess of Downshire, 7 September
	Birth of Marianne Austen, later Knight (MK), 15 September
	Birth of Lord George Hill, posthumous son of Arthur Hill, 2nd Marquess of Downshire, December
1802	JA accepts and next day refuses proposal of marriage from Harris Bigg-Wither of Manydown
	Mary Sandys, widow of 2nd Marquess of Downshire, created Baroness Sandys in her own right

1803	Arrest and execution in Dublin of Robert Emmet, following failed rebellion
	Birth of Charles Austen, later Knight (CBK), son of Edward and Elizabeth, March
	JA's novel *Susan,* later known as *Northanger Abbey*, sold to Crosky & Co., publishers
1804	Birth of Louisa Austen, later Knight, daughter of Edward and Elizabeth, 13 November
	JA thought to be engaged in writing *The Watsons* and *Lady Susan*
1805	Death of Rev. George Austen at Bath; JA ceases writing
	Birth of Caroline Austen, daughter of James and Mary, at Steventon, 18 June
1806	JA, CEA and their mother move to Southampton, lodging with Francis Austen and his wife
	Birth of Cassandra Jane Austen, later Knight, 16 November
1807	Austens move to Castle Square, Southampton
1808	Death of Elizabeth Austen, wife of Edward, following the birth of Brook John, 10 October
1809	MK and EKR sent away to school in Wanstead, 30 January
	Austens arrive in Chawton, 5 April; JA makes unsuccessful attempt to have *Lady Susan* published
	Arthur Hill, 3rd Marquess of Downshire, comes of age; commits himself to efficient management
1810	*Sense and Sensibility* accepted for publication
1811	Beginning of the Regency period
	Publication of *Sense and Sensibility*, September
	Arthur Hill, 3rd Marquess of Downshire, marries Lady Maria Windsor, eldest daughter of 5th Earl of Plymouth, 25 October
1812	Death of Catherine Knight, adoptive mother of Edward Austen
	Edward Austen's family takes the name of Knight
	JA sells copyright of *Pride and Prejudice* to Egerton
	Birth of Arthur Wills Blundell Sandys Trumbull Windsor Hill, later 4th Marquess of Downshire, 6 August

1813	Publication of *Pride and Prejudice*, 28 January
	Knights spend four months at Chawton; JA returns with Knights to Godmersham, via London
1814	Publication of *Mansfield Park*, 9 May
	Anna Austen marries Rev. Benjamin Lefroy, 8 November
1815	*Persuasion* begun, 8 August
	Illness of Henry Austen, nursed back to health by JA, October
	Publication of *Emma*, December
	Persuasion completed
1816	JA begins to feel unwell
	Failure of Austen, Maunde and Tilson, March: Henry Austen bankrupt; Edward suffers great financial loss
	Henry Austen enters the Church
1817	Death of James Leigh Perrot, 28 March; omission of Mrs Austen and her daughters grieves JA
	JA makes her will, April
	Edward Knight travels with EKR and George to Paris, May; EKR meets her future husband, Edward Royds Rice
	CEA travels with JA to Winchester in hope of cure, 24 May; William Knight and Henry Austen accompany them; JA and CEA stay at 8 College Street, attended by Mr Lyford; Mary Lloyd Austen helps CEA nurse JA; CBK visits from Winchester College
	JA dies, 18 July; buried in Winchester Cathedral, 24 July
	EKR coming out into society postponed until August following JA's death
	Posthumous publication of *Northanger Abbey* and *Persuasion*, December, dated 1818
1818	Lords George and Augustus Hill begin their Grand Tour of Europe
	EKR marries Edward Royds Rice, of Dane Court, Kent, 6 October
	MK enters society following EKR's marriage; her cousin JEAL, still an impecunious undergraduate at Oxford, falls in love with her; dissuaded by his father, James Austen

1819 Death of James Austen; JEAL and his family leave Steventon;
    Henry Austen holds the living until William Knight comes of
    age to take it over
    Birth of Edward Bridges Rice, son of EKR; MK in attendance

1820 Accession of George IV, formerly Prince Regent
    Henry Austen marries as his second wife Eleanor Jackson, niece to
    Mr Papillon, former Rector of Chawton
    FCK marries Sir Edward Knatchbull of Mersham le Hatch, Kent,
    24 October; Cassandra Knight (aged 16) to share
    governess with Sir Edward's daughter, Mary Dorothea
    MK takes over household management of Godmersham Park,
    aged nineteen

1822 MK refuses proposal of marriage from Rev. John Billington,
    November
    William Knight takes over Steventon living John Knight goes to
    school at Winchester; Henry Knight in 8th Light Dragoons;
    Edward Knight Jr Captain in East Kent Militia

1823 Formation in Ireland of Catholic Association, under Daniel
    O'Connell
    Edward Austen Knight supervises building of new Rectory at
    Steventon

1824 Birth of Elizabeth Louisa Rice (Louisa), daughter of EKR
    Birth of Fanny Elizabeth Knatchbull, first child of FCK

1825 William Knight marries Caroline Portal
    Birth of Marianne Sophia Rice, daughter of EKR

1826 Edward Knight Jr elopes to Scotland with Mary Dorothea
    Knatchbull, FCK's stepdaughter and Cassandra's former
    schoolfellow, 13/14 May

1827 Death of Mrs George Austen (née Cassandra Leigh), March
    Cassandra Knight meets Lord George Hill (LGH) in London,
    while staying with FCK
    Cassandra refuses a proposal from a Mr Burrows, June; LGH
    proposes, August; Cassandra accepts, but engagement called

off after opposition by LGH's mother, Lady Downshire

John Knight joins his regiment in Cork

1828 Duke of Wellington Prime Minister

Thomas Lefroy, former friend of JA, founds club to preserve 'integrity of the Protestant constitution'

Francis Austen marries, as second wife, Martha Lloyd, sister of Mary

Louisa Knight refuses proposal from Sir William Young

1829 Peel introduces Catholic Relief Bill, 5 March, enacted 5 April

Daniel O'Connell not permitted to take his seat in House of Commons

Louisa Knight receives proposal from George C. Oxenden

1830 Accession of William IV, 26 June

Daniel O'Connell first Catholic to take his seat in House of Commons

End of Louisa's relationship with George C. Oxenden

1831 Tumultuous Rising Act, following agrarian unrest in Ireland

LGH becomes MP for Carrickfergus, Co. Antrim, 1831–32

1833 Publication by Bentley of Collected Edition of JA's Novels (the Steventon Edition)

Henry Austen's revised *Memoir* published with *Sense and Sensibility*

Louisa Knight refuses proposal from Captain Stracey

LGH Comptroller of the Lord Lieutenant's Household in Dublin

Death of Sophia Knight, née Cage, wife and cousin of Henry Knight

1834 Melbourne dismissed; Peel forms Tory government

Cassandra Knight briefly engaged, July–August, to Musgrave Alured Harris; family disapproval ends engagement

LGH resumes his addresses August; marries Cassandra, 21 October, St George's, Hanover Square; newly married couple spend Christmas with Knights at Godmersham

1835	Peel resigns; Melbourne PM
	Death of Lady Salisbury (née Lady Emily Hill), maternal aunt of LGH, by fire at Hatfield House, 22 November
	Birth of Norah Hill, first child of Lord and Lady George Hill, at Godmersham, December
1836	Poor Relief Act in England, 31 July
	Death of Lady Downshire, LGH's mother
	Death of Jane Leigh Perrot; James Edward Austen inherits Scarlets; takes name of Austen Leigh
1837	Accession of Queen Victoria
	Birth of Arthur Blundell George Sandys Hill, 13 May
	Marriage of Arthur, later 4th Marquess of Downshire, to Caroline Cotton, daughter of 1st Viscount Combermere, 23 August
	George Knight marries Hilaire, Countess Nelson
1838	Extension of Poor Relief Act to Ireland, and Tithe Rent Act
	LGH begins purchase of estate at Gweedore, Co. Donegal
	Death of George Austen, brother of JA (b. 1766), in care since childhood
	CBK leaves Godmersham to become Rector of Chawton
	Death of Mary Knight (née Knatchbull), wife of Edward Knight Jr, following birth of William Brodnax
1839	Irish Poor Law Unions (Workhouses) come into existence
	Birth of Augustus Charles Edward Hill, son of Lord and Lady George, at Godmersham, 9 March
1840	First great meeting to press for repeal of the Union, Castlebar, Co. Mayo, 26 July
	Edward Knight Jr marries, as second wife, Adela Portal
1842	Daniel O'Connell Lord Mayor of Dublin
	Founding of *The Nation*
	Opening of LGH's Gweedore Hotel in Donegal
	Death of Cassandra, Lady George Hill, following birth of Cassandra Jane Louisa at Gartlee, Letterkenny, Donegal, 14/15 March 1842; Louisa and CBK go to Donegal for funeral

and burial of Cassandra at Conwal Cemetery, Letterkenny

Louisa takes charge of Hill children; LGH goes to London in April; takes house in summer at Updown, Kent, where Louisa continues to tend the children

Birth of James McFadden, future parish priest of Gweedore, at Carrigart, Co Donegal

1843 Arrest of Daniel O'Connell; William Smith O'Brien joins the Repeal Association

LGH, in London at first anniversary of Cassandra's death, taken ill and obliged to stay some days at house of FCK

1844 Daniel O'Connell imprisoned, January

Agrarian movemement ('Molly Maguires') active in Leitrim, Longford and Roscommon

Death of Henry Knight, June

Death of Mary Austen (née Lloyd), August

Birth of Montagu George Knight, son of Edward and Adela Knight, 26 October

Birth of Arthur Wills Blundell Trumbull Sandys Roden Hill, future 5th Marquess of Downshire

1845 Visit to Gweedore Hotel by John Mitchel, Charles Gavan Duffy and John O'Hagan

Widespread failure of potato harvest in Ireland, leading to Great Famine

Death of CEA at Portsmouth, home of her brother Francis; JA's letters and MSS distributed among family members

LGH publishes *Facts from Gweedore*, account of his work in Donegal

Louisa Knight spends all summer in Ireland with Hill children

Death of 3rd Marquess of Downshire, following riding accident

1846 Lord John Russell, PM, upholds policy of laissez-faire in Ireland despite widespread famine

Establishment of Famine Relief Commission; LGH, as chairman, requests further aid for tenants

Louisa Knight in Donegal and Godmersham with Hill children; commited to building of Glebe House for Protestant tenants of Gweedore

FCK asks former Godmersham governess, Miss Dorothy Chapman, to patronise LGH's *Facts from Gweedore* to augment Louisa's efforts

Birth of Lord Arthur Hill, 2nd son of 4th Marquess of Downshire

1847 Irish Confederation formed under William Smith O'Brien

LGH launches appeal for Famine Relief

Marriage of LGH and Louisa Knight at Wandsbeck, Denmark, 11 May

1848 John Mitchel sentenced to fourteen years' transportation; Gavan Duffy and Smith O'Brien also transported

William Knight's three daughters die of scarlet fever

Henry Rice, son of EKR, dies of cholera in Barbados, aged 27

1849 Queen Victoria visits Dublin

Thomas Carlyle visits Ballyare, Gweedore Hotel and Bunbeg as part of Irish tour

Birth of George Marcus Wandsbeck Hill, 9 April, Dublin

FCK leaves Mersham le Hatch for Provender, following death of Sir Edward Knatchbull, 24 May

Fanny Margaretta Rice, daughter of EKR, marries George Finch-Hatton, 10th Earl of Winchilsea

1850 Founding of Tenant League, 10 August

Death of Henry Austen, brother of JA

Hill family at Godmersham all summer

1851 Census shows depopulation of Ireland of 19.85% since 1841, following Great Famine

Debate, House of Lords, over validity of LGH's marriage to Louisa

Marianne Sophia Rice refuses her cousin, Edward Knatchbull-Hugesssen, son of FCK

1852 Potato blight in Ireland

Thomas Lefroy Lord Chief Justice in Ireland

Death of Edward Austen Knight at Godmersham, November

Death of Charles Austen, JA's brother, of cholera, serving on
Irawaddy River

JEAL Rector of Bray

1853   Edward Knight Jr lets Godmersham; MK goes first to Donegal to
the Hills, then to live with CBK at Chawton Rectory

John Knight marries Margaret Pearson

Death of Henry Rice, son of EKR

1854   Philip and Brodnax Knight, sons of Edward Knight Jr, at
Sebastopol; death of Ernest Knight of cholera; Cecil Rice, son
of EKR, at battle of Balaclava

1855   George Howard, Earl of Carlisle, sworn in as Lord Lieutenant

MK begins her *Garden Book*, 16 April

Death of Maria, widow of 3rd Marquess of Downshire, 7 April

1857   Indian Mutiny: Arthur Hill, Somerset Ward (veteran of Crimean
War and future husband of Norah Hill), Philip and Brodnax
Knight all serving in India

Marianne Sophia Rice marries T. Emilius Bayley ('Derby')

1858   Founding of Fenian movement (Irish Republican Brotherhood, or
IRB) in Dublin by James Stephens

Louisa Hill spends spring in Dublin with children; Norah and
Cassandra Hill spend summer at Castle Ward, as guests of Lord
and Lady Bangor, parents of Somerset Ward

1859   Marriage of Norah Hill to Capt. the Hon. Somerset Ward, 8th
Regiment of Foot, 26 April

1860   Walter Rice, son of EKR, serving in Ireland

1861   Beginning of American Civil War

Visit to Ireland by Queen Victoria and Prince Albert

1862   Edward Royds Rice, husband of EKR, paralysed after fall

Commission of Montagu Knight as Ensign, 21st Hampshire Rifle
Volunteers, 21 July

1863   Henry Knight, son of Edward and Adela Knight, visits Hills in
Donegal

Cecil Rice, son of EKR, again in India

Montagu Knight made Lieutenant

1864   Richard Chenevix Trench, future father-in-law of Arthur Hill, consecrated Archbishop of Dublin

Death of William Smith O'Brien, former Young Ireland leader, father of Cassandra Hill's friend Charlotte Grace O'Brien

MK on extended visit to EKR at Dane Court

Edward Bridges Rice marries Cecilia Harcourt

Anna Austen Lefroy writes *Recollections of Aunt Jane*

1865   End of American Civil War

Death of Sir Francis Austen, last remaining sibling of JA

Morland Rice, son of EKR, marries Caroline York

Cecil Rice, son of EKR, marries Frances Napier

1867   Failure of Fenian Rising; suspension of habeas corpus until March

Death of George Knight, JA's 'itty Dordy', August

Death of CBK at Chawton, 13 October; MK goes to live with John and Margaret Knight at Highway House, Bentley, Hants

Birth of Marcia Rice, daughter of Cecil, granddaughter of EKR

Caroline Austen writes *My Aunt Jane: A Memoir*

1868   Disraeli becomes PM, followed by Gladstone; Gladstone proposes disestablishment of Church of Ireland

Death of 4th Marquess of Downshire, 6 August

1869   Disestablishment of Church of Ireland (Irish Church Act)

FCK writes letter to MK deploring inferior social standing of JA and CEA

1870   Gladstone's first Land Act; beginning of Home Rule Movement under Issaac Butt (Home Government Association)

JEAL publishes *Memoir of Jane Austen*

1871   Arthur Hill marries Helen Emily Trench, daughter of Richard Chenevix Trench, Archbishop of Dublin, 16 February

JEAL's *Memoir* goes into 2nd edition, with *Lady Susan*, *The Watsons* and cancelled chapter of *Persuasion*

1872   Anna Austen Lefroy dies, aged seventy-nine, 1 September

	JEAL uses proceeds from *Memoir* to place memorial tablet to JA in Winchester Cathedral
1873	Home Governement Association conference in Dublin; change of name to Irish Home Rule League
	Death of William Knight, rector of Steventon
	Montagu Knight made Captain, 26 June
1874	Disraeli becomes Prime Minister
	Edward Knight Jr sells Godmersham to John Cunliffe Lister Kaye
	Death of JEAL, aged seventy-five
1875	Election of Charles Stewart Parnell as MP for Meath; allies himself with members disagreeing with Issac Butt
	Auction at Godmersham of furniture and effects
1876	Death of John Mitchel, aged sixty
	Birth of Arthur Fitzgerald Sandys Hill, 6th Baron Sandys, 4 December
	Death of Emma, wife of JEAL
1877	Parnell replaces Isaac Butt as president of Home Rule Confederation of Great Britain
1878	Assassination at Mulroy Bay, Donegal of William Sydney Clements, 3rd Earl of Leitrim, April
	Death of John Knight, youngest son of Edward and Elizabeth Knight, 10 January
	Death of Edward Royds Rice
	LGH becomes gravely ill: all his children sent for;
	MK goes to Ireland to be with Louisa
1879	Wettest year on record; harvest disastrous, worst since Great Famine of 1840s
	LGH dies at Ballyare, Co Donegal, 6 April; buried with Cassandra in Conwal Cemetery, Letterkenny; his eldest son, Captain Arthur Hill, inherits
	Edward Knight Jr dies, aged eighty-five, 5 November; Montagu Knight inherits Chawton
1880	MK pays extended visit to EKR at Dane Court

	Caroline Austen dies, November
	Lord Arthur Hill, 2nd son of 4th Marquess, MP for Co. Down
1881	Land Law (Ireland) Act, legalising 'the 3Fs' – fair rent, fixity of tenure and free sale of tenant's interest – and establishing Land Commission and Land Court, April
	Parnell arrested, October; imprisoned Land League leaders issue No-Rent Manifesto
	Arthur Hill clashes with tenants in Gweedore over rents; Gweedore Hotel boycotted
1882	Parnell released on parole, April; withdrawal of No-Rent Manifesto
	Phoenix Park murders of Chief Secretary, Lord Frederick Cavendish and Under-secretary Thomas Burke, May
	Arrears of Rent (Ireland) Act and Labourers' Cottages & Allotments Act, August
	Death of FCK, Christmas morning, in her ninetieth year. Her son Lord Brabourne finds correspondence with JA and original MS of *Lady Susan*
	Birth of Andrew Edward Somerset Mulholland, son of Norah Ward, later killed at Ypres; MK present at his birth
1883	Execution of 'Invincibles' convicted of Phoenix Park Murders, May–June
	Labourers (Ireland) Act, August
1884	MK goes to Donegal to live with Louisa and Cassandra Hill; begins correspondence with Montagu and Florence Knight
	Birth of Eva Norah Mulholland, daughter of Norah Ward
	Death of EKR; her unmarried daughters have to move from Dane Court when their brother inherits
	Publication of Lord Brabourne's edition of Jane Austen's letters, in two volumes, December
1885	Gladstone's government defeated on budget, June; Lord Salisbury, grandson of LGH's aunt Lady Salisbury (née Lady Emily Hill), forms caretaker government

Purchase of Land (Ireland) Act provides loans required for tenant purchase

1886   Salisbury rejects Gladstone's proposal for bipartisan approach to Home Rule

Irish Unionist Party formed under E.J. Saunderson, future father-in-law of Fanny Ward's daughter, Eva Mulholland

Death of Richard Chenevix Trench, father-in-law of Arthur Hill

1887   Arthur Hill obliged to reinstate evicted tenants at Gweedore, and to offer reduced rents

MK writing from Ballyare expresses view that 'rebels' should be punished 'severely and immediately'

FCK's son, Cecil Knatchbull Hugessen, visiting Donegal, writes to his sister, describing tenant unrest

1888   MK visiting Norah in Strangford, Co. Down, on her way to England via Scotland for annual family visit

Louisa Hill's health causing increasing concern

1889   Murder in Gweedore of Inspector William Martin (cousin of Violet Martin, 'Ross' of writing partnership Somerville and Ross), February

Cassandra Hill at Isle O'Valla, Strangford with Norah Ward; Somerset Ward concussed following incident when he was dragged by a runaway horse

Louisa Hill's illness worsens; MK postpones annual trip to England until July

Louisa dies in MK's absence, 29 July; buried at Tully, close to Ballyare

1890   Captain O'Shea's divorce action against his wife Katharine, November; Parnell named as correspondent

Parnell re-elected as Chair of Irish Parliamentary Party, but party splits; Catholic hierarchy call on faithful to reject Parnell; Gladstone declines to continue support for Home Rule with Parnell as leader

Arthur Hill examines his accounts, September, to determine

	whether MK and his sister Cassandra Hill may continue to live at Ballyare
	Montagu Knight offers home to MK, if Arthur asks her to leave Donegal; invitation not extended to his cousin, Cassandra Hill
1891	Parnell marries Katherine O'Shea, June
	Purchase of Land (Ireland) Act, August
	Death of Parnell, October
	Brabourne sells ten of JA's letters
1892	General Election: Gladstone forms last administration, July
	MK with George and Cassandra Hill at Moville, Donegal; Ballyare redecorated in spring
	Death of Walter Rice, son of EKR
1893	Anti-Home Rule marches in Belfast, April
	Gaelic League founded
	Cassandra Hill ill; stays with her brother Arthur outside Dublin
	Death of Cecil Rice, son of EKR
	Death of Lord Brabourne; his heirs sell sixty-four letters by JA and two by CEA
1894	Gladstone retires, March; succeeded as PM by Lord Roseberry
	Sharp decline in health of MK
1895	Roseberry resigns as PM, June; succeeded by Salisbury
	MK receives from Montagu Knight Jane Austen's *Charade Book*, July; no longer remembers her as author
	Death of MK, 4 December, at Ballyare; buried beside Louisa, at Tully, near Ballyare House
1896	Land Law (Ireland) Act, empowering Land Court to sell bankrupt estates to tenants, August
	Poor potato harvest; severe shortages over winter 1896 into following spring
	Death of Edward Bridges Rice, eldest son of EKR
1897	*The Nation* ceases publication, June, to be succeeded by *The Weekly Nation.*
	Death of Morland Rice, son of EKR

1899   Outbreak of Boer War (1899–1902)
1900   Ballyare House sold
1901   Visit to Ireland by Queen Victoria
        Death of Cassandra Hill at *Fáilte*, Foxrock, Co. Dublin, former
            home of Charlotte Grace O'Brien

BIBLIOGRAPHY

UNPUBLISHED MATERIAL

Austen, Mary Lloyd. Pocketbooks. Hampshire Record Office, Winchester, Hants.

Austen Leigh, James Edward. Diaries, 1820 and 1821. Hampshire Record Office, Winchester, Hants.

Billington Family Archive. Centre for Kentish Studies, Kent.

Corder, Jane. 'Akin to Jane; Family Genealogy of Jane Austen's Siblings and Descendants'. MS, privately compiled, 1953. Jane Austen's House Museum, Chawton, Hants.

Famine Relief Commission Papers 1845–1847. National Archives of Ireland, Dublin.

Gweedore Hotel Book, 1, 1842–1859. Donegal County Archives, Three Rivers Centre, Lifford, County Donegal.

Gweedore Hotel Book, 2, 1873–1895. An Chúirt, Gweedore Hotel and Heritage Centre, Gweedore, County Donegal.

Hill, Lord George. Downshire Papers. Granard Papers: Correspondence, etc. to 1954. Public Record Office of Northern Ireland, Belfast.

Knatchbull, Fanny Catherine. Pocketbooks; Letters from Fanny Catherine Knatchbull to Miss Chapman; Letters to Fanny Catherine Knatchbull from siblings, 1858–60. Centre for Kentish Studies, Kent.

Knight, Charles Bridges. Diaries. Jane Austen's House Museum, Chawton, Hants.

Knight, Marianne. Letters to Montagu and Florence Knight of Chawton House; 'Letters from Aunt May'; *Garden Book*, 1853–76; 'Letters belonging to Aunt May'; Letters from Marianne Knight to Montagu Knight, 20 December 1891 to 22 July 1895. Hampshire Record Office, Winchester, Hants.

Papers of Pamela, Lady Campbell and her family. National Library of Ireland, Dublin.

Papers relating to the compilation of material for James Edward Austen Leigh's Memoir, National Portrait Gallery, London.

Rice Archive: Uncatalogued papers of the Rice family, including letters to Elizabeth Knight Rice from her family. Centre for Kentish Studies, Kent.

Saunderson Papers (contains miscellaneous papers of the Hill family). Public Record Office of Northern Ireland, Belfast.

Scrapbooks of the Knight Family of Chawton. Hampshire Record Office, Winchester, Hants.

Ward, Capt. the Hon. Somerset. Correspondence with Capt. Arthur Hill. Saunderson Papers. Public Record Office of Northern Ireland, Belfast.

PUBLISHED MATERIAL

A List of All the Officers of the Army and Royal Marines on Full and Half-Pay; with an Index and a Succession of Colonels. The Fifty-First Edition. War Office, 1803.

Aalen, F.H. and Hugh Brody. *Gola: the Life and Last Days of an Island Community.* Cork: Mercier Press, 1969.

Austen, Caroline. *My Aunt Jane Austen: A Memoir.* London and Colchester: The Jane Austen Society, 1952.

Austen, Jane. *The Cambridge Edition of the Works of Jane Austen.* Edited by Janet Todd. Cambridge: Cambridge University Press, 2005.

—— *Letters of Jane Austen.* Edited with an Introduction and Critical Remarks by Edward, Lord Brabourne. London: Richard Bentley and Son, 1884.

—— *Jane Austen's Letters.* Edited by Deirdre Le Faye. Oxford, 1995. Reprint, London: The Folio Society, 2003.

Austen Leigh, James Edward. *A Memoir of Jane Austen.* Edited by R.W. Chapman. Oxford, 1926. Reprint, London: The Folio Society, 1989.

Austen Leigh, Mary Augusta. *James Edward Austen Leigh: A Memoir by his Daughter.* Privately printed, 1911.

———— *Personal Aspects of Jane Austen.* London: John Murray, 1920.

Austen Leigh, William, and Montagu George Knight. *Chawton Manor and its Owners: A Family History.* London: Smith, Elder & Co., 1911.

Austen Leigh, William, and Richard Arthur Austen Leigh. *Jane Austen: Her Life and Letters, A Family Record.* London: Smith, Elder & Co., 1913.

Austen Leigh, William, Richard Arthur Austen Leigh, and Deirdre Le Faye. *Jane Austen: A Family Record.* Revised and enlarged edition. London: The British Library, 1989.

Beckett, J.C. *The Making of Modern Ireland, 1603–1923.* London: Faber and Faber, 1966.

———— *A Short History of Ireland.* London: The Cresset Library, 1986.

Bowen, Elizabeth. *The Mulberry Tree: Writings of Elizabeth Bowen,* ed. Hermione Lee. London: Virago, 1986.

Boycott, Owen. 'Cause of Austen's Death Not Universally Acknowledged'. *Guardian* (London), December 1, 2009.

Brewer, John. 'England: The Big Change'. Review of *A Mad, Bad and Dangerous People? England 1783–1846,* by Boyd Hilton. *The New York Review of Books* 55, no. 11 (2008): 54–58.

Butler, Marilyn. *Maria Edgeworth: A Literary Biography.* Oxford: The Clarendon Press, 1972.

Carleton, William. *The Black Prophet: A Tale of Irish Famine.* 1899. Reprint, Shannon: Irish University Press, 1972.

Carlyle, Thomas. *Reminiscences of My Irish Journey in 1849.* London: Sampson Low, Marston, Searle & Rivington, 1882.

Cecil, David. *The Cecils of Hatfield House.* London: Constable & Co., 1973.

———— *A Portrait of Jane Austen.* 1978. Reprint, London: Constable, 1989.

Chapman, R.W. *Jane Austen: Facts and Problems.* 1948. Reprint, Oxford: Oxford University Press, 1970.

Connolly, S.J. 'Mass Politics and Sectarian Conflict, 1823–30'. *A New History of Ireland,* 5: *Ireland Under the Union, 1. 1801–1870,* ed. W.E.Vaughan. Oxford: The Clarendon Press, 1989. 74–106.

Daly, Mary E. *The Famine in Ireland.* 1994. Reprint, Dundalk: Dundalgan Press, for the Historical Association of Ireland, 1994.

Day, Angélique and Patrick McWilliams, eds. *Ordnance Survey Memoirs of Ireland, Volume Thirty-Eight: Parishes of County Donegal I, 1833–5.* Belfast: The Institute of Irish Studies, 1997.

—— *Ordnance Survey Memoirs of Ireland, Volume Thirty-Nine: Parishes of County Donegal II, 1835–6.* Belfast: The Institute of Irish Studies, 1997.

Day, Malcolm. *Voices from the World of Jane Austen.* London: David and Charles, 2007.

Donnelly, Jr, James S. 'Landlords and Tenants'. *A New History of Ireland, 5: Ireland Under the Union, I. 1801–1870,* ed. W.E.Vaughan. Oxford: The Clarendon Press, 1989. 332–49.

—— *The Great Irish Potato Famine.* 2001. Reprint, Thrupp, Gloucestershire: Sutton Publishing, 2002.

Dooley, Terence. *The Big Houses and Landed Estates of Ireland: A Research Guide.* Dublin: Four Courts Press, 2007.

Dorian, Hugh. *The Outer Edge of Ulster: A Memoir of Social Life in Nineteenth-Century Donegal,* ed. Breandán Mac Suibhne and David Dickson. Dublin: Lilliput Press, 2000.

Drabble, Margaret. Introduction to *Lady Susan, The Watsons and Sanditon.* Harmondsworth: Penguin English Library, 1974. 8–31.

Dudley Edwards, R., and T. Desmond Williams. *The Great Famine: Studies in Irish History, 1845–52.* Dublin: Lilliput Press, 1994.

Edgeworth, Maria. *Castle Rackrent.* 1800. Reprint, Oxford: Oxford University Press, 1964.

Egremont, Max. *The Cousins: The Friendship, Opinions and Activities of Wilfrid Scawen Blunt and George Wyndham.* London: Collins, 1977.

Evans, E. Estyn. 'Donegal Survivals'. *Antiquity* 13 (1939): 207–22.

—— 'The Northern Heritage'. *Aquarius* 4 (1971): 51–6.

—— Introduction to *Facts from Gweedore, Compiled from the Notes of Lord George Hill, M.R.I.A., A Facsimile Reprint of the Fifth Edition, 1887.* Reprint, Belfast: Institute of Irish Studies, 1971.

Ferris, Tom. *Irish Railways: A New History.* Dublin: Gill & Macmillan, 2008.

Figes, Orlando. *Crimea: The Last Crusade*. London: Allen Lane, 2010.

Foster, R.F. *Modern Ireland, 1600–1972*. London: Allen Lane, Penguin, 1988.

—— *Paddy and Mr Punch: Connections in Irish and English History*. London: Allen Lane, Penguin, 1993.

Gray, Peter. *Famine, Land and Politics: British Government and Irish Society, 1843–1850*. Dublin: Irish Academic Press, 1999.

Gwynn, Denis. *Young Ireland and 1848*. London and Cork: Blackwell, Ltd., and Cork University Press, 1949.

Gwynn, Stephen, ed. *Charlotte Grace O'Brien: Selections from Her Writings and Correspondence, with a Memoir by Stephen Gwynn*. Dublin: Maunsel and Co., Ltd., 1909.

—— *Highways and Byways in Donegal and Antrim, with Illustrations by Hugh Thomson*. London: Macmillan, 1928.

Hammond, M.C. *Relating to Jane: Studies on the Life and Novels of Jane Austen, with a Life of her Niece Elizabeth Austen/Knight*. London: Minerva Press, 1998.

Hill, Constance. *Jane Austen: Her Homes and Her Friends*. London and New York: John Lane, 1902.

Hill, Lord George. *Facts from Gweedore, with Useful Hints to Donegal Tourists*. Dublin: Philip Dixon, Hardy and Sons, 1845.

Hillan King, Sophia. "'Pictures Drawn from Memory': William Carleton's Experience of Famine'. *The Irish Review* 17/18 (1995): 80–9.

Hurlburt, William Henry. *Ireland Under Coercion: The Diary of an American*. Edinburgh: David Douglas, 1888.

Jenkins, Elizabeth. 'Some Notes on Background: Address Given at the Annual General meeting of the Jane Austen Society, 1980'. *The Jane Austen Society: Collected Reports* 3 (1985): 166.

—— *Jane Austen: A Biography*. 1938. Reprint, London: Victor Gollancz, 1986.

Kee, Robert. *The Laurel and the Ivy: The Story of Charles Stewart Parnell and Irish Nationalism*. London: Hamish Hamilton, 1993.

Kelly, Matthew. 'With Bit and Bridle'. *Review of Eighteenth-Century Ireland: The Isle of Slaves,* by Ian McBride. *London Review of Books* 32, no. 15 (2010): 12–13.

Kerr, Paul. *The Crimean War.* London: Channel Four, Boxtree, 1997.

Killen, John, ed. *The Decade of the United Irishmen: Contemporary Accounts, 1791–1801.* 1997. Reprint, Belfast: Blackstaff Press, 1998.

—— ed. *The Famine Decade: Contemporary Accounts, 1841–1851.* Belfast: Blackstaff Press, 1995.

Kinealy, Christine and Trevor Parkhill. *The Famine in Ulster: The Regional Impact.* Belfast: Ulster Historical Foundation, 1997.

Knatchbull, Timothy. *From a Clear Blue Sky.* London: Hutchinson, 2009.

Le Faye, Deirdre. 'The Nephew Who Missed Jane Austen'. *Notes and Queries* NS 31/4, December (1984): 471–2.

—— *Fanny Knight's Diaries: Jane Austen Through Her Niece's Eyes.* 2000. Reprint, Chawton, Hants: The Jane Austen Society, 2003.

—— *A Chronology of Jane Austen and Her Family.* Cambridge: Cambridge University Press, 2006.

Lucas, Victor. 'Jane Austen's Don Juan'. *The Jane Austen Society: Collected Reports* 4 (1989): 255–63.

McFadden, Rev. James. *The Present and the Past of the Agrarian Struggle in Gweedore: With Letters on the Railway Extension in Donegal.* Londonderry: The Derry Journal, 1889.

MacGill, Patrick. *Glenmornan.* 1918. Reprint, Dingle, Kerry: Brandon, 1983.

Mackail, J.W., and Guy Wyndham. *Life and Letters of George Wyndham.* London: Hutchinson & Co., n.d.

Maguire, W.A. *A Century in Focus: Photography and Photographers in the North of Ireland, 1839–1939.* Belfast: The Blackstaff Press, 2000.

—— *The Downshire Estates in Ireland, 1801–1845: The Management of Irish Landed Estates in the Early Nineteenth Century.* Oxford: The Clarendon Press, 1972.

—— ed. *Letters of a Great Irish Landlord: A Selection from the Estate Correspondence of the Third Marquess of Downshire, 1809–45.* Belfast: HMSO for the Public Record Office of Northern Ireland, 1974.

Malcomson, A.P.W. 'The Gentle Leviathan; Arthur Hill, 2nd Marquess of Downshire, 1753–1801'. *Plantation to Partition: Essays in Ulster History in Honour of J.L. McCracken,* ed. Peter Roebuck. Belfast: Blackstaff Press, 1981. 102–118.

—— *The Pursuit of the Heiress: Aristocratic Marriage in Ireland, 1740–1840.* Belfast: Ulster Historical Foundation, 2006.

Moran, Gerard. *Radical Irish Priests, 1660–1970.* Dublin: Four Courts Press, 1998.

Murphy, David. *Ireland and the Crimean War.* Dublin: Four Courts Press, 2002.

New Annual Army List for 1843. London: John Murray, 1843.

New Annual Army List for 1853. London: John Murray, 1853.

New Annual Army List for 1861. London: John Murray, 1861.

Nicolson, Nigel. *Godmersham Park, Kent: Before, During, and Since Jane Austen's Day.* Chawton, Hants: The Jane Austen Society, 1996.

Nolan, William, Liam Ronayne, and Mairead Dunlevy, eds. *Donegal History and Society: Interdisciplinary Essays on the History of an Irish County.* Templeogue, Dublin: Geography Publications, 1995.

Ó Corráin, Donnchadh, and Tomás O'Riordan, eds. *Ireland 1815–1870: Emancipation, Famine and Religion.* Dublin: Four Courts Press, 2011.

O'Raghallaigh, Liam. 'Captain Boycott: Man and Myth'. *History Ireland* 19, no. 1 (2011): 28–31.

Oxenden, G.C. *Poems, Etc.* 1829. Reprint, Breinigsville, PA: Legacy Reprint Series, 2010.

Rankin, Peter, ed. *Ballywalter Park.* Belfast: Ulster Architectural Society, 1985.

Robertson, Nora. *Crowned Harp: Memories of the Last Years of the Crown in Ireland.* Dublin: Allen Figgis & Co., Ltd., 1960.

Selwyn, David, ed. *Fugitive Pieces, Trifles Light as Air: The Poems of James Edward Austen Leigh, Nephew and Biographer of Jane Austen.* Winchester: The Jane Austen Society, 2006.

Somerville-Large, Peter. *The Irish Country House: A Social History.* London: Sinclair-Stevenson, 1995.

Sutherland, Kathryn. Introduction to *A Memoir of Jane Austen and Other Family Recollections*. 2001. Reprint, Oxford: Oxford University Press, 2008. xiii–li.

Tillyard, Stella. *Aristocrats: Caroline, Emily, Louisa and Sarah Lennox 1740–1832*. London: Chatto & Windus, 1994.

—— *Citizen Lord: Edward Fitzgerald 1763–1798*. London: Chatto & Windus, 1997.

—— 'The Madness of the Regency.' *BBC History Magazine*, February 2011.

Tomalin, Claire. *Jane Austen: A Life*. London: Viking, 1997.

Tynan, Katharine. *The Middle Years*. London: Constable & Co., 1916.

Vaughan, W.E. *Landlords and Tenants in Mid-Victorian Ireland*. Oxford: The Clarendon Press, 1994.

—— *Landlords and Tenants in Ireland, 1848–1904*. 1984. Revised edition, Dundalk: Dun Dalgan Press, 1994.

Vickery, Amanda. *The Gentleman's Daughter: Women's Lives in Georgian England*. New Haven: Yale Nota Bene, Yale University Press, 2003.

—— *Behind Closed Doors: At Home in Georgian England*. New Haven: Yale University Press, 2009.

—— 'Do Not Scribble'. Review of *The Pen and the People: English Letter-Writers 1660–1800*, by Susan Whyman. *London Review of Books* 32, no. 21 (2010): 34–6.

Viveash, Chris. 'James Edward Austen at Oxford'. *The Jane Austen Society Report* 5 (2008): 114–23.

Wall, Maureen. 'County Donegal in 1845: Excerpts from the Journal of John O'Hagan, giving an account of a tour in Ulster in the summer of 1845, presented with an introductory note, by Maureen Wall.' *Donegal Annual* (1970): 161–177.

Welland, Freydis Jane, and Eileen Sutherland, eds. *Life in the Country, with Quotations by Jane Austen and Silhouettes by Her Nephew James Edward Austen Leigh*. 2005. Reprint, London: The British Library, 2008.

Whelan, Kevin. *The Tree of Liberty: Radicalism, Catholicism and the Construction of Irish Identity, 1760–1830*. Cork: Cork University Press, 1996.

Wilson, *Almost Another Sister: The Family Life of Fanny Knight,*
   Jane Austen's Favourite Niece. Kent: Kent Arts and Libraries, 1990.
Woodham-Smith, Cecil. *The Great Hunger: Ireland 1845–9*. London:
   Hamish Hamilton, 1962.

NOTES

INTRODUCTION

1 William Austen Leigh and Richard Arthur Austen Leigh, *Jane Austen: Her Life and Letters, A Family Record* (London: Smith, Elder & Co., 1913).

2 R.W. Chapman, *Jane Austen: Facts and Problems* (1948; reprint, Oxford: Oxford University Press, 1970), 132–4.

3 Jane Austen (hereafter JA) to Cassandra Elizabeth Austen (hereafter CEA), 15 June 1808. Deirdre Le Faye, ed. *Jane Austen's Letters* (1995; reprint, London: The Folio Society, 2003), no. 52.

4 The needlecase and slippers are displayed at Jane Austen's House Museum, Chawton, Alton, Hants.

5 Chris Viveash, 'James Edward Austen at Oxford,' *The Jane Austen Society Report* (2008): 114–23.

6 Amanda Vickery, *The Gentleman's Daughter: Women's Lives in Georgian England* (New Haven and London: Yale Nota Bene, Yale University Press, 2003), 54.

7 Stella Tillyard, 'The Madness of the Regency,' *BBC History Magazine* 12, no. 2 (February 2011): 52 . See also John Brewer, 'England: The Big Change', review of *A Mad, Bad and Dangerous People? England 1783–1846* by Boyd Hilton in *The New York Review of Books* 55, no. 11 (26 June 2008): 54–8.

8 *Ibid.*

9 Matthew Kelly, 'With Bit and Bridle', review of *Eighteenth-Century Ireland: The Isle of Slaves*, by Ian McBride, *London Review of Books* 32, no. 15 (5 August 2010): 13

10 *Ibid.*

CHAPTER 1

1 Elizabeth Jenkins, *Jane Austen: A Biography* (1938; London: Victor Gollancz, 1986), 45.

2 Jane Austen, *Pride and Prejudice* (1813; Cambridge: Cambridge University Press, 2006), 186. All subsequent references to JA's novels are to this edition, *The Cambridge Edition of the Works of Jane Austen*, under the general editorship of Janet Todd, with the exception of *Lady Susan, The Watsons* and *Sanditon,* for which the Penguin English Library edition of 1974, with an introduction by Margaret Drabble, has been used.

3 James Edward Austen Leigh, *A Memoir of Jane Austen* (1870, 2nd enlarged ed. 1871; rev. ed., Oxford: Clarendon Press, 1926, ed. R.W. Chapman; reprint, London: the Folio Society, 1989), 77–8; Mary Augusta Austen Leigh (hereafter MAAL), *Personal Aspects of Jane Austen* (London: John Murray, 1920), 23; 51.

4 Claire Tomalin, *Jane Austen: A Life* (London: Viking, 1997), 11–20.

5 *Ibid.,* 14.

6 *Ibid.,* 180–2.

7 MK to Montagu George Knight, 28 September 1890, Knight Family Archive, 39M89/F124/15, HRO, Winchester, Hants.

8 Nigel Nicolson, *Godmersham Park, Kent: Before, During and Since Jane Austen's Day* (Chawton, Hants: The Jane Austen Society, 1996), 13.

9 William Austen Leigh, Richard Arthur Austen Leigh and Deirdre Le Faye, *Jane Austen: A Family Record* (London: The British Library, 1989), 40–1.

10 *Ibid.,* 15.

11 Lady Bridges to Mrs Fielding, 2 March 1791, quoted in Margaret Wilson, *Almost Another Sister: The Family Life of Fanny Knight, Jane Austen's Favourite Niece* (Kent: Kent Arts & Libraries, 1990), 6.

12 Nicolson, *Godmersham Park, 7.*

13 Catherine Knight to Edward Austen, later Knight, Knight Family Archive, HRO, 39M89/ F111/1–2. See also Deirdre Le Faye, *A Chronology of Jane Austen and her Family* (Cambridge: Cambridge University Press, 2006), 202.

14 JA to CEA, 8 January 1799. Deirdre Le Faye, ed. *Jane Austen's Letters* (1995; reprint, London: The Folio Society, 2003), no. 17.

15 JA to CEA, 27 October 1798, Le Faye, *Letters*, no. 10.

16 JA to CEA, 27 August 1805, Le Faye, *Letters*, no 46. Sophia Cage, daughter of the former Fanny Bridges, sister of Edward Austen's wife Elizabeth. She later married Henry Knight, and died in 1833. A third sister, Sophia Bridges, married William Deedes of Sandling. See Austen Leigh, Austen Leigh and Le Faye, *A Family Record*, 66.

17 George Austen (1765–1838) suffered from fits, and remained in care in a neighbouring village throughout his life. See Tomalin, *Life*, 5–6.

18 JA to CEA, 1 October 1808, Le Faye, *Letters*, no. 56.

19 Tomalin, *Life*, 135.

20 JA to CEA, 18 December 1798, Le Faye, *Letters*, no. 14.

21 Mrs Austen's income of £460 could, in today's terms, be worth approximately £15,000.

22 JA to CEA, 20 June 1808, Le Faye, *Letters*, no. 53

23 Tomalin, *Life*, 267; Jenkins, *Biography*, 133.

24 Elizabeth Bridges Austen died in 1808, four years before the change of name from Austen to Knight.

25 Austen Leigh, Austen Leigh and Le Faye, *Family Record*, 161–2.

26 *Ibid.*

27 Wilson, *Almost Another Sister*, 13.

28 *Ibid.*, 8.

29 Henry Austen was still a Captain in the 33rd Regiment of Foot, under Cornwallis as Colonel and Arthur Wellesley as Lieutenant Colonel in March 1801, having begun his service there on 1 March 1798. *A List of All the Officers of the Army and Royal Marines On Full and Half-Pay, with An Index and A Succession of Colonels* (London: The War Office, 10 January 1803), 145.

30 Jenkins, *Biography*, 228; Tomalin, *Life*, 153.

31 MK to Fanny Catherine Knatchbull (FCK), 31 October 1867, Knatchbull Family Archive, Centre for Kentish Studies (hereafter CKS), Maidstone, Kent, Knatchbull Family Archive, U951/C113/7.

32 JA to CEA, 20–22 February 1807, Le Faye, *Letters*, no. 51.

33 Elizabeth Bridges Austen to Elizabeth (Lizzy) Austen, later Knight and Rice (EKR), 2 September 1807, CKS, Rice Archive EK/U116/10/2 (uncatalogued), Hammond no. 112.

34 JA to CEA, 15–17 June 1807, Le Faye, *Letters*, no. 52.

35 JA to CEA, 20–22 June 1808, Le Faye, *Letters*, no. 53.

36 JA to CEA, 30 June–1 July 1808, Le Faye, *Letters*, no. 55.

37 *Ibid.*

38 JA to CEA, 1–2 October 1808; 7–9 October 1808, Le Faye, *Letters*, nos. 56 and 57.

39 FCK, 10 October 1808, Pocket Books, CKS, Knatchbull Archive, U951/F24/5.

40 JA to CEA, 13 October 1808, Le Faye, *Letters*, no. 58.

41 JA to CEA, 15–16 October 1808, Le Faye, *Letters*, no. 59.

42 JA to CEA, 7–9 October 1808, Le Faye, *Letters*, no. 57.

43 JA to CEA, 15–16 October 1808, Le Faye, *Letters*, ed., no. 59.

44 *Ibid.*

45 JA to CEA, 24–25 October 1808, Le Faye, *Letters*, no. 60.

46 JA to CEA, 10–11 January 1808, Le Faye, *Letters*, no. 64.

47 JA to CEA, 24 January 1809, Le Faye, *Letters*, no. 66.

48 JA to CEA, 30 January 1809, Le Faye, *Letters*, no. 67.

49 Susanna Sackree to Miss Dorothy Chapman, 18 February 1809, CKS, Knatchbull Archive, U951/C107/12; Le Faye, *Chronology*, 366.

50 FCK, 17 June 1809, Pocket Books, CKS, Knatchbull Archive, U951/F24/6; Le Faye, *Chronology*, 370.

51 FCK, 20 October 1809, Pocket Books, CKS, Knatchbull Archive, U951/F24/6; Le Faye, *Chronology*, 373.

52 FCK, 31 December 1810, Pocket Books, CKS, Knatchbull Archive, U951/F24/7; Le Faye, *Chronology*, 394.

53 JA to CEA, 30 April 1811, Le Faye, *Letters*, no. 72.

54 FCK, 9 November 1812, Pocket Books, CKS, Knatchbull Archive, U951/F24/9; Le Faye, *Chronology*, 432.

55 JA to CEA, 30 April 1811, Le Faye, *Letters*, no. 72.

56 Tomalin, *Life*, 237.

57 Le Faye, *Chronology*, 360.

58 JA to CEA, 20 November 1808, Le Faye, *Letters*, no. 61.

59 Austen Leigh, Austen Leigh and Le Faye, *Family Record*, 154–5.

60 *Ibid.*, 155.

61 *Ibid.*, 113.

62 JA is believed to have abandoned work on the fragment known as *The Watsons*, written in Bath during 1804, after the death of her father in 1805. See Margaret Drabble, 'Introduction', *Lady Susan*, *The Watsons* and *Sanditon* (Harmondsworth: Penguin, 1974), 16.

63 JA to Francis Austen, 3 July 1813, Le Faye, *Letters*, no. 86.

64 Charlotte-Maria Beckford, née Middleton, 1875, quoted in Deirdre Le Faye, letter to *Times Literary Supplement*, 3 May 1985, 495.

65 *Ibid.* Charlotte-Maria may have been correct in her assessment as the name Middleton is used in *Sense and Sensibility* for the well-intentioned, if intrusive, Sir John.

66 Caroline Austen, *My Aunt Jane Austen: A Memoir* (London and Colchester: the Jane Austen Society, 1991), 6–7.

67 Charlotte-Maria Beckford, in Le Faye to *TLS*, 3 May 1985, 495.

68 JA to CEA, 4 February 1813, Le Faye, *Letters*, no. 80.

69 JA to CEA, 31 May 1811, Le Faye, *Letters*, no. 74.

70 Austen Leigh, Austen Leigh and Le Faye, *Family Record*, 158.

71 Caroline Austen, *My Aunt Jane Austen*, 6–7.

72 James Edward Austen Leigh, *Memoir*, 78.

73 JA to Martha Lloyd, 29–30 November 1812, Le Faye, *Letters*, no. 77.

74 FCK, 6 December 1812, Pocket Books, CKS, Knatchbull Archive, U951/F24/9; Le Faye, *Chronology*, 435.

75 FCK, 21 April 1813, Pocket Books, CKS, Knatchbull Archive, U951/F24/10; Austen Leigh, Austen Leigh and Le Faye, *Family Record*, 178.

76 FCK to Miss Chapman, October 1813, CKS, Knatchbull Archive, U951/C109/2.

77 Elizabeth Jenkins, 'Some Notes on Background', Address Given at the Annual General Meeting of the Jane Austen Society, 1980, *Collected Reports* 2 (1966–1985), 166.

78 *Ibid.*

79 Constance Hill, *Jane Austen; Her Homes & her Friends* (London and New York: John Lane, 1902), 202.

80 *Ibid.*

81 Jenkins, *Biography*, 164.

82 FCK, 5 June 1813, Pocket Books, CKS, Knatchbull Archive, U951/F24/10; Le Faye, *Chronology*, 447.

83 JA to CEA, 24 May 1813, Le Faye, *Letters*, no. 85.

84 FCK to Miss Chapman, October 1813, CKS, Knatchbull Archive, U951/C109/2.

85 JA to Francis Austen, 3 July 1813, Le Faye, *Letters*, no. 86.

86 Edward, 1st Lord Brabourne, ed., *Letters of Jane Austen*, 2 vols. (London: Richard Bentley and Son, 1884), 1: 26.

87 Deirdre Le Faye, 'The Nephew Who Missed Jane Austen', *Notes and Queries*, NS 31/4, December 1984, 472.

88 JA to Francis Austen, 25 September 1813, Le Faye, *Letters*, no. 90.

89 JA to CEA, 15–16 September 1813, Le Faye, *Letters*, no. 87.

90 *Ibid.*

91 *Ibid.* See also Victor Lucas, 'Jane Austen's Don Juan' in The Jane Austen Society Reports for 1989, *Collected Reports*, 4, 255–63.

92 JA to CEA, 16 September 1813, Le Faye, *Letters*, no. 88.

93 Tomalin, *Life*, 241.

94 JA to CEA, 11–12 October 1813, Le Faye, *Letters*, no. 91.

95 JA to CEA, 30 November 1814, Le Faye, *Letters*, no. 114.

96 Wilson, *Almost Another Sister*, 40.

97 FCK to Miss Chapman, 13 February 1814, CKS, Knatchbull Archive, U951/C109/3.

98 FCK to Miss Chapman, 13 August 1814, CKS, Knatchbull Archive, U951/C109/4. As if the preparation of her sisters for society were not enough for a young woman of twenty-one, Fanny had the anxiety in July 1815 of the likely loss of an eye by her youngest brother John, then almost seven, following an incident involving an arrow. 'My little darling's eye,' she wrote to Miss Chapman, in distress. '[There is] ... hardly any chance of his regaining the sight' (FCK to Miss Chapman, 18 July 1815, CKS, Knatchbull Archive, U951/C109/5).

99 FCK to Miss Chapman, 29 May 1815, CKS, Knatchbull Archive, U951/C109/6.

100 JA to CEA, 17–18 October 1815, Le Faye, *Letters*, no. 121.

101 David Cecil, *A Portrait of Jane Austen* (London: Constable, 1978; reprint, 1989), 182.

102 Tomalin, *Life*, 254.

103 Austen Leigh, Austen Leigh and Le Faye, *Family Record*, 194–5.

104 Caroline Austen, *My Aunt Jane Austen*, 47–8.

105 JA to James Edward Austen, later James Edward Austen Leigh (JEAL), 16 December 1816, Le Faye, *Letters*, no. 146.

106 Cecil, *Portrait*, 183. Theories of the source of her symptoms have included Addison's Disease, cancer of the lymphatic system, and tuberculosis caught from cattle. See also Owen Bowcott, 'Cause of Austen's Death Not Universally Acknowledged', *Guardian*, 1 December 2009, 13.

107 Tomalin, *Life*, 264.

108 Drabble, 'Introduction', *Lady Susan, The Watsons, Sanditon*, 24.

109 JA to Charles Austen, 6 April 1817, Le Faye, *Letters*, no. 157.

110 FCK to Miss Chapman, 4 March 1817, CKS, Knatchbull Archive, U951/C109/7. Sophia Cage, their cousin, would marry Henry Knight in 1832.

111 JA to FCK, 20–21 February 1817, Le Faye, *Letters*, no. 151.

112 JA to FCK, 13 March 1817, Le Faye, *Letters*, no. 153.

113 *Ibid.*

114   Jenkins, *Biography*, 133.

115   JA to FCK, 23–25 March 1817, Le Faye, *Letters*, no. 155.

116   JA to Anne Sharp, 22 May 1817, Le Faye, *Letters*, no. 159.

117   *Ibid.*

118   JA to JEAL, 27 May 1817, Le Faye, *Letters*, no. 160.

119   JEAL, *Memoir*, 155.

120   CEA to FCK, 29 July 1817, Le Faye, *Letters*, CEA/3.

121   FCK, 20 July 1817, Pocket Books, CKS, Knatchbull Archive, U951/F24/19.

122   FCK to Miss Chapman, 10 August 1817, CKS, Knatchbull Archive, U951/C109/8.

CHAPTER 2

1   Evelyn, Viscountess Templetown (née Finch-Hatton), in Jane Corder, *Akin to Jane: Family Genealogy of Jane Austen's Siblings and Descendants, 1760–1953*, MS compiled 1953, Jane Austen's House Museum (JAHM), Chawton, Hants, 51. Second copy lodged at College of Arms, London.

2   *Ibid.*

3   *Ibid.*

4   Margaret Wilson, *Almost Another Sister: The Family Life of Fanny Knight, Jane Austen's Favourite Niece* (Kent: Kent Arts & Libraries, 1990), 107.

5   Corder, *Akin to Jane*, 51.

6   M.C. Hammond, *Relating to Jane: Studies on the Life and Novels of Jane Austen with a Life of her Niece Elizabeth Austen/Knight.* (London; Minerva Press, 1998), 196.

7   Corder, *Akin to Jane*, 52.

8   Elizabeth Austen to EKR, 2 September 1807, CKS, Rice Archive, EK-U116 (uncatalogued), Hammond no. 1/2.

9   JA to CEA, 15–17 June 1808. Deirdre Le Faye, ed. *Jane Austen's Letters* (1995; reprint, London: The Folio Society, 2003), no. 52.

10   Mary Augusta Austen Leigh (MAAL), *James Edward Austen Leigh: A Memoir by his Daughter*, privately printed, 1911, 11.

11   *Ibid.*, 70.

12   JA to JEAL, 16–17 December 1816, Le Faye, *Letters*, no. 146.

13   *Ibid.* The silhouette of Jane Austen known as 'L'Aimable Jane', entitled on its first appearance in JEAL's *Memoir* as 'L'Amiable Jane', as Jane spelled it in her letter, is thought to have been executed by James Edward. See R.W.Chapman, *Jane Austen: Facts and Problems* (Oxford: Clarendon Press, 1948), 214.

14   MAAL, *James Edward Austen Leigh: A Memoir*, 22.

15   *Ibid.*

16   Chris Viveash, 'James Edward Austen at Oxford', *The Jane Austen Society Report* (2008): 115.

17   MAAL, *James Edward Austen Leigh: A Memoir*, 28.

18   *Ibid.*, 23.

19   *Ibid.*, 24.

20   Viveash, 'James Edward Austen at Oxford', 115.

21   Caroline Austen to JEAL, 4 May 1819, HRO, Austen Leigh Family Archive, 23 M93/86/3; *Chronology*, 599.

22   MAAL, *James Edward Ausen Leigh: Memoir*, 18.

23   JEAL, 'Lines accompanying a pearl pin, addressed to William Heathcote on Friday May 17th: 1822. On which day he came of age', *Fugitive Pieces: Trifles Light as Air: The Poems of James Edward Austen Leigh, Nephew and Biographer of Jane Austen*, ed. David Selwyn (Winchester: The Jane Austen Society, 2006), 74; MAAL, *James Edward Austen Leigh: Memoir*, 26.

24   Claire Tomalin, *Jane Austen: A Life* (London: Viking, 1997), 276.

25   MAAL, *James Edward Austen Leigh: Memoir*, 31; 39.

26 Deirdre Le Faye, *A Chronology of Jane Austen and her Family* (Cambridge: Cambridge University Press, 2006), 655.

27 FCK to Miss Chapman, 25 March 1819, CKS, Knatchbull Archive, U951/C109/9. Mrs Deedes of Sandling had been Sophia Leigh, sister of Mrs George Austen, née Cassandra Leigh.

28 Hammond, *Relating to Jane*, 230–2. This child was Edward Bridges Knight (1819–1902).

29 FCK to Miss Chapman, 13 December 1819, CKS, Knatchbull Archive, U951/C109/10.

30 Wilson, *Almost Another Sister*, 54.

31 FCK to Miss Chapman, 18 September 1820, CKS, Knatchbull Archive, U951/C109/11.

32 Wilson, *Almost Another Sister*, 50.

33 *Ibid.*, 53.

34 *Ibid.*, 54.

35 *Ibid.*, 49.

36 *Ibid.*, 48.

37 *Ibid.*, 52.

38 FCK to Miss Chapman, 18 September 1820, CKS, Knatchbull Archive, U951/C109/11.

39 FCK to Miss Chapman, 1 December 1820, CKS, Knatchbull Archive, U951/C109/13.

40 Hammond, *Relating to Jane*, 240. This child was Henry Rice (1821–1848).

41 Wilson, *Almost Another Sister*, 56.

42 *Ibid.*, 58.

43 FCK to Miss Chapman, 2 September 1821, CKS, Knatchbull Archive, U951/C109/14.

44 FCK to Miss Chapman, 9–12 March 1822, CKS, Knatchbull Archive, U951/C109/16.

45 FCK, 19 November 1822, Pocket Books, CKS, Knatchbull Archive, U951/F24/19. See also Billington Family Archive, CKS, U1045/F1-15. John Billington would marry Maria Wyndham in 1829, and remain a family friend of the Knights at Godmersham. His son George Moyle Billington would later distinguish himself in the Crimea.

46 Hammond, *Relating to Jane*, 240–1.

47 Wilson, *Almost Another Sister*, 70.

48 Tomalin, *Life*, 275.

49 'When William Knight married Caroline Portal in [1825] old Mrs Austen commented, "… Well, my dear, only think of old Joe Portal's daughter marrying my grandson!" Joe Portal was the grandson of a French emigré but he had married a Miss Hasker, whose parents kept a marine store and clothing shop in Portsmouth, a connection which made him and his family socially suspect.' Hammond, *Relating to Jane*, 217–8.

50 Hammond, *Relating to Jane*, 245.

51 Wilson, *Almost Another Sister*, 71.

52 *Ibid.*, 70.

53 FCK, 31 December 1824, Pocket Books, CKS, Knatchbull Archive, U951/F24/21.

54 FCK, December 1825, Pocket Books, CKS Knatchbull Archive, U951/F24/22.

55 FCK, January 1826, Pocket Books, CKS, Knatchbull Archive, U951/F24/23.

56 FCK, 13–14 May 1826, Pocket Books, CKS, Knatchbull Archive, U951/F24/23.

57 *Ibid.*, 17 May 1826.

58 Wilson, *Almost Another Sister*, 72; Le Faye, *Chronology*, 630.

59 Le Faye, *Chronology*, 630.

60 *Ibid.*

61 FCK, 13–14 May 1826, Pocket Books, CKS, Knatchbull Archive, U951/F24/23.

62 Wilson, *Almost Another Sister*, 73.

CHAPTER 3

1 William Austen Leigh and Montagu George Knight, *Chawton Manor and its Owners: A Family History* (London: Smith, Elder & Co., 1911), 173.

2 *Ibid.*, 172; Jane Corder, *Akin to Jane: Family Genealogy of Jane Austen's Siblings and Descendants, 1760–1953*, MS compiled 1953,

Jane Austen's House Museum, Chawton, Hants, 121.

3   FCK, 7 June 1827, Pocket Books, CKS, Knatchbull Archive, U951/F24/24.

4   FCK, 8 May 1827, Pocket Books, CKS, Knatchbull Archive, U951/F24/24.

5   *Ibid.*, 17 May 1827. Lady Salisbury, the former Lady Mary Amelia (Emily) Hill (1750–1835) married James Cecil, 1st Marquess of Salisbury in 1773. A powerful and flamboyant figure, she died in a tragic accident when fire broke out in her apartments at Hatfield House on 22 November 1835. The young Charles Dickens, reporting the fire, was so struck by it that he included an account in the novel he was then writing. See *The Adventures of Oliver Twist* (1837; Oxford: Oxford University Press, 1981), 368–70.

6   *Ibid.*, 26 June 1827. Fanny spells his name in both forms, but eventually settles for 'Burrows' in her yearly summary: 'Mr Burrows, son of Sir B. Burrows proposed to Cass & was refused.' FCK, 31 December 1827, Pocket Books, CKS, Knatchbull Archive, U951/F24/24.

7   Jane Austen, *Persuasion* (1818; reprint, ed. Janet Todd and Antje Blank, Cambridge: Cambridge University Press, 2006), 197-207.

8   FCK, 11 August 1827, Pocket Books, CKS, Knatchbull Archive, U951/F24/24.

9   FCK, 27 August 1827, Pocket Books, CKS, Knatchbull Archive, U951/F24/24.

10 *Ibid.*, 29 August 1827.

11 Capt. John Hart to Viscountess Forbes, 17 September 1834, Public Record Office of Northern Ireland (hereafter PRONI), Granard Papers, Register of Irish Archives, K/3/1; A.P.W. Malcolmson, *The Pursuit of the Heiress* (Belfast; Ulster Historical Foundation, 2006), 174.

12 FCK, 31 December 1827, Pocket Books, CKS, Knatchbull Archive, U951/F24/24.

13 Richard James Lane, *Lord George Hill*, National Portrait Gallery, London, NPG/ D22025/17-C-10.

14 Corder, *Akin to Jane*. The Marquess, or Marquess, of Downshire was also styled as 'Earl and Viscount of Hillsborough, Viscount Kilwarlin and Baron Hill of Kilwarlin, in Ireland. Earl of Hillsborough, Viscount Fairford and Baron Harwich in Great Britain'.

15 W.A. Maguire, *The Downshire Estates in Ireland: 1801–1845* (Oxford: The Clarendon Press, 1972), 1–8.

16 Malcolmson, *Pursuit of the Heiress*, 121; PRONI, Downshire Papers, D/3880, 'Continental Disbursements on Account of Lords Augustus and George Hill', 21 November 1818-10 December 1819.

17 See Maguire, *Downshire Estates*, 86–7: 'The considerable property in Ireland –namely the estates at Dundrum in county Down and Edenderry in King's county – which [Lady Downshire] brought to the family was to be security for the raising of portions for the younger children of the marriage: £20,000 if one child, £30,000 if two, £40, 000 if three or more ... It was left to her to decide on the divisions of the portions for the younger children.'

18 *Ibid.*, 6. See also A.P.W. Malcolmson, 'The Gentle Leviathan: Arthur Hill, 2nd Marquess of Downshire, 1753–1801', in *Plantation to Partition: Essays in Ulster History in Honour of J.L. McCracken*, ed. Peter Roebuck (Belfast: Blackstaff Press, 1981), 102.

19 Maguire, *Downshire Estates*, 6.

20 *Ibid.*, 9; 80.

21 *Ibid.*, 121.

22 *Ibid.*, 122.

23 *Lady Susan, The Watsons, Sanditon*, ed. Drabble, 166.

24 *Pride and Prejudice* (1813; Cambridge: Cambridge University Press, 2006), 173.

25 FCK, 31 December 1828, Pocket Books, CKS, Knatchbull Achive, U951/F24/25.

26 Margaret Wilson, *Almost Another Sister: The Family Life of Fanny Knight, Jane*

Austen's Favourite Niece (Kent: Kent Arts & Libraries, 1990), 27.

27 JA to CEA, 23–24 August 1814. Deirdre Le Faye, ed. *Jane Austen's Letters* (1995; reprint, London: The Folio Society, 2003), no. 105.

28 M.C. Hammond, *Relating to Jane: Studies on the Life and Novels of Jane Austen with a Life of her Niece Elizabeth Austen/Knight.* (London; Minerva Press, 1998), 247.

29 Margaret Wilson to Sophia Hillan, 17 June 2010.

30 'Pourquoi Pas', in *Poems, Etc. By George Chichester Oxenden* (1829; Breinigsville, PA: Legacy Reprint Series, 2010), 59–60.

31 FCK, Pocket Books, CKS, Knatchbull Archive, U951/F24/ 26; U951/F24/27.

32 The silhouette is on display, JAHM. See also Jane Austen Society, *Collected Reports*, 3, 299–300.

33 Diaries of Charles Bridges Knight (CBK) 1832–1847, MS in 13 volumes, numbered 2–15, held at JAHM.

34 CBK, 30 January 1832, Diaries, 2, JAHM.

35 CBK, 26 January 1835, Diaries, 8, JAHM. In Corder, *Akin to Jane*, Brook John Knight is described as 'Captain, Unattached List' in June 1835; he exchanged to, first, the 48th Regiment of Foot (July 1835), then the 51st Regiment of Foot (1837), and was on the unattached list, on half-pay, by October 1837. He exchanged to the 6th Dragoon Guards in February 1839, and was by August 1844 again on half-pay in the Staff Corps.

36 CBK, 20 September 1832, Diaries, 3, JAHM.

37 CBK, 18 March 1832, Diaries, 2, JAHM.

38 CBK, 12 July 1833, Diaries, 6, JAHM.

39 CBK, 16 May 1832, Diaries, 2, JAHM.

40 CBK, 15 May 1833, Diaries, 6, JAHM.

41 CBK, 23 August 1823, Diaries, 3, JAHM.

42 CBK, 5 October 1832, Diaries, 3, JAHM.

43 CBK, 17 May 1832, Diaries, 2; 27 April 1833, Diaries, 5, JAHM.

44 CBK, 26 January 1833, Diaries, 5, JAHM.

45 CBK, 23 April 1832, Diaries, 2, JAHM.

46 CBK, 19 July 1833, Diaries, 6, JAHM.

47 CBK, 23 May 1833, Diaries, 6, JAHM.

48 CBK, 25 February 1832, Diaries, 2, JAHM.

49 CBK, 5 March 1835, Diaries, 8, JAHM.

50 Nora Robertson, *Crowned Harp; Memories of the Last Years of the Crown in Ireland* (Dublin: Allen Figgis & Co. Ltd., 1960), 74.

51 'Hillsborough House Twelfth Night Ball', *Newry Commercial Telegraph*, 15 January 1828.

52 FCK, 31 December 1829, Pocket Books, CKS, Knatchbull Archive, U951/F24/26.

53 Lord George Hill (LGH) to Lord Downshire, PRONI, Downshire Papers, D/671/C/348/2.

54 Maguire, *Downshire Estates*, 10–12.

55 LGH to Lord Downshire, 1828–1844, PRONI, D/671/C/348/1–25.

56 See S.J. Connolly, 'Mass Politics and Sectarian Conflict, 1823–30', in *A New History of Ireland, 5: Ireland Under the Union, 1, 1801–1870* (Oxford: Oxford University Press, 1989), 106.

57 Maguire, *Downshire Estates*, 11.

58 Maguire, *Downshire Estates*, 10; PRONI, Downshire Papers, D/3880.

59 *Gweedore Hotel Book*, 1, 123. MS in 2 volumes, volume 1 held at Donegal County Archives, Lifford, County Donegal, P/46,: volume 2 in possession of Patricia Doherty, at An Chúirt, Gweedore Court Hotel and Heritage Centre, Gweedore, County Donegal, formerly the Gweedore Hotel.

60 He was a member of the Royal Irish Academy in Dublin, founded in 1785, and possessed an extensive library of ancient and mediaeval Irish texts. These include handwritten transcriptions of, among others, Gaelic poet Brian Merriman's eighteenth-century epic *The Midnight Court* in 'A Collection of Ossianic poems

and tales, Ulster tales and poems, including Cúirt an Mhéodhan Oidche'. Scribe: Muiris Ó Riagáin, Doneraile, c. 1817–27 [From the library of Lord George Hill], Manuscripts Reading Room, National Library of Ireland, MS G.1.121.

61 *Gweedore Hotel Book*, 1, 123, Donegal County Archives, Lifford, County Donegal.

CHAPTER 4

1 CBK, 21 October 1834, Diaries, 8, JAHM.

2 *Ibid.*

3 Claire Tomalin, *Jane Austen: A Life* (London: Viking, 1997), 180–2.

4 Harris Family Archive, CKS, U624/C6; C23/1–15; Margaret Wilson to Sophia Hillan, 17 June 2010.

5 FCK, 10 July – 1 August 1834, Pocket Books, CKS, Knatchbull Archive, U951/F24/31.

6 Caroline Austen to Emma Austen (later Austen Leigh), 10 August 1834, HRO, Austen Leigh Family Archive, 23M93/87/3; Deirdre Le Faye, *A Chronology of Jane Austen and her Family* (Cambridge: Cambridge University Press, 2006), 650.

7 *Ibid.*

8 JA to CEA, 20–22 June 1808. Deirdre Le Faye, ed. *Jane Austen's Letters* (1995; reprint, London: The Folio Society, 2003), no. 53.

9 FCK, 31 December 1834, Pocket Books, CKS, Knatchbull Achive, U951/F24/31.

10 Lushington Family Tree, CKS, Harris Archive, U624. Anne Elizabeth Harris (1780–1856) married Stephen Rumbold Lushington (1776–1868). Their daughter, Mary Anne, married James Wildman of Chilham Castle.

11 FCK, 19–21 August 1834, Pocket Books, CKS, Knatchbull Archive, U951/F24/31.

12 Captain John Hart to Viscountess Forbes, 17 September 1834, PRONI, Granard Papers, Register of Irish Archives, K/3/1.

13 CBK, 17 October 1834, Diaries, 8, JAHM.

14 CBK, 18 October 1834, Diaries, 8, JAHM.

15 CBK, 19 October 1834, Diaries, 8, JAHM.

16 CBK, 20 October 1834, Diaries, 8, JAHM.

17 *Ibid.*

18 See Malcolm Day, *Voices from the World of Jane Austen* (London; David and Charles, 2007), 137–142 for discussion of various qualities of carriage and conditions of travel.

19 CBK, 20 October 1834, Diaries, 8, JAHM.

20 CBK, 21 October 1834, Diaries, 8, JAHM.

21 *Ibid.*

22 *Ibid.*

23 *Ibid.*

24 *Ibid.*

25 Lord George's brother, Lord Downshire, had two daughters, Ladies Charlotte and Mary Hill, then nineteen and seventeen.

26 'In spite of her sense of rank, she was not a dignified figure, especially at this stage of her career.' David Cecil, *The Cecils of Hatfield House* (London: Constable & Co., 1973), 192.

27 CBK, 21 October 1834, Diaries, 8, JAHM. The diary before this, vol. 7, in which CBK may have given details of Cassandra's engagement to Musgrave Harris and explained why it was 'such a shocking thing' is one of two missing from the collection at Jane Austen's House. It is not known whether they are still in existence.

28 CBK, 22 October, 1834, Diaries, 8, JAHM.

29 *Ibid.*

30 *Ibid.*

31 CBK, October – November 1834, Diaries, 8, JAHM.

32 CBK, 19 November 1835, Diaries, 9, JAHM; January 1836, 10, JAHM.

33 Inventory of clothing and linen belonging to Lady George Hill, 1834, CKS, Knatchbull Archive, U951/C132/2.

34 *Ibid.*

35 CBK, 12 December 1834, Diaries, 8, JAHM.

36 CBK, 29 December 1835, Diaries, 9, JAHM.

37 CBK, 25 January 1835, Diaries, 10, JAHM.

38 W.A. Maguire, *The Downshire Estates in Ireland: 1801–1845* (Oxford: The Clarendon Press, 1972), 88.

39 Estyn Evans, introduction to *Facts from Gweedore, Compiled from the Notes of Lord George Hill, M.R.I.A., A facsimile Reprint of the Fifth Edition, 1887* (Belfast: Institute of Irish Studies, 1971), vi.

40 Le Faye, *Chronology*, 657.

41 Margaret Wilson, *Almost Another Sister: The Family Life of Fanny Knight, Jane Austen's Favourite Niece* (Kent: Kent Arts & Libraries, 1990), 106.

42 CBK, 31 December 1837, Diaries, 11, JAHM; JA to CEA, 9 December 1808, *Letters*, ed. Le Faye, no. 62.

43 Sir Edward Knatchbull to FCK, 18 March 1838, CKS, Knatchbull Archive, U951/C128/14.

44 JA to Anna Austen, 10–18 August 1814, Le Faye, *Letters*, no. 104.

45 Lord George Hill, *Facts from Gweedore, with Useful Hints to Donegal Tourists* (Dublin: Philip Dixon, Hardy and Sons, 1845), 25.

46 Aidan Manning, *Donegal Poitín: A History* (Letterkenny: Donegal Printing Company, 2002), 216–8.

47 Hill, *Facts from Gweedore* (1845), 25.

48 Evans, Introduction, *Facts from Gweedore* (1971), vii–viii. See also E.R.R. Green, 'The Western Seaboard', in R. Dudley Edwards and T. Desmond Williams, *The Great Famine: Studies in Irish History 1845–52* (Dublin: Lilliput Press, 1994), 113–4.

49 Evans, Introduction, *Facts from Gweedore* (1971), viii.

50 Tom Ferris, *Irish Railways; A New History*

(Dublin: Gill and Macmillan, 2008), 115ff.

51 Lord George Hill to Lord Marcus Hill, 30 June 1839, PRONI, Downshire Papers, D671/C/348/19.

52 Hill, *Facts from Gweedore* (1845), 9.

53 F.H. Aalen and Hugh Brody, *Gola: The Life and Last Days of an Island Community* (Cork: Mercier Press, 1969), 34.

54 Hill, *Facts from Gweedore* (1845), 9.

55 FCK to Miss Chapman, 9 October 1838, CKS, Knatchbull Archive, U951/C109/20.

56 CBK, January–March 1841, Diaries, 13, JAHM.

57 LGH to Lord Downshire, 15 March 1842, PRONI, Downshire Papers, D671/C/348/20.

CHAPTER 5

1 *Persuasion*, 199.

2 In Irish, Beal Atha Daire. Legend has it that 'Turlogh Mac Suibhne ... was defeated by O'Donnell and O'Doherty at Fearsad Mhor ... was followed and overtaken at Beal Atha Daire where he was slain, "and they say it was his old age and inability to walk that was the cause of his slaying".' Seamus McGee, *Ramelton* (Ramelton Historical Research Association, 1994), 11. Lord George's house, built in the Georgian era, about 1780, and surrounded by a park of 200 acres, was described in the *Ordnance Survey of 1833–5* as 'a good whitewashed house of two storeys high'. It contained examples of archaeological survivals from the Bronze age within its grounds, undoubtedly of interest to the antiquarian in Lord George. See Angélique Day and Patrick McWilliams, eds., *Ordnance Survey Memoirs of Ireland*, 38 (Belfast: The Institute of Irish Studies, 1997), 89; Brian Lacy et al., *Archaeological Survey of County Donegal*, (Lifford: Donegal County Council, 1983), 64.

3   Lord George Hill, *Facts from Gweedore, with Useful Hints to Donegal Tourists* (Dublin: Philip Dixon, Hardy and Sons, 1845), 6.

4   Estyn Evans, introduction to *Facts from Gweedore, Compiled from the Notes of Lord George Hill, M.R.I.A., A facsimile Reprint of the Fifth Edition*, 1887 (Belfast: Institute of Irish Studies, 1971), xii.

5   LGH to Lord Downshire, 15 March 1842, PRONI, Downshire Papers, D671/C/348/20.

6   FCK, 17 March 1842, Pocket Books, CKS, Knatchbull Archive, U951/F24/39.

7   Cassandra is buried in Conwal Church of Ireland Cemetery in Letterkenny, County Donegal. Her inscription reads: 'Sacred to the memory of Cassandra Jane, the beloved wife of Lord George Augusta Hill who died March 15th 1842. Aged Thirty-Five years. "The Lord gave and the Lord hath taken away, blessed be the name of the Lord".'

8   FCK, 28 March 1842, Pocket Books, CKS, Knatchbull Archive, U951/F24/39.

9   FCK, 30 March 1842, Pocket Books, CKS, Knatchbull Archive, U951/F24/39.

10   FCK, 7 April 1842, Pocket Books, CKS, Knatchbull Archive, U951/F24/39.

11   CBK, 11 April 1842, Diaries, 13, JAHM.

12   FCK, 29 April 1842, Pocket Books, CKS, Knatchbull Archive, U951/F24/39.

13   FCK, 2 May 1842, Pocket Books, CKS, Knatchbull Archive, U951/F24/39.

14   FCK, 13 May 1842, Pocket Books, CKS, Knatchbull Archive, U951/F24/39.

15   FCK, 16 May 1842, Pocket Books, CKS, Knatchbull Archive, U951/F24/39.

16   FCK, 31 December 1842, summary of the year, Pocket Books, CKS, Knatchbull Archive, U951/F24/39.

17   FCK, August 1842, Pocket Books, CKS, Knatchbull Archive, U951/F24/39; Updown was near Betteshanger in Kent. Built in the early eighteenth century, it had a small,

handsome park. Margaret Wilson to Sophia Hillan, 18 September 2010.

18   FCK, December 1842, Pocket Books, CKS, Knatchbull Archive, U951/F24/39.

19   FCK, September – November 1842, Pocket Books, CKS, Knatchbull Archive, U951/F24/40.

20   FCK, May 1845, Pocket Books, CKS, Knatchbull Archive, U951/F24/42. It is not clear whether Louisa travelled to Ireland between 1842 and 1845, as no direct reference is made to it by FCK.

21   FCK, December 1845, Pocket Books, CKS, Knatchbull Archive, U951/F24/42.

22   LGH to Lord Downshire, 25 May 1842, PRONI, Downshire Papers, D671/C/348/23.

23   LGH, *Facts from Gweedore* (1845), 35–6.

24   *Gweedore Hotel Book*, 25 May 1842, 1, 36, Donegal County Archives, Lifford, County Donegal. A second volume, discovered in an attic during renovations of the original building, is held at An Chúirt, Gweedore Court Hotel and Heritage Centre (formerly the Gweedore Hotel), Gweedore, County Donegal. No other volumes are known to have survived.

25   October 1844, *GHB*, 1, Donegal County Archives, Lifford, County Donegal.

26   Lord Downshire, 31 August 1842, *GHB*, 1, Donegal County Archives, Lifford, County Donegal.

27   Anon., 1843, *GHB*, 1, Donegal County Archives, Lifford, County Donegal.

28   Hill, *Facts from Gweedore* (1845), 36.

29   A plaque in the church which Lord George built in Bunbeg describes him as a 'self-denying Christian [who] devoted his life and fortune to civilise Gweedore, and to raise its people to a higher social and moral level'.

30   Lord Downshire, 23 October 1844, *GHB*, 1, Donegal County Archives, Lifford, County Donegal. See also Maguire, *Downshire Estates*, 42–3, for Lord Downshire's criteria

for valuation of his tenants' property in 1844.

31 John Killen, ed., *The Famine Decade: Contemporary Accounts 1841–1851* (Belfast: Blackstaff Press, 1995), 28.

32 Peter Somerville-Large, *The Irish Country House: A Social History* (London: Sinclair-Stevenson, 1995), 250.

33 *Persuasion*, 268.

34 Roy Foster, *Modern Ireland, 1600–1972* (London and New York: Allen Lane, Penguin, 1988), 31n, 327–8.

35 See also Foster, *Modern Ireland*, 291; 310–16; Dudley Edwards and Williams, *The Great Famine*, 83; J.C. Beckett, *The Making of Modern Ireland, 1603–1923* (London: Faber and Faber, 1966), 331–35.

36 Frances Anne Edgeworth, *A Memoir of Maria Edgeworth* (London, 1867, 3 vols.), 3, 85; quoted in Oliver McDonagh, 'Politics, 1830–45', *New History of Ireland*, 5, 1: 1801–1870, 194.

37 Foster, *Modern Ireland*, 320.

38 William Carleton, *The Black Prophet: A Novel of Irish Famine* (1847: reprint from 1899 edition, Shannon: Irish University Press, 1972), vii.

39 *Ibid.*, 227.

40 *Ibid.*, 299.

41 Lord John Russell to Lord Lansdowne, October 1846, G.P. Gooch, ed., *The Later Correspondence of Lord John Russell 1840–1878* (London: Longmans, Green and Co, 1925), 151.

42 Foster, *Modern Ireland*, 320; Cormac O'Grada, *Ireland Before and After the Famine; Explorations in Economic History, 1800–1925* (Manchester and New York: Manchester University Press, 1993), 127.

43 Margaret Wilson, *Almost Another Sister: The Family Life of Fanny Knight, Jane Austen's Favourite Niece* (Kent: Kent Arts & Libraries, 1990), 104.

44 JA to FCK, 20–1 February 1817. Deirdre Le Faye, ed. *Jane Austen's Letters* (1995;

reprint, London: The Folio Society, 2003), no. 151; Le Faye, 'The Nephew Who Missed Jane Austen', *Notes and Queries*, NS 31/4 (December 1984): 471–2.

45 CBK, 5–31 May 1843, Diaries, 13, JAHM.

46 CBK, 23 March 1845, Diaries, 14, JAHM.

47 William Austen Leigh and Montagu George Knight, *Chawton Manor and its Owners: A Family History* (London: Smith, Elder & Co, 1911), 171. The Jane Austen Society had been founded by Dorothy Darnell in 1940 to gain possession of Chawton Cottage with the intention of making it a museum. It was finally purchased in 1947 by Thomas Edward Carpenter, in response to an appeal published in *The Times* in December 1946, and was administered by the Jane Austen Memorial Trust, set up by Mr Carpenter in memory of his son who had been killed in action. The house was formally opened in 1949. See Elizabeth Jenkins, Introduction, *Collected Reports of the Jane Austen Society, vol. 2, 1949–1965*.

48 FCK to Miss Chapman, 17 September 1845, CKS, U951/C109.

49 Maguire, *Downshire Estates*, 8.

50 21 February 1845, *GHB*, 1, Donegal County Archives, Lifford, County Donegal.

51 30 May 1845, *GHB*, 1, Donegal County Archives, Lifford, County Donegal.

52 19 August 1845, *GHB*, 1, Donegal County Archives, Lifford, County Donegal.

53 Maureen Wall, 'County Donegal in 1845: Excerpts from the Journal of John O'Hagan, giving an account of a tour in Ulster in the summer of 1845, presented, with an introductory note, by Maureen Wall,' *Donegal Annual*, 1970, 167.

54 *Ibid.*, 167. The Young Irelanders, thinkers and writers, Catholic and Protestant, had broken with O'Connell over the question of university education in Ireland – they favouring secular education, O'Connell a system based on religious segregation. At the time of their visit to Gweedore, Mitchel and his colleagues had formed the

Irish Confederation, under the leadership of William Smith O'Brien, 'by birth and possession amongst the most distinguished of the Protestant gentry'. Denis Gwynn, *Young Ireland and 1848* (Oxford: Blackwell Ltd, and Cork: Cork University Press, 1949), 18. See also *Ireland 1815–1870: Emancipation, Famine and Religion*, ed. Donnchadh Ó Corráin and Tomás Ó Ríordan (Dublin: Four Courts Press, 2011), 27–8. Smith O'Brien's daughter Charlotte Grace would later prove a loyal friend to Cassandra Hill, youngest daughter of Lord George and Cassandra.

55 'In April Lord Downshire died suddenly in Ireland ... 15 May Lord G. Hill & his 4 children & Louisa went to Ireland ... 19th December Lord G. Hill returned to Godmersham & published his book, "Facts from Gweedore". FCK, Summary, 31 December 1845, Pocket Books, CKS, Knatchbull Archive, U951/F24/42.

56 FCK to Miss Chapman, 31 January 1846, Pocket Books, CKS, Knatchbull Archive, U951/C109/25.

57 FCK to Miss Chapman, February 1846, Pocket Books, CKS, Knatchbull Archive, U951/C109/26.

58 FCK to Miss Chapman, 10 February 1846, Pocket Books, CKS, Knatchbull Archive, U951/C109/27.

59 The *Illustrated London News* made the point, four years later in 1849, that 'few of [the landowners] have it in their power to be merciful or generous to their poorer tenantry ... they are themselves engaged in a life and death struggle with their creditors'. *Illustrated London News*, 3 October 1849, quoted in Ó Corráin and O'Ríordan, *Ireland 1815–1870*, 73.

60 LGH to Famine Relief Commission, 13 September 1846, stamped by Relief Commission, RLFC/3/2/7/12, National Archives of Ireland, Dublin.

61 The Hill children were quarantined at Godmersham with measles and mumps during the spring of 1846, and spent the summer in recuperation at Dover, in a house lent by the Rices, while Lord George commuted between England and Ireland. FCK to Miss Chapman, 25 April 1846, CKS, Knatchbull Archive, U951/C109/29; 19 June 1846, CKS, U951/C109/31.

62 FCK to Miss Chapman, 30 November 1846, CKS, Knatchbull Archive, U951/C109/32.

63 See Famine Relief Commission Papers 1845–1847, National Archives of Ireland, RLFC3/2/7/12. Description reads: 'Lord George Hill, chairman, requesting further aid, justifying the sale of food at below cost price, because of the district's remoteness and the people's great need and requesting that seed be provided for the committee at one of the western Donegal ports rather than at Longford. Encloses certified subscription lists, including some for soup kitchens at Stranacorcragh, and Dunlewey. Also includes printed appeal for subscriptions to supplement the funds already provided by Hill.' The similarity in tone and layout of this appeal to Lord George's earlier plea for funds to build a glebe house indicates his grasp of the power of the media in garnering support, and the involvement of Louisa shows how quickly she developed an astute understanding of advertising.

64 Foster, *Modern Ireland*, 327; J.C. Beckett, *A Short History of Ireland* (London: The Cresset Library, 1986), 136–7.

65 See Foster, *Modern Ireland*, 328.

66 Louisa Knight (Lady George Hill) to FCK, 1847, CKS, Knatchbull Archive, U951/C109/35.

67 J.C. Beckett, *The Making of Modern Ireland, 1603–1923* (London: Faber and Faber, 1966), 350.

68 Captain John Knight, 17 September 1847, *GHB*, 1, Donegal County Archives, Lifford, County Donegal.

69 FCK to Miss Chapman, August 1847, CKS, Knatchbull Archive, U951/C109/34.

70   *Ibid.*

71   CBK, 18 May 1847, Diaries, 14, JAHM.

72   CBK, 12 March 1835, Diaries, 8, JAHM.

73   Fanny's approval is indicated in a letter to Miss Chapman, 'I am … very glad to learn your favourable opinion of my sister's marriage. It is a subject upon which people differ so much that I seldom introduce the subject unasked, but it is of course a satisfaction to know when our friends see it in the same light as we do ourselves.' 11 September 1847, CKS, Knatchbull Archive, U951/C109/36.

74   CBK, 9 January 1836, Diaries, 9, JAHM.

75   Despite his lack of enthusiasm for the marriage, Charles Knight's diaries for the following years indicate that he was later fully reconciled with his sister and Lord George Hill. See CBK, Diaries, 15, 14 August 1847 – 24 March, 1851.

76   FCK to Miss Chapman, 25 August 1847, CKS, Knatchbull Archive, U951/C109/34.

77   *Ibid.*

78   Margaret Wilson to Sophia Hillan, re second reading of the Marriages Bill in the House of Lords, 25 February 1851.

79   12 June 1846, Protection of Life (Ireland) Bill, Adjourned Debate, House of Commons. http://hansard.millbanksystems.com/commons/1846.

80   Thomas Carlyle, Preface, *Reminiscences of My Irish Journey in 1849* (London: Sampson Low, Marston, Searle, and Rivington, 1882), v.

81   *Ibid.*, 223.

82   *Ibid.*, 229–30.

83   *Ibid.*, 230.

84   M.C. Hammond, *Relating to Jane: Studies on the Life and Novels of Jane Austen with a Life of her Niece Elizabeth Austen/Knight.* (London; Minerva Press, 1998), 247; 292.

85   Carlyle, *Reminiscences*, 231.

86   *Ibid.*

87   *Ibid.*, 236–43.

88   CBK, 31 December 1835, Diaries, 9, JAHM.

89   Cecil Woodham-Smith, *The Great Hunger* (London, Hamish Hamilton, 1962), 24.

90   *Ibid.*, 266.

91   Carlyle, *Reminiscences*, 251.

92   *Ibid.*, 253.

93   FCK to Miss Chapman, July 1846, CKS, Knatchbull Archive, U951/C109/33.

94   *Persuasion*, 199.

CHAPTER 6

1   MK to FCK, 23 July 1849, CKS, Knatchbull Archive, U951/C113/6.

2   Margaret Wilson, *Almost Another Sister: The Family Life of Fanny Knight, Jane Austen's Favourite Niece* (Kent: Kent Arts & Libraries, 1990), 87–9.

3   FCK moved to the Hugessen family home at Provender, close to Faversham in Kent, where her husband had lived during his father's lifetime. 'Fanny was expected to live there and to leave it to her eldest son.' Wilson, *Almost Another Sister*, 90.

4   JA to CEA, 3 January 1801. Deirdre Le Faye, ed. *Jane Austen's Letters* (1995; reprint, London: The Folio Society, 2003), no. 29.

5   MK to FCK, 23 July 1849, CKS, Knatchbull Archive, U951/C113/6. John's friend 'Mr Hill' is not identified but, since no name or indication of acquaintance is made by Marianne, seems unlikely to be a member of the Hill family to whom the Knights had by 1849 been related for fifteen years.

6   M.C. Hammond, *Relating to Jane: Studies on the Life and Novels of Jane Austen with a Life of her Niece Elizabeth Austen/Knight.* (London; Minerva Press, 1998), 299; 271. George Finch-Hatton was a descendant of the poet Anne Finch, Countess of Winchilsea (1661–1720). One of the descendants of the marriage between Lizzy's daughter Fanny Margaretta and George Finch-Hatton was Denys Finch-

Hatton (1887–1931), later the lover of Karen, Baroness Blixen who, as Isak Dinesen, wrote of their affair in her memoir, *Out of Africa*. Another is Anna Chancellor, who played Caroline Bingley in the 1995 BBC production of *Pride and Prejudice*.

7   Louisa Rice to Edward Rice, 1852, quoted in Jane Corder, *Akin to Jane: Family Genealogy of Jane Austen's Siblings and Descendants, 1760–1953*, MS compiled 1953, Jane Austen's House Museum, Chawton, Hants, 287–8.

8   Edward Austen Knight to Edward Knight Jr, June 1822, HRO, Knight Archive, 39M89/F111/5.

9   *Ibid.*, Postscript, 1835.

10 George Oxenden to MK, 1838, HRO, Knight Archive, 39M89/F117/ 2–5.

11 CBK, 11 October 1835, Diaries, 9.

12 Jane Austen, *Lady Susan, The Watsons, Sanditon*, ed. Drabble, 208–9.

13 CBK, 10 October 1835, Diaries, 9.

14 Morland Rice to Edward Rice, 18 September 1850, Rice Archive, CKS, EKU116/ uncatalogued, Hammond no. 1/40. Morland Rice does not seem to have been a naturally unkind man, yet it was noted in the family that he tended, especially after two severe head injuries, to be rather more disconcertingly sharp than accorded with his essential good nature, demonstrated by his kindness to his grandfather. See Hammond, *Relating to Jane*, 282–6.

15 Louisa Rice, 1850, quoted in Hammond, *Relating to Jane*, 291–2.

16 EKR to Caroline Cassandra Rice, May 1850, quoted in Hammond, *Relating to Jane*, 247–8. Charlotte was Henry Knight's daughter, born in 1837 to his second wife, Charlotte Northey.

17 William Austen Leigh and Montagu George Knight, *Chawton Manor and its Owners: A Family History* (London: Smith, Elder & Co, 1911), 172.

18 FCK to Miss Chapman, 2 March 1853, CKS, Knatchbull Archive, U951/C109/53.

19 *Ibid.*

20 *Ibid.*

21 *Ibid.*

22 *Ibid.*

23 Marianne Sophia Rice to Louisa Rice, 1853, CKS, Rice Archive, EK-U116 (uncatalogued), Hammond no. 1/65.

24 Caroline Cassandra Rice to Louisa Rice, 1853, CKS, Rice Archive, EK-U116 (uncatalogued), Hammond no. 1/184.

25 FCK to Miss Chapman, 30 June 1853, CKS, Knatchbull Archive, U951/C109/54.

26 *Ibid.*

27 Godmersham Park was let to Carnegie Jervis, 'who succeeded his grandfather as 3rd Viscount St Vincent in 1859'. Nigel Nicolson, *Godmersham Park, Kent: Before, During and Since Jane Austen's Day* (Chawton, Hants: The Jane Austen Society, 1996), 27.

28 John Knight to CBK, 1 September 1853, HRO, Knight Archive, 39M89/F125/1. Apart from his entry in the *Gweedore Hotel Book* in 1847, only two letters from John have survived, each characterised by his own particular style of spelling, grammar and punctuation. The second was written after Charles Knight died in 1867.

29 'Release of Miss Knight's Annuity', *Godmersham House Book*, HRO, Knight Archive, 18M61/Box A/Bundle 5.

30 *The Garden Book of Marianne Knight*, HRO, Knight Archive, 18M61/Box 88/46.

31 Paul Kerr, *The Crimean War* (London: Channel Four, Boxtree, 1997), 10.

32 'The conflict certainly had a religious spark, a fight between rival Latin and Greek Orthodox priests inside the Church of the Holy Sepulchre on Good Friday 1846, which left 40 dead. And it is abundantly true that Russian Orthodoxy saw the Holy Lands as an extension of their spiritual

motherland and the French Catholics had a religious heritage they were prepared to defend militarily.' David Hearst, review of Orlando Figes, *Crimea: The Last Crusade* (London: Allen Lane, 2010), *Guardian*, 30 October 2010, 9.

33 *Ibid.*

34 *Ibid.*

35 Cecil Rice to Louisa Rice, November 1854, from Hammond, *Relating to Jane*, 356.

36 George Moyle Billington to Rev. and Mrs John Billington, 28 March 1856, CKS, Billington Archive, U1045/F9. See Kerr, *The Crimean War*, 40, and David Murphy, *Ireland and the Crimean War* (Dublin: Four Courts Press, 2002).

37 *Ibid.*

38 *The New Annual Army List for 1861* (London: John Murray, 1861), 351.

39 Murphy, *Ireland and the Crimean War*, 230.

40 Hammond, *Relating to Jane*, 362.

41 Louisa Hill to FCK, 27 January 1858, CKS, Knatchbull Archive, U951/C113/8.

42 Norah Hill to Louisa Rice, 20 January 1858, CKS, Rice Archive, EK-U116 (uncatalogued) , Hammond no. 1/84.

43 Figes, *Crimea: The Last Crusade*, 454.

44 Cecil Rice, December 1856, quoted in Hammond, *Relating to Jane*, 366–7.

45 *Ibid.*, 367.

46 25 February 1851, Marriages Bill, House of Lords, debates. http://hansard.millbanksystems.com/lords/1851/feb/25/marriages-bill.

47 Pamela Fitzgerald was born at Hamburg in 1796, to Lord Edward Fitzgerald and his wife Pamela (née Sims). She married Sir Guy Campbell on 21 November 1820. The youngest of their eleven children, Madeline, became the mother of George Wyndham (1863–1913), Chief Secretary for Ireland (1900–1905). See *Papers of Pamela, Lady Campbell and Her Family*, National Library of Ireland, Dublin, Collection List no. 88 (MSS 40, 024-40, 021, Accession no. 6048).

48 William Austen Leigh, Richard Arthur Austen Leigh and Deirdre Le Faye, *Jane Austen: A Family Record* (London: The British Library, 1989), 247. See also Edward, 1st Lord Brabourne, ed., *Letters of Jane Austen*, 2 vols. (London: Richard Bentley and Son, 1884), 1: 79–80.

49 *Ibid.*, 248.

50 *Ibid.*

51 *Ibid.*

52 See George Moore, *A Drama in Muslin* (London: Vizetelly, 1886).

53 Louisa Hill to FCK, 27 January 1858, CKS, Knatchbull Archive, U951/C113/8.

54 Norah Hill to Louisa Rice, 20 January 1858, CKS, Rice Archive, EK-U116 (uncatalogued), Hammond no. 1/84.

55 William Knight to FCK, 27 March 1858, CKS, Knatchbull Archive, U951/C113/2.

56 Louisa Hill to FCK, CKS, Knatchbull Archive, U951/C113/9.

57 *Ibid.*

58 Lord Carlisle to Lady Campbell, 21 June 1858, Dublin, National Library of Ireland (Manuscripts), MS 40, 028/6.

59 Hammond, *Relating to Jane*, 263, 310.

60 Isle O'Valla is at Ballyculter, south of Strangford at Cloghy, in County Down. The house, which is now a ruin, was opened in 1817 as a Charter School.

61 Edward Knight to FCK, 1 January 1858, CKS, Knatchbull Archive, U951/C113/1.

62 Hammond, *Relating to Jane*, 308. Margaret Hammond suggests these references are to Edward Knight's children Elizabeth Adela, born 1841, and Charles, then twelve. Elizabeth, another Lizzy, was later to be a particular favourite of Marianne's. 'Derby' was the pet name of Emilius Bayley, husband of Marianne Sophia Rice.

63 *Ibid.*, 310.

CHAPTER 7

1 The 'Big House' in Ireland, usually the home of a member of the landed gentry, was not the same as a Great House, belonging to a member of the aristocracy. 'The paradox of these big houses', as the novelist Elizabeth Bowen (1899–1973), herself the daughter of one of the finest examples, Bowen's Court in Cork, wrote in 1940, 'is that often they are not big at all … [They] would be only called "big" in Ireland – in England they would be country houses, no more.' See Elizabeth Bowen, 'The Big House', in *The Mulberry Tree: Writings of Elizabeth Bowen*, ed. Hermione Lee (London: Virago, 1986), 25–30.

2 Brendan Mac Suibhne, 'Soggarth Aroon and Gombeen-Priest: Canon James MacFadden (1842–1917)', in *Radical Irish Priests 1660–1970*, ed. Gerard Moran (Dublin: Four Courts Press, 1998), 152–3.

3 *Ibid.*

4 Thomas Carlyle, *Reminiscences of my Irish Journey in 1849* (London: Sampson Low, Marston Searle and Rivington, 1882), 246

5 Peter Gray, *Famine, Land and Politics: British Government and Irish Society 1843–1850* (Dublin: Irish Academic Press, 1999), 140.

6 Brendan Mac Suibhne, 'Agrarian Improvement and Social Unrest: Lord George Hill and the Gaoth Dobhair Sheep War', in W. Nolan, L. Ronayne and M. Dunleavy, eds., *Donegal History and Society* (Dublin: 1995), 557.

7 See C.W.P. MacArthur, ed. 'Memoirs of a Land Agent, Part 2,' *Donegal Annual* 47 (1995): 62–3, for one first-hand account by a Donegal land agent, Daniel Swiney, of Lord George's protecting his interests.

8 W.E. Vaughan, *Landlords and Tenants in Mid-Victorian Ireland* (Oxford: Clarendon Press, 1994), 221.

9 'A question of general interests which arises is the apparent anomaly of the existence in this depressed area of the Ulster custom of tenant right, which is believed to have originated in the special circumstances of the Ulster plantation, when protestant settlers build their houses and improved their holdings at their own expense. The Ulster Custom not only gave tenants some security of tenure, but, it is generally held "promoted a spirit of manliness and independence and encouraged industry and respect for the law".' Estyn Evans, introduction to *Facts from Gweedore, Compiled from the Notes of Lord George Hill, M.R.I.A., A facsimile Reprint of the Fifth Edition, 1887* (Belfast: Institute of Irish Studies, 1971), xvi.

10 Mac Suibhne, 'Agrarian Improvement and Social Unrest', 565.

11 W.E. Vaughan, 'The Derryveagh Evictions, 1861', in *Donegal: The Making of a Northern County* (Dublin: Four Courts Press, 2007), 229.

12 Mac Suibhne, 'Agrarian Improvement and Social Unrest' n. 47, 579.

13 *Ibid.*, 576.

14 *Ibid.*, 231.

15 Louisa Hill to Henry Knight, 20 August 1863, HRO, Knight Archive, 39M89/F121/13. According to the *Ordnance Survey Memoirs*, 'The Fort Stewart ferry, the property of Sir James Stewart, is well-conducted and worth 400 pounds per annum. Laden carts, carriages, horses, cattle and passengers are passed over with the greatest expedition. The tolls are collected on the Tully side, 3d for a man, 5d for a horse. Good cattle and other boats are constantly ready on each side [of] the water.' Angélique Day and Patrick McWilliams, eds., *Ordnance Survey Memoirs of Ireland*, 38 (Belfast: The Institute of Irish Studies, 1997), 90.

16 M.C. Hammond, *Relating to Jane: Studies on the Life and Novels of Jane Austen with a Life of her Niece Elizabeth Austen/Knight.* (London; Minerva Press, 1998), 320.

17 Her niece Elizabeth (Lizzie) Bradford, née Knight, was then living in India. Like her brother Montagu, she remained close to Marianne after she left Chawton for Ireland, and may have sent this recipe, if it was not brought back by one of the nephews who served in India during the Mutiny.

18 Godmersham House Book, HRO, Knight Archive, 'Release of Miss Knight's Annuity', 18M61/Box A, Bundle 5.

19 *The Garden Book of Marianne Knight*, HRO, Knight Archive, 18M61/Box 88/46.

20 Margaret Knight to EKR, with postscript by John Knight, 18 October 1867, CKS, Rice Archive, EK-U116 (uncatalogued), Hammond no. 1/131.

21 *Ibid.*

22 *Ibid.*

23 FCK to Miss Chapman, 2 May 1853, CKS, Knatchbull Archive, U951/C109/53.

24 Margaret Wilson, *Almost Another Sister: The Family Life of Fanny Knight, Jane Austen's Favourite Niece* (Kent: Kent Arts & Libraries, 1990), 106.

25 John Knight to EKR, CKS, Rice Archive, EK-U116 (uncatalogued), Hammond no. 1/131.

26 MK to FCK, 31 October 1867, HRO, Knight Archive, 39M89/C113/7.

27 James Edward had become James Edward Austen Leigh on his inheritance of the Leigh Perrot estate in 1836.

28 Anna Lefroy to JEAL, December 1864, HRO, Austen Leigh Archive, 23M93/97/4.

29 MAAL, *James Edward Austen Leigh: A Memoir by his Daughter,* privately printed, 1911, 261–2.

30 Louisa Knatchbull-Hugessen to JEAL, 12 July 1869, 'Letters re Memoir', National Portrait Gallery, London.

31 *Ibid.* Fanny's letters from Jane Austen remained unpublished until after her death in 1882, when her eldest son, Lord Brabourne, found them, publishing them in two volumes in 1884.

32 Wilson, *Almost Another Sister*, 112.

33 FCK to MK, 23 August 1869, first published in *Cornhill Magazine*, vol. 163, numbers 973–8, Winter 1947/8–Spring 1949, 72–3. Marcia Rice, daughter of Cecil and granddaughter of Lizzy, thought this letter might have been occasioned by family discussion about Jane Austen. Wilson, *Almost Another Sister*, 111. The identification of Marianne as the recipient was first made by Margaret Wilson.

34 Hammond, *Relating to Jane*, 428.

35 Nigel Nicolson, *Godmersham Park, Kent: Before, During and Since Jane Austen's Day* (Chawton, Hants: The Jane Austen Society, 1996), 27–8.

36 Wilson, *Almost Another Sister*, 116.

37 EKR to Louisa Rice, 24 July 1874, quoted in Hammond, *Relating to Jane*, 428–9.

38 Caroline Cassandra Rice to Louisa Rice, July 1874, CKS, Rice Archive, EKU116/ (uncatalogued), Hammond no. 1/144, quoted in Hammond, *Relating to Jane*, 430.

39 EKR to Louisa Rice, 29 July 1874, quoted in Hammond, *Relating to Jane*, 429.

40 EKR to Louisa Rice, July 1874, CKS, Rice Archive, EK-U116/(uncatalogued), Hammond no. 1/144. Lizzy did eventually forgive her brother. See Hammond, *Relating to Jane*, 432. A letter to Edward Royds Rice from J.F. Harvey, one of the staff on the Godmersham Estate, describes Mr Harvey's buying from the auction, which took place in the spring of 1875, a clock and dressing table which he thought the Rices would like to have. 'The sale of the Estate is regarded by myself and I may say by every Tenant and Labourer on the property with deep regret, a feeling in which I am sure you and Mrs Rice deeply sympathise.' J.F. Harvey to Edward Royds Rice, 4 May 1875, CKS, Rice Archive, EK-U116 (uncatalogued), Hammond no.1/145.

41   The second edition of JEAL's *Memoir* included not only *Lady Susan*, *The Watsons* and a summary of *Sanditon* but also the cancelled chapter of *Persuasion*. See Deirdre Le Faye, *A Chronology of Jane Austen and her Family* (Cambridge: Cambridge University Press, 2006), 691.

42   Wilson, *Almost Another Sister*, 116–7.

43   EKR to Walter Rice, 1878, CKS, Rice Archive, EK-U116/(uncatalogued), Hammond no. 1/312.

44   J.C. Beckett, *The Making of Modern Ireland* (London: Faber and Faber, 1966), 335.

45   See Donnchadh Ó Corráin and Tomás Ó Riordan (eds), *Ireland 1815–1870: Emancipation, Famine and Religion* (Dublin: Four Courts Press, 2011), 30: 'The failed uprising of 1848 seemed to mark the end of the radical politics of Young Ireland, but some had escaped to France and America ... In 1858, James Stephens returned from Paris to Ireland where he established a new revolutionary organisation known as the Fenian Brotherhood (or IRB). A parallel branch was formed in America by John O'Mahony. From the outset, the Fenians were opposed to constitutional tactics, believing that British rule could only be ended by armed insurrection. The Catholic bishops, led by Archbishop Paul Cullen, were implacably opposed to the Fenians.'

46   Robert Kee, *The Laurel and the Ivy; The Story of Charles Stewart Parnell and Irish Nationalism* (London: Hamish Hamilton, 1993), 30–1; Max Egremont, *The Cousins: The Friendship, Opinions and Activities of Wilfrid Scawen Blunt and George Wyndham* (London: Collins, 1977), 95.

47   See Liam O'Raghallaigh, 'Captain Boycott: Man and Myth', in *History Ireland* 19, no.1 (January/February, 2011): 28–31.

48   A.P.W. Malcomson, *Virtues of a Wicked Earl: The Life and Legend of William Sydney Clements, 3rd Earl of Leitrim (1806-78)* (Dublin: The Four Courts Press, 2008), 341.

49   *Ibid.*, 217.

50   *Ibid.*, 255.

51   *Ibid.*, 271.

52   Lord George had not given up all hope of making a difference in a distant land. In 1878, just months before his death, he encouraged a group from Donegal to join a party of settlers setting out for Katikati on the shore of Tauranga Harbour in New Zealand, where his neighbour, George Vesey Stewart of Martray, Co. Tyrone, had arranged with the government that land would be granted 'on conditions of occupation and improvement'. Part of the plan seems to have been that a new depot for the Donegal Knitting Company should be set up at Katikati, to the benefit of Lord George's tenants in Gweedore. The scheme does not appear to have been continued by Arthur Hill after his father's death. See Donald Harman Akenson, *Half the World from Home: Perspectives on the Irish in New Zealand 1860-1950*, (Wellington: Victoria University Press, 1990); Alan Mulgan, 'George Vesey Stewart', http://www.teara.govt.nz/en/1966/stewart-george-vesey/1/ and Kay Carter, 'Lord and Lady George Hill', 2 February 2001, http://boards.ancestry.com/surnames.hill/4160/mb.ashx.

53   Death Certificate of Lord George Hill, 17 April 1879, transcribed from Death Register no. 4, 9, Donegal Ancestry, Ramelton, County Donegal.

54   The Land League was founded in Dublin on 21 October 1879, with Charles Stewart Parnell, leader of the Irish Parliamentary Party, as its president. Its secretaries were Michael Davitt, Thomas Brennan and Andrew Joseph Kettle, its treasurers Patrick Egan, Joseph Gillis Biggar and William Henry O'Sullivan. See T.W. Moody, F.X. Martin, F.J. Byrne, eds., *A New History of Ireland, 8: A Chronology of Irish History to 1976* (Oxford: Clarendon Press, 1982), 351.

55 Maria Edgeworth, in her novel *Castle Rackrent* (1800) has her narrator Thady, steward to the reckless and profligate Rackrent family, say of his own son, an attorney, 'Jason Quirk, though he be my son, I must say was a good scholar from his birth and a very 'cute lad – I thought to make him a priest, but he did better for himself.' Edgeworth adds in a note: 'It was customary amongst those of Thady's rank, in Ireland, whenever they could get a little money, to send their sons abroad to St Omer's, or to Spain, to be educated as priests. Now they are educated at Maynooth.' Maria Edgeworth, *Castle Rackrent*, (1800: reprint, Oxford: Oxford University Press, 1964), 22, 108.

56 Michael Logue, Bishop of Raphoe in Donegal (1879–1887) and Cardinal and Archbishop of Armagh (1887–1923) was his cousin: Daniel McGettigan, Bishop of Raphoe (1861–1870) and Archbishop of Armagh (1870–1887) was an uncle.

57 Terence Dooley, *The Big Houses and Landed Estates of Ireland: A Research Guide* (Dublin: Four Courts Press, 2007), 43–4. Donegal was one of the nine counties of the historic province of Ulster, as were Cavan and Monaghan.

58 W.E. Vaughan, *Landlords and Tenants in Ireland, 1848–1904* (Dundalk: Dun Dalgan Press, 1984, revised 1994), 33.

59 James S. Donnelly, Jr, 'Landlords and Tenants,' in *A New History of Ireland, 5: Ireland Under the Union I: 1801–1870*, 332–49.

60 R.F. Foster, *Paddy and Mr Punch: Connections in Irish and English History* (London: Allen Lane and Penguin, 1993), 65–6.

61 *Ibid.*, 66.

62 Edgeworth, *Castle Rackrent,* 20.

63 Griffith's valuation, set by Sir Richard John Griffith (1784–1878) was carried out between 1852 and 1865, following the Valuation (Ireland) Act of 1852.

Replacing the Poor Law Valuation, it set the assessment of rates for administration of the Poor Law, but was not intended to set the letting value of land. The Land League's instruction to its members was that rent above Griffith's Valuation should be withheld if not acceptable. See D.J. Hickey and J.E. Doherty, *A New Dictionary of Irish History from 1800* (Dublin: Gill & Macmillan, 2003), 194.

64 Somerset Ward, G.F. Ward, J.E.A. Ward, Henry Lyle Mulholland, *GHB*, 2, 23–25 May 1881. An Chúirt, the Gweedore Court Hotel, Gweedore, County Donegal. Written below, without a signature, are the words: 'What about the three loaves the above truculent scribe begged & received from the … [scored out] … when undergoing ...' No entries appear to have been made between 1 August 1878 and 30 August 1880, suggesting that the hotel may have been out of operation for some time, not only after boycotting was adopted, but also during the period of Lord George's final illness in 1878–9.

65 The 1881 Land Act, introduced under Gladstone and passed in August, 'virtually conceded the basic demands of the Land League agitation, popularly known as the "three Fs": fair rent, to be assessed by arbitration; fixity of tenure, while the rent was paid; freedom for the tenant to sell his right of occupancy at the best market price.' Beckett, *The Making of Modern Ireland*, 390.

66 Capt. the Hon. Somerset Ward to Capt. Arthur Hill, 27 May 1881, PRONI, Saunderson Papers, T2996/11/1.

67 *Ibid.*

68 *Ibid.*

69 'Passive resistance' was the phrase used by the Land League in its 'No Rent Manifesto', 18 October 1881, signed by, among others, Parnell, Davitt and Dillon: 'Against the passive resistance of the entire population military power has no weapon.' See Richard Aldous and Niamh Puirseil, *We Declare:*

Landmark Documents in Ireland's History (London: Quercus, 2008), 91.

70 The Marquess of Conyngham had given an abatement of 33 per cent. See Ward to Hill, 29 May 1881, PRONI, Saunderson Papers, T2996/11/4.

71 Ward to Hill, 28 May 1881, PRONI, Saunderson Papers, T2996/11/2.

72 *Ibid.*

73 *Ibid.*

74 Ward to Hill, 29 May 1881, PRONI, Saunderson Papers, T2996/11/3.

75 Ward to Hill, 29 May 1881, PRONI, Saunderson Papers, T2996/11/4.

76 *Ibid.*

77 *Ibid.*

CHAPTER 8

1 Jane Corder, *Akin to Jane: Family Genealogy of Jane Austen's Siblings and Descendants, 1760–1953*, MS compiled 1953, Jane Austen's House Museum (JAHM), Chawton, Hants, 51. Second copy lodged at College of Arms, London., 117–18.

2 M.C. Hammond, *Relating to Jane: Studies on the Life and Novels of Jane Austen with a Life of her Niece Elizabeth Austen/Knight.* (London: Minerva Press, 1998), 313–5. The opinion of their brother's kind treatment of his sisters, quoted by Hammond, was expressed by Walter Rice, father of Marcia, writing to his brother Ernest on the day before leaving Dane Court for the last time.

3 MK to Montagu Knight, 11 October 1884, HRO, Knight Archive, 39M89/F124/1. No surviving letters from MK suggest that she was permanently based in Ireland before 1884. Almost all the letters of her correspondence with the Knights of Chawton and the Rices of Dane Court (1884–1895) are from Ballyare House in Donegal; any which are from elsewhere, including those from Norah Ward's

house in Strangford, indicate that MK was permanently based in Donegal.

4 The series of land acts began in 1860 and continued until 1923. Throughout the 1880s there were further Acts not only in 1881 (Land Law [Ireland] Act, providing for fair rent, free sale, fixity of tenure and the establishment of the Land Commission), but also in 1882 (Settled Land Act, empowering the Land Commission to cancel arrears of less than £30); 1885 (Lord Ashbourne's Land Purchase Act, making available a loan fund for tenant purchase); 1887 (Land Law [Ireland] Act providing for the extension of the Act of 1881 to leaseholders); and 1888 (Land Purchase Act giving further extensions of facilities for purchase).

5 MK to Montagu Knight, 11 October 1884, HRO, 39M89/F124/1. Norah Ward Jr had married Henry Lyle Mulholland in 1881. The child she was expecting when this letter was written, Andrew Mulholland, would die at Ypres in September 1914.

6 See correspondence concerning Cassandra Hill's interest in establishing a convalescent home in Ramelton, PRONI, Saunderson Papers, T2996/17/2.

7 Stephen Gwynn, *Highways and Byways in Donegal and Antrim, with Illustrations by Hugh Thomson* (London: Macmillan, 1928), 142.

8 Amanda Vickery, 'Do Not Scribble', *London Review of Books*, 32, no. 21 (4 November 2010): 36.

9 Corder, *Akin to Jane*, 118. Ballyare is, in fact, in County Donegal, not Antrim, as Marcia Rice mistakenly supposed.

10 Cecil Knatchbull-Hugessen to Eva Knatchbull-Hugessen, 29 August 1887, CKS, Knatchbull Archive, U951/C114/1.

11 Robert Kee, *The Laurel and the Ivy: The Story of Charles Stewart Parnell and Irish Nationalism* (London: Hamish Hamilton, 1993), 524–5.

12 *Ibid.*

13 Terence Dooley, *The Big Houses and Landed Estates of Ireland: A Research Guide* (Dublin: Four Courts Press, 2007), 50.

14 Patrick MacGill, in a thinly-veiled portrait of McFadden (renamed Father Devaney), has him declare in his novel *Glenmornan* that 'the Irish people and the Catholic Church are one and the same', almost directly quoting words McFadden used in addressing an 1884 reunion of Donegal emigrants living in Glasgow. See Patrick MacGill, *Glenmornan* (1918, reprint Brandon, 1983), 293; Dooley, *The Big Houses,* 165.

15 Rev. James McFadden, P.P., *The Present and the Past of the Agrarian Struggle in Gweedore: With Letters on the Railway Extension in Donegal* (Londonderry: *The Derry Journal*, 1889), 57. The 'Coercion Act' referred to was the Criminal Law and Procedure (Ireland) Act (Crimes Act) of 19 July 1887, which preceded official government condemnation of the Land League as a dangerous organisation.

16 *Ibid.,* 163–4.

17 'Evictions in Gweedore,' *The Derry Journal,* 13 August 1886, 8.

18 'Notes from Speech of the Revd. James McFadden P.P. Gweedore,' National Archives, C.S.O.R.P. 1889/11318, Glenveigh, 4 Jan. 1888, Stephen Cooley, Constable to Sgt. Orr, Plan of Campaign Meeting Derryart Chapel, quoted in Dooley, *The Big Houses,* 167.

19 Katharine Tynan, *The Middle Years* (London: Constable & Co., 1916), 86. Blunt, a cousin of George Wyndham, future Chief Secretary, wanted to become 'fully acquainted with this [Home Rule] branch of the Irish question'. 'It stood me … in good stead that I was an English landlord myself,' he wrote, 'and no ignoramus, as nearly all the Radical supporters of Home Rule in the House of Commons were, in agricultural matters.' To him, Fr McFadden was 'wise … and filled with an unconquerable energy … a shrewd man

of business … President and everything else of the League, at mortal feud with the landlords'. See Wilfrid Scawen Blunt, *The Land War in Ireland: Being a Personal Narrative of Events, in Continuation of 'A Secret History of the English Occupation of Egypt'* (London: Stephen Swift and Co., Ltd., 1912), 41; 55.

20 *Ibid.* The name Donegal is an anglicisation of the Irish '*Dún na nGall*', or 'Fort of the Strangers'.

21 William Henry Hurlburt, *Ireland Under Coercion: the Diary of an American* (Edinburgh: David Douglas, 1888), 85.

22 *Ibid.,* 97

23 *Ibid.,* 104.

24 William Limerick Martin (1847–1889), though born in Tulla, County Clare, was a member of the Martin family of Ross, in Galway. He was a cousin of Violet Martin who, as Martin Ross, wrote critically acclaimed novels and short stories with her cousin, Edith Somerville, including the novel *The Real Charlotte* (1894), which addresses the issue of land agitation and the rise of the new middle classes.

25 Martin's body was later taken to the Gweedore Hotel, where the inquest was held on 4 February 1889.

26 Tynan, *The Middle Years,* 87–8.

27 *Ibid.*

28 Hugh Dorian, *The Outer Edge of Ulster: A Memoir of Social Life in Nineteenth-Century Donegal,* ed. Breandán Mac Suibhne and David Dickson (Dublin: Lilliput Press, 2000), 43–5.

29 J.C. Beckett, *The Making of Modern Ireland* (London: Faber and Faber, 1966), 403.

30 T.W. Moody, F.X. Martin, F.J. Byrne, eds., *A New History of Ireland, 8: A Chronology of Irish History to 1976* (Oxford: Clarendon Press, 1982), 361.

31 *Ibid.,* 362. This was the Act condemned by Father McFadden in his speech of 4 January 1888 to the tenants of Gweedore.

32 MK to Florence Knight, 4 February 1887, HRO, Knight Archive, 39M89/F124/20.

33 See Knight Family Scrapbooks, HRO, Knight Archive, 78M89/6.

34 Maria Edgeworth to Charles Sneyd Edgeworth, quoted in Marilyn Butler, *Maria Edgeworth: A Literary Biography* (Oxford: The Clarendon Press, 1972), 454.

35 MK to Florence Knight, 4 February 1887, HRO, Knight Archive, 39M89/F124/20.

36 MK to Florence Knight, 10 April 1888, HRO, Knight Archive, 39M89/F124/2.

37 *Ibid.*

38 MK to Florence Knight, 5 May 1888, HRO, Knight Archive, 39M89/F124/3.

39 MK to Florence Knight, 25 June 1888, HRO, Knight Archive, 39M89/F124/4.

40 *Ibid.*

41 MK to Florence Knight, 9 July 1888, HRO, Knight Archive, 39M89/F124/6.

42 MK to Florence Knight, 8 May 1899, HRO, Knight Archive, 39M89/F124/7.

43 *Ibid.*

44 MK to Florence Knight, 10 June 1889, HRO, Knight Archive, 39M89/F124/8.

45 MK to Montagu Knight, 29 June 1889, HRO, Knight Archive, 39M89/F124/9.

46 MK to Florence Knight, 10 July 1889, HRO, Knight Archive, 39M89/F124/9.

47 *Ibid.*

48 MK to Montagu Knight, 17 September 1889, HRO, Knight Archive, 39M89/F124/10.

49 Death Certificate of Lady George Hill, 29 July 1889, transcribed from Death Register no. 7, 15, Donegal Ancestry, Ramelton, County Donegal. The death was registered on 15 August 1889, with Fanny Hopkins as witness. Louisa's name was wrongly transcribed as Louisa Jane Hill, and corrected by the registrar. Cause of death was 'senile decay and cerebral haemorrhage, one day, certified'.

50 MK to Montagu Knight, 17 September 1889, HRO, Knight Archive, 39M89/F124/10.

51 *Ibid.*

52 *Ibid.*

53 FCK, 12 March 1843, Pocket Books, CKS, Knatchbull Archive, U951/F24/40.

54 MK to Montagu Knight, 28 September 1889, HRO, Knight Archive, 39M89/F124/15.

55 MK to Edward Bridges Rice, 21 September 1889, CKS, Rice Archive, EK-U116 (uncatalogued), Hammond no.1/232. Edward Bridges Rice died in 1902, only seven years after Marianne.

56 *Ibid.*

57 *Ibid.*

58 Misses Lawrence, Miss Janet Glaze, Miss Macdonell, Miss Irvine, all with London addresses, 13 September 1889, *GHB*, 2, An Chúirt, Gweedore Court Hotel and Heritage Centre, County Donegal. Written underneath in another hand is: 'One would suppose [illegible] was too near the hotel.' Written over the words 'too near' in yet another hand is the phrase: 'The nearer the Church the further from God.'

59 Traditionally, tenants' rents were paid twice a year, on 1 May and 1 November, the 'Gale Days'.

60 MK to Florence Knight, sent 18 November 1889, HRO, Knight Archive, 39M89/F124/11/2.

61 *Ibid.*

62 'Sept. 8Th 1890. Miss Knight, Miss Hill & Mr Hill, Hotel very comfortable. Ballyare House, Ramelton.' entry in *GHB*, 2, An Chúirt, Gweedore Court Hotel and Heritage Centre, Gweedore, County Donegal.

63 MK to Florence Knight, 3 February 1890, HRO, Knight Archive, 39M89/F124/17.

64 MK to Florence Knight, 13 July 1890, HRO, Knight Archive, 39M89/F124/13.

65 MK to Florence Knight, 28 November 1890, HRO, Knight Archive, 39M89/F124/16.

66 MK to Florence Knight, 28 January 1891, HRO, Knight Archive, 39M89/F124/19.

67 MK to Florence Knight, 7 April 1891, HRO, Knight Archive, 39M89/F124/21.

68 MK to Florence Knight, 8 June 1891, HRO, Knight Archive, 39M89/F124/23.

69 MK to Florence Knight, 16 July 1891, HRO, Knight Archive, 39M89/F124/24.

70 MK to Florence Knight, 28 December 1891, HRO, Knight Archive, 39M89/F32/1.

71 MK to Florence Knight, 25 July 1892, HRO, Knight Archive, 39M89/F124/25.

72 MK to Florence Knight, April 1893, HRO, Knight Archive, 39M89/F124/32.

73 MK to Florence Knight, 15 May 1893, HRO, Knight Archive, 39M89/F124/33.

74 MK to Florence Knight, 15 September 1893, HRO, Knight Archive, 39M89/F32/2.

75 MK to Montagu Knight, 15 September 1894, HRO, Knight Archive, 39M89/F32/4.

76 MK to Edward Bridges Rice, 20 February 1895, CKS, Rice Archive, EK-U116 (uncatalogued), Hammond no.1/373. Edward Bridges Rice survived Marianne by only seven years. He 'died in his sleep by the fire on his eighty-third birthday'. Hammond, *Relating to Jane*, 265.

77 Cassandra Hill to Edward Bridges Rice, 20 February 1895, CKS, Rice Archive, EK-U116 (uncatalogued), Hammond no.1/374. 'Cecy' was Cecilia, Edward Rice's wife.

78 It is not clear whether Montagu sent MK an original MS of JA's charades or, which may be more likely, a copy of *A Collection of Charades*, privately published by the Austen Leigh family in June 1895, shortly before this letter of thanks was sent by MK. See Deirdre Le Faye, *A Chronology of Jane Austen and her Family* (Cambridge: Cambridge University Press, 2006), 698.

79 MK to Montagu Knight, 22 July 1895, HRO, Knight Archive, 39M89/F32/6.

80 JEAL, *Memoir*, 155.

81 The death certificate of Marianne Knight, registered eight days after her death, in the 'District of Ramelton in the Union of Milford in the County of Donegal' describes her as a 'female', 'spinster' and 'gentlewoman', who died at the age of ninety-four of 'senile decay and asthemia'. Her nephew Augustus Hill is registered as having been present at the death, at Ballyare, on 4 December 1895. Death register no. 7, 98, Donegal Ancestry, Ramelton, County Donegal. A memorial window dedicated to Marianne in St Nicholas' Church, Chawton, mistakenly gives the year of her death as 1896. 'Asthemia', a condition recently suffered by astronauts, has been defined as 'a kind of agitated depression, where they became irritable, couldn't sleep, and started to withdraw from their colleagues … a normal response to a confined environment'. 'The Biggest Challenge for Astronauts is Living Together,' *Guardian*, 23 November, 2000.

82 'Tully' is an anglicisation of the Irish word '*tulach*', meaning 'a hill or mound'. See Patrick. S. Dineen, ed., *Foclóir Gaedhilge agus Béarla, an Irish-English Dictionary* (Dublin: The Educational Company for the Irish Texts Society, 1927), 1276.

POSTSCRIPT

1 Elizabeth Bowen, 'The Big House,' in *The Mulberry Tree: Writings of Elizabeth Bowen*, ed. Hermione Lee (London: Virago, 1986), 29.

2 Stephen Gwynn ed., *Charlotte Grace O'Brien: Selections from Her Writings and Correspondence, with a Memoir by Stephen Gwynn* (Dublin: Maunsel and Co., Ltd, 1909), 47.

3 Stephen Gwynn, *Highways and Byways in Donegal and Antrim, with Illustrations by Hugh Thomson* (London: Macmillan & Co. Ltd., 1928), 146–7.

4 Ballyare House was sold in 1900 to William Russell, and stayed in his family until 1974 when it was bought by Ian Smith. In 1981

it was purchased by Andy O'Loughlin and since 1989 is the property of Roy and Noreen Greenslade.

5   Gwynn, *Highways and Byways*, 146–7.

6   Cassandra Hill is registered as 'Head of Family' in the Census of Ireland, 1901, with 'income derived from mortgage on land and dividends', www.census. nationalarchives.ie/reels/naio003737225.

7   Gwynn, *Highways and Byways*, 119.

8   Death Certificate, 21 August 1901, District of Rathdrum, Dublin.

9   Estyn Evans, 'The Northern Heritage,' *Aquarius*, 4 (1971): 54.

10   *Ibid.*

11   Death Certificate, 25 March 1901, District of Stillorgan, Dublin.

12   Capt. the Hon. Somerset Ward to Capt. Arthur Hill, 29 May 1881, PRONI, Saunderson Papers, T2996/11/3.

13   Elizabeth Malcolm, 'Family History,' *Ballywalter Park*, series ed. Peter Rankin (Belfast: Ulster Architectural Society, 1985), 35–6.

14   Col Saunderson did not change his mind about Father McFadden, and was supported in this by his parliamentary colleague, Edward Carson. 'Carson has just made a magnificent speech, which has completely vindicated all I said about McFadden', PRONI, Saunderson Papers, T2996/2/B/442.

15   MK to Florence Knight, 28 November 1890, HRO, Knight Archive, 39M89/F124/16.

16   Lord Dunleath, 'A Dinosaur That Defied Extinction', *Ballywalter Park*, 9.

17   Lord Dunleath, 'Not A Botanical Golf Course', *Ballywalter Park*, 30–1.

18   *Ibid.*, 31.

19   Timothy Knatchbull, *From a Clear Blue Sky* (London: Hutchinson, 2009), 369. Timothy Knatchbull is a direct descendant of Edward Knight, through Fanny, Lady Knatchbull.

20   *Ibid.*, Introduction, xiii.

21   *Ibid.*, 367.

PICTURE ACKNOWLEDGEMENTS

The editor and publisher gratefully acknowledge permission to include the following copyright material

Ballyare House, County Donegal, reproduced by kind permission of Brendan Meegan

Chawton Great House, sourced from G.F. Prosser, *Select Illustrations of Hampshire* (1833), Hampshire Record Office, 728.8, reproduced with thanks to Hampshire Record Office

Chawton Rectory, c.1803, artist unknown, reproduced with thanks to Jane Austen's House Museum, Jane Austen Memorial Trust

Edward Austen Knight (1768–1852) at the time of his Grand Tour (oil on canvas), English School, (19th century) / Jane Austen Society, on loan to Chawton House Library, UK

Edward Knight (1794–1879), sourced from *Akin to Jane*, ed. Joan Corder (Private circulation, 1953), reproduced with thanks to Jane Austen's House Museum, Jane Austen Memorial Trust

Elizabeth and Marianne Knight, 1805 (on ivory), reproduced with thanks to Jane Austen's House Museum, Jane Austen Memorial Trust

Elizabeth Austen Knight, n.d. (from an ivory pounce box), reproduced with thanks to Jane Austen's House Museum, Jane Austen Memorial Trust

Godmersham Park, Seat of Thomas Knight, Esq., 1785, artist unknown. Engraving by William Watts (1752–1851) as part of his 'Seats of the Nobility and Gentry' series, produced in 1779–86. With thanks to Godmersham Park Heritage Centre

Gweedore Hotel, Co. Donegal, c.1890, by William Lawrence [4576 W.L.] With thanks to Mícheál Ó Domhnaill and Tony McHugh of Comharchumann Fordartha, Derrybeg.

Isle O'Valla, Strangford, reproduced by kind permission of Rhoma Buchanan

Hill Family Crest, sourced from *Akin to Jane*, ed. Joan Corder (Private circulation, 1953), reproduced with thanks to Jane Austen's House Museum, Jane Austen Memorial Trust

Knights of Chawton Family Crest, sourced from *Akin to Jane*, ed. Joan Corder (Private circulation, 1953), reproduced with thanks to Jane Austen's House Museum, Jane Austen Memorial Trust

Knights of Godmersham Family Crest, sourced from *Akin to Jane*, ed. Joan Corder (Private circulation, 1953) reproduced with thanks to Jane Austen's House Museum, Jane Austen Memorial Trust

L'Aimable Jane, silhouette of Jane Austen by an unknown artist (3181) © National Portrait Gallery, London

Lord George Hill by Richard James Lane (D22025) © National Portrait Gallery, London

'Lord George Hill, Memorial Plaque' from Bunbeg Church, Donegal, reproduced by kind permission of Brendan Meegan

Louisa Hill, c.1860 (daguerreotype), reproduced with thanks to Jane Austen's House Museum, Jane Austen Memorial Trust

Marianne Knight, c.1880, by an unknown artist, reproduced with thanks to Jane Austen's House Museum, Jane Austen Memorial Trust

Marianne Knight and Louisa Hill – Gravestones, Tully, Donegal, reproduced by kind permission of Kevin McLean

'Marianne Knight's letter to Montagu Knight', 22 July 1885, Hampshire Record Office: 39M89/F32/6, reproduced with thanks to Hampshire Record Office

'Marianne Knight's review of Gweedore Hotel', 1890, from the Gweedore *Hotel Book*

Mr Montagu G. Knight, D.L., J.P., sourced from *Hampshire at the Opening of the Twentieth Century* (W.T. Pike and Co, 1905), Hampshire Record Office: 920, reproduced with thanks to Hampshire Record Office

New Mill, Bunbeg, Day and Haghe lithographers, from a sketch by Lady Harriet Clive. Sourced from Lord George Hill, *Facts from Gweedore* (1845). Thanks to Mícheál Ó Domhnaill and Tony McHugh of Comharchumann Fordartha, Derrybeg.

Norah Ward, 1887, by H. Christabelle Deanes, reproduced with thanks to Lord and Lady Dunleath

Rev. Charles Bridges Knight, sourced from *Akin to Jane*, ed. Joan Corder (Private circulation, 1953), reproduced with thanks to Jane Austen's House Museum, Jane Austen Memorial Trust

'Silhouette of Marianne, Louisa and Cassandra Knight', c.1829, author unknown, with thanks to Jane Austen's House Museum, Jane Austen Memorial Trust

'Silhouette of the Knight and Austen Family', William Wellings, a silhouette portrait of the Knight family and the Austen family playing chess, signed C. Welling fecit 1783, Chawton House Library

Somerset Ward, 1887, by H. Christabelle Deanes, reproduced with thanks to Lord and Lady Dunleath

Sophia Hillan, author photograph, 2004 © Bobbie Hanvey, reproduced with thanks to Bobbie Hanvey

Every effort has been made to trace and contact copyright holders before publication. If notified, the publisher will retify any errors or omissions at the earliest opportunity.

INDEX

~~~~~~~~~~~~~~~~~